3/9

# Understanding
# Social Inequality

Volume        earch

# RECENT VOLUMES IN . . .
# SAGE LIBRARY OF SOCIAL RESEARCH

# Understanding
# Social Inequality

## Modeling Allocation
### Processes

Hubert M. Blalock, Jr.

Sage Library of Social Research 188

**SAGE** PUBLICATIONS
*The International Professional Publishers*
Newbury Park   London   New Delhi

*For information address*:

SAGE Publications, Inc.
2455 Teller Road
Newbury Park, California 91320

SAGE Publications Ltd.
6 Bonhill Street
London EC2A 4PU
United Kingdom

SAGE Publications India Pvt. Ltd.
M-32 Market
Greater Kailash I
New Delhi 110 048 India

Printed in the United States of America

**Library of Congress Cataloging-in-Publication Data**

Blalock, Hubert M.
    Understanding social inequality : modeling allocation processes/
Hubert M. Blalock, Jr.
        p.    cm.   (Sage library of social research : v. 188)
    Includes bibliographical references (p.    ) and index.
    ISBN 0-8039-4339-3 (c). ISBN 0-8039-4340-7 (p)
    1. Equality. 2. Distributive justice. 3. Resource allocation.
4. Decision-making. I. Title. II. Series.
    HM146.B584 1991
305—dc20                                                91-22015CIP

**FIRST PRINTING, 1991**

Sage Production Editor:  Judith L. Hunter

# Contents

# Figures

*To Andrew Blalock Lyon, who in
his first year of life is just
beginning to understand and cope
with the complexities of
allocation processes.*

# *Preface*

This is a book about social inequality and stratification processes, a subject in which I have long been interested. It has a somewhat unusual focus, however, in that it is specifically designed to fill what I consider to be a major theoretical gap in the literature. Most empirical studies of stratification deal primarily with *resultants* of stratification processes, such as educational, occupational, or income inequalities, other forms of heterogeneity, or clusterings of units into social strata or interest groups.

Nowhere did this become more clear to me than when I served as a member of the group of social scientists on the National Academy of Sciences' Committee on the Status of Black Americans. In producing the book, *A Common Destiny: Blacks and American Society* (Jaynes and Williams, 1989), we found substantial hard data showing trends in black-white inequalities of different sorts, but very little involving the independent variables responsible for these trends. To be sure, there were anecdotal accounts and considerable speculation concerning the actual social processes producing these results, and indeed our interpretations were heavily based on this kind of unreliable information. But hard data relating to causal factors were generally missing. And in the chapters that dealt with various kinds of racial inequalities, human actors were virtually absent.

Social surveys are useful in obtaining selected information about attitudes or perspectives on social processes, including distributive justice, but they do not catch such processes in operation. Similarly, we obtain information about racial or ethnic separation, as for example in the form of residential segregation, and we refer to "white flight." We may even interview respondents concerning the reasons they provide for withdrawing from a given residential area or for aspiring to and applying for certain jobs rather than others. But we seldom either witness the actual behaviors involved or even seriously theorize about the kinds of multiple party social interactions that jointly affect the outcomes we can more readily observe. At best, we look only at one party at a time.

Thus there are very substantial gaps in both our empirical data and in our theories about the underlying social processes that generate the inequalities or heterogeneity that we readily observe about us. More correctly, we *do* have theories about these processes, but these are very one-sided and typically focus only on the behaviors of those parties we wish to blame for the phenomenon in question. Given large data gaps, our intellectual and disciplinary biases are then permitted to fill the holes by encouraging us to make overly simplistic assumptions about highly complex, multi-party interactive processes. We often blame whites or other dominant groups almost entirely for educational, occupational, or income inequalities in our own society. Blaming the "victim" is definitely not only out of fashion in American sociology, but it is virtually a taboo subject as well.

Similarly, other kinds of elites, such as white males, corporation executives, bankers, or political leaders are presumed to impact on whatever nonelites are being studied, whereas the behaviors of the latter are assumed to have negligible effects on such elites. Feedback processes are typically ignored in favor of recursive models in which the causation is virtually always assumed to flow from relatively more powerful actors to weaker ones. Children, for example, do not influence either their parents or their teachers, only their peers.

This is perhaps an oversimplification in order to make a point. That point is that serious data gaps do not simply result from complications in data collection or a lack of faith in unreliable information. They are also likely to be patterned in such a way as to reflect not only disciplinary boundaries and intellectual fads but, perhaps even more importantly, our ideological biases as well. If certain things are best left unsaid, this is also likely to mean that we will not study them or collect data designed to answer potentially embarrassing questions. Much better to say, for example, that we lack the data to compare the academic preparation or actual qualifications of black and white job candidates, or the amount of effort they have put into the learning process, than to introduce such factors into an empirical analysis. Much more respectable to assert that unequal rates of occupational advancement are based on "racism," or the discriminatory policies of employers, than to attempt to apportion the responsibility among several actors, including the workers themselves. And so any preexisting gaps in the empirical information we have are never filled.

The present book does not attempt to fill such empirical gaps, since such an effort would necessarily require the considerable work of large numbers of persons, as well as—perhaps—major changes in the ways we are organized to collect data. Instead, our focus will be on the task of locating where such gaps are likely to be through an effort to construct a set of delimited theories and causal models of some of the social processes that have been responsible for producing important kinds of social inequalities. As a still further restriction of our focus, we shall delimit our theories to what may be referred to as *allocation processes* through which individuals are assigned or sorted into positions by a series of microlevel decisions, both by persons serving in more or less formal allocator positions and by the prior and contemporary actions of those potentially interested in competing for these positions.

I strongly believe that authors should attempt to state their own value premises and biases, not only for the benefit of readers but also so as to inhibit themselves, perhaps ever so slightly, from letting such biases creep into their analyses. My own tendencies as a liberal sociologist are to assume that powerful or dominant parties are primarily responsible for most kinds of inequalities and that, though not necessarily acting in a conspiratorial manner, such elites are usually well aware of what they are doing, namely attempting to hold back certain categories of persons either to exploit them or at least to prevent their turning the tables and becoming dominant parties themselves.

I believe that such a liberal bias is also characteristic of much of the sociological literature, in general, and the race relations literature, in particular. I also believe, however, that such biases are no more pronounced than those evidenced in the general population and that tend to work in the opposite direction, namely that of continually blaming the victim and of seeing inequalities as primarily stemming from individual behavioral and motivational differences, rather than system-level factors or discriminatory behaviors by members of dominant groups. There is a sense, then, in which liberal and conservative biases tend to balance one another.

Yet when we do empirical research and construct explanatory models or theories, we need to compensate intellectually for whatever biases we may have, so that we do not omit variables or data that might prove embarrassing. We give our "opponents'" explanations a fair chance, rather than either ignoring them altogether or more or less deliberately failing to collect the data necessary to falsify our own theories while supporting those that we would prefer not to believe. A very important value premise to which I subscribe, then, is that scientific integrity must override whatever personal biases a writer may have.

There is a very practical reason, as well, for adhering to this position. If we do not make an honest effort to include variables and hypotheses we would prefer not to examine, our work will not be credible to those who do not share our biases. It is my perception that this is precisely the situation in which sociology, as an academic discipline, now finds itself. Our rather obvious biases color our explanations, so much so that we are often not taken seriously. I hold to the position that our long-term intellectual impact will be far greater if we attempt to purge our explanations of such biases, in an honest effort to approximate the "value neutrality" objective that supposedly characterizes the ideal scientific effort. I believe that those who take the opposite stance—namely that since value-free science represents an impossible goal we should therefore make no pretense of endorsing it—do the profession a disservice by almost deliberately undermining our credibility.

My interest in allocation processes was initiated by reading the pioneering work of my former colleague, Gerhard Lenski, whose book *Power and Privilege* (1966) discussed a wide variety of societies in which goods were allocated by powerful actors to ordinary people in very different ways and in varying amounts. In complex industrial societies, such as our own, such allocation processes are of course far more complicated than in simple horticultural socie-ties, so much so that Lenski's account deals only with very macro processes. I was left puzzled about precisely how the sorting process takes place in such industrial societies. Of course we all are familiar in a general way with how students are passed along from one grade level to the next, apply for and sometimes are accepted into jobs, and are then either promoted through the ranks or are bypassed or blocked from further advancement. We also know that decisions are being made by certain officials who make choices among a number of candidates, and whose personal biases may or may not be permitted to operate. But we lack general theories about how such allocating systems actually work, how candidates self-select themselves into positions, and how earlier allocation deci-sions impact on current ones.

My own thinking on the subject also owes much to Paul H. Wilken, with whom I collaborated over a number of years in producing the general work, *Intergroup Processes: a Micro-Macro Perspective* (1979). In that work we wrote several chapters dealing with the subject of racial discrimination, where we argued that allocation processes could not be easily separated from the suppos-edly simple notion of discrimination and that minority behaviors and other factors needed to be included in reasonably complete causal models, even if one merely wishes to *measure* racial discrimination. The basic reason is that our data are given to us in the form of inequalities, whereas discrimination refers to a kind of behavior that is typically defined, theoretically, in such a way that causal assumptions are inherently built into the definition itself. Many of the ideas developed in the present work stem from this initial formulation, and so I am indebted to Wilken who helped to provide me with numerous insights during this stage in my own thinking.

I am also indebted to three of my current colleagues, Karen Cook, Judith Howard, and Wesley Wager, for their help in my literature search in related areas. In general, however, I discovered very little material directly relevant to most of the discussion and models that form the core of the book. Perhaps this is because I did not look carefully enough, but I made the self-conscious decision, at some point, to strike out much more on my own than to conduct a very extensive and intensive literature search. The reader will therefore soon discover many fewer citations and references than I would have preferred to provide.

Finally, I would like to express my appreciation to April Ryan for the superb work in preparing the figures for this book.

# Why Study Allocation Processes?

The fundamental problem with which we shall be concerned in this book is that of how individuals are allocated to positions of various kinds by means of a series of decision processes at various points in their life cycles. Social scientists in general, and sociologists in particular, have long been deeply concerned with questions about social differentiation and inequality, as well as the nature of class systems that have been developed in all but the simplest of human societies. Often, this concern is with social structures and how these may differ from one setting or time period to another. Macro-level sociological theories with a historical thrust also offer more dynamic explanations of social stratification or differentiation, but usually without accompanying discussions of the more micro-level decision processes that, when aggregated, actually produce these phenomena.

The basic assumption underlying the present work is that it is human actors, making decisions and exercising control over others, whose behaviors it is that result in the sorting of persons into positions, as well as determining the nature of the positions themselves, the perquisites and power that attach to them, and the criteria that are used to determine which individuals occupy which positions. This is not to imply a psychological reductionist position, since actors will be constrained and otherwise influenced by setting or structural variables which, in turn, will be partly influenced by prior decision processes.

For the most part, our focus will be on developing contextual-effect types of models in which micro dependent variables are influenced by a combination of other micro variables and macro setting variables. The assumption is that macro processes cannot be adequately understood without first specifying such micro processes (Blalock, 1989a). Given this delimited focus, we shall therefore not attempt a detailed macro analysis of the system variables themselves.

As we shall note in connection with the illustrative case of the concept of discrimination, social scientists often tend to neglect or gloss over micro-level allocative decision processes, either because they are taken for granted or because scholars simply lack the data necessary to study them. Obviously, historical analyses of stratification systems must rely on available records that usually shed much more light on *products* or resultants—such as occupational distributions, inequalities in education, income or wealth, or spatial segregation—than they do on the micro-level processes that have generated them.

Sometimes there are contemporary documents such as personal diaries that may describe such processes from a particular point of view, but these will generally provide a very incomplete picture of what has actually taken place at the micro level. Records may tell us how many peasants there were in a given locale, what taxes were collected, crop yields and acreage planted, prison sentences handed out, or battle casualty figures. Archaeologists must, of course, rely on even more scanty evidence if they wish to infer such things as religious beliefs, power struggles among individuals or between clans, the division of labor, and so forth. Information about social processes is often either totally lacking or must be filtered through the reports of a small number of interested parties. Social surveys and participant observation are simply not available to social historians as sources of micro-level information.

In the case of very simple societies such as hunting and gathering bands or even horticultural societies, we can undoubtedly gain a reasonably accurate gross picture of the nature of these micro-level processes, especially if we are willing to rely on eye-witness reports or anthropological accounts of contemporary societies presumed to be highly similar to the many others that existed in the past. Lenski (1966), indeed, makes a convincing argument concerning the nature of the distributive systems in such societies. Usually, our interest does not center so much on explaining fine-grained differences among such societies as it does in comparing their typical characteristics with those societies, such as our own, that are drastically different from them.

In the case of complex social systems, however, it becomes much more difficult to account for structural differences without also examining the more micro- or individual-level processes that undergird them *unless* one makes the fundamental assumption either that individual behaviors are nearly completely determined by structural factors or that, if not, individual differences may be simply canceled out in some sort of aggregation process. The writer, however, totally rejects this kind of simplifying assumption unless it can be justified on empirical rather than a priori grounds. As we shall see, the presumption that one may use highly aggregated data to make justifiable inferences about individual behaviors depends on a set of strong assumptions that will rarely be met. The proper methodological stance, it will be argued, is to begin one's theory-building and data-collecting efforts by working at the micro and contextual-effects levels, and only *then* to determine whether or not aggregating operations can be theoretically justified on the basis of the empirical evidence.

This implies that in studying social stratification and differentiation it is advisable to examine first the nature of the micro processes that are involved, showing how such processes may result in racial or ethnic inequalities, a sexual division of labor, residential or organizational segregation, social mobility patterns, and a number of other phenomena commonly studied by social scientists interested in social stratification. What makes this strategy difficult, however, are very substantial data gaps, including the fact that many social processes either cannot be directly observed or have not been adequately described in historical documents. A second major difficulty, and one we shall attempt to address in the present work, is that theories about such processes are also rudimentary and diffuse, involving large numbers of implicit or untested assumptions. It is no surprise, then, that stratification studies tend to focus much more heavily on structural or static characteristics of social systems, rather than the processes that underlie them.

There will of course be a number of different kinds of actors involved in any complex social process, but we shall focus primarily on two types. First, there will be a set of competitors for positions, locations in space, school grades, or parental attention and care. Second are those who make allocation decisions that apportion scarce goods or resources among such competitors. The competitors will, in turn, react to these allocation decisions and will undoubtedly base their own earlier decisions concerning entry into the pool of eligible candidates partly on the perceived outcomes of prior allocation decisions. Thus we shall be concerned with the actions and reactions of both kinds of parties under varying circumstances.

There are a wide variety of allocation situations that involve most if not all of the factors that enter into discussions of social stratification, mobility, and status attainment. Parents allocate time, energy, support, and advice among their children. Teachers do likewise with their students and in addition assign grades and make other decisions that may affect the nature of the tracks or academic programs that such students later enter. College admissions officers select applicants from an explicit set of candidates who have made the prior decision as to whether or not to apply. Usually, such students have made multiple applications, so that they may or may not elect to accept any awards that have been made. Employers decide which persons to hire and which workers to promote, but again usually do so only after candidates have permitted their names to be considered. Banks select among candidates for home mortgages, often steering applicants of a given race or ethnic category into particular neighborhoods.

Rather than focus on each of such highly specific types of allocation situations, we shall attempt to formulate a more general theory involving sets of *variables* that influence allocation decisions. Allocator roles will vary in terms of clarity of expectations and the degree to which trained specialists have been delegated to make final decisions. The power that competitors have over the allocators will also vary. Sometimes recipients will later be in a position to become allocators themselves or even to gain authority over them. Losers may organize to challenge the system or to influence third parties to do so. Some competitors may have special advantages in these regards, or they may belong to the same social groups as the allocators themselves. Allocators will sometimes be in a position to avoid close surveillance and may be provided considerable autonomy with respect to the choice of evaluation criteria to use. Such criteria may be objective or highly diffuse and subject to considerable debate. Norms regarding the conditions under which allocation decisions are challenged by losers may or may not be accepted by all parties.

Allocators also have their own personal agendas and biases that often need to be taken into consideration. In many instances those persons who make the actual allocation decisions are merely agents acting on behalf of certain principals to whom they are supposedly responsible. As agents, however, their interests may only partly coincide with those of their principals. In particular, they will often make decisions that are designed either to simplify their own efforts or to help assure themselves of continued employment. Sometimes they deliberately make use of biased procedures that have been endorsed by their employers. At other times, they do so but with the implicit understanding that, if discovered, their principals will deny their own knowledge of these actual practices, as contrasted with those ideal ones that have been officially endorsed.

As noted, allocating agents are sometimes closely supervised or are subject to surveillance by parties looking out for the interests of certain sets of competitors. On other occasions, allocators may have a more or less free hand in using whatever criteria they may **choose. Competitors may or may not be aware of all such criteria** or the weights that are used in combining them to make favorable or unfavorable decisions. Furthermore, their *beliefs* concerning the allocation process in use may or may not be accurate, and yet their future behaviors may depend much more upon such beliefs than on actual processes or outcomes. They may come to believe that there are either high or low levels of procedural and distributive justice, or perhaps a high level of the one but a low level of the other.

Thus there are a number of complex sorting processes going on over a substantial portion of a person's lifetime, but the candidates are by no means passive actors in these processes. They make decisions concerning their own preparation for future competitions and whether or not to join any given pool of applicants. These self-selective processes, if unobserved or ignored in data analyses, are especially likely to lead investigators to incorrect conclusions whenever reliance is placed on highly aggregated data. In particular, if investigators must rely almost totally on outcome measures they must make a number of very strong assumptions concerning the operation of missing variables. In order to illustrate the implications of such assumptions, let us turn to the example of how discrimination is inferred on the basis of inequalities or other measures involving aggregated outcome data.

## INDIRECT MEASUREMENT: THE EXAMPLE OF DISCRIMINATION

To illustrate our general point, consider the very important notion of discrimination, as this term is employed in the race relations literature. Like many other words ending in "-tion," the concept of discrimination sometimes refers only to a resultant or product, but more frequently to the act or process of discriminat-*ing*. Unfortunately, however, our data usually come to us in the form of observed *inequalities* or similar notions such as that of residential separation, differential associations, or perceptions or beliefs about discrimination. Yet, our theoretical interests typically focus on the causal mechanisms or processes that have produced these inequalities, segregation, or beliefs.

If one examines theoretical definitions of discrimination one finds a variety of features that usually include some notion of intent or the basis for differential treatment, as well as one of "relevance" (Blalock and Wilken, 1979). A prototype definition would be that discrimination (the act) involves the differential treatment of persons "based on" (or caused by) race, religion, gender, or some other social category, rather than criteria that are "really" relevant to the choices being made. Consider the following such definitions:

> Differential treatment solely on the grounds of race, religion, national origin, ethnic group, class, age, or sex. . . . (Yinger, 1965, p. 27)

> The effective injurious treatment of persons on grounds rationally irrelevant to the situation. . . . (Antonovsky, 1960, p. 81)

> Discrepancy in treatment between candidates who are identical in all "relevant" characteristics. . . . (Pascal and Rapping, 1972, p. 120)

> . . . Overt action in which members of a group are accorded unfavorable treatment on the basis of their religious, ethnic, or racial membership. (Vander Zanden, 1972, p. 26)

> . . . Any behavior on the part of an individual which leads to unequal treatment on the basis of race or ethnicity. (Farley, 1988, p. 9)

How does one know on the basis of observed inequalities, say, between blacks and whites, whether or not there has been actual discrimination? Most operational definitions entail a kind of residualizing process, the rationale for which is seldom fully justified. If there are occupational or income differentials, for example, one may introduce very imperfect controls for years of formal schooling or perhaps work experience, and if racial inequalities persist even after such controls have been applied, the adjusted differentials are then attributed to "discrimination," or perhaps even "employer discrimination." Other possible causes for these differentials are ignored, perhaps with the justification that proper controls for such variables could not be made because of data unavailability. Let us take a closer look at what is going on here, since the problem is a very general one and constitutes the core of our argument in favor of a more intensive study of actual allocation processes.

What is often only implicitly recognized when we make the intellectual leap from product back to process, or in this case from observed inequalities to discriminatory or biased allocation procedures, is that causal assumptions must inevitably be made by the theorist-investigator. When one controls for years of schooling, for example, one is assuming that "education" is a primary "relevant" cause of occupational and income inequalities and that before one jumps to the conclusion that racial differences are due to discrimination, one needs to control for education. This is indeed a reasonable assumption, as far as it goes. But what about additional causes that cannot be controlled? And what if "years of schooling" is a very imperfect indicator of true education, as this notion is being defined by the employer or other allocating agent?

Sociologists and economists are fond of speaking about "returns to education," implying that if the regression equations for blacks and whites (or men and women) are not the same, then the "returns" are different and there is evidence favoring the assumption of discrimination. But what measure of education is commonly used to measure such returns? Years of formal schooling completed is typically employed, the assumption being that black and white high school graduates, for example, have "equivalent" educations. In a different context, however, the very same authors who employ such a measure will turn around and argue that blacks are receiving educations that are inferior to those of whites, meaning that a single year's "investment" of education is indeed not the same for blacks and whites. They may not even have "invested" the same amount of effort, attentiveness, or hours of homework during each year of formal schooling, to say nothing of the differential impacts of their peers and teachers. How, then, can the control for years of schooling be justified? Usually, on the grounds that it is the only available information.

But it is not. There is evidence, for example, that black students' scores on objective tests place them well behind their white counterparts, perhaps by as much as three or four years by the time they have graduated from high school. If so, then perhaps black high school graduates should be compared with whites completing the ninth grade. And how about so-called functional illiterates, who may possibly be detected in an interview situation or one requiring the filing of written applications? The assumption of equal years of schooling presumes that all those with formal degrees are equally "educated." Perhaps it is true that all students have invested the same amount of time in school if they have completed the same grade levels, and that therefore years of schooling is a proper measure to use if one is examining returns to education. From the standpoint of an employer who is using education as a predictor of future performance, motivation, and ability, however, such an assumption is totally unreasonable and other educational indicators will be relevant to the allocation decision.

A similar argument can be made in the opposite direction, namely that such things as scores on objective examinations, grades received in school, disciplinary records, and so forth are also racially biased and therefore should not be used in making a totally nondiscriminatory decision. The simple truth is that unless one has available considerably more information, there will be no way to decide. It is here where simplifying assumptions and biases enter into both measurement and allocation processes, as well as the judgments one makes as to whether or not allocators' decisions have been discriminatory or biased. Unfortunately, it is often the case that substantial disagreements will occur whenever anyone attempts to make this leap from observed "factual" information about differences back to the underlying processes that have produced this fallible information.

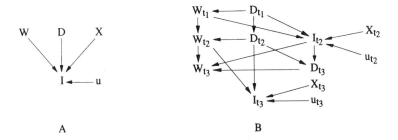

**Figure 1.1.** Naive and More Realistic Models Relating Inequality to Discrimination

To broaden the argument consider what we may term the simple, naive causal model of Figure 1.1A representing what is the commonly employed rationale for the residualizing type of operational definition of discrimination. We have the measured variable $I$ representing a given kind of inequality, say between black and white incomes. This inequality is assumed to have been produced by discrimination $D$ plus several explicitly controlled causes, $W$ and $X$, say formal education and years of work experience. A residual term $u$ is then added to represent the effects of all other uncontrolled causes of inequality. If a linear regression model has been used to infer discrimination, the model also involves the highly convenient assumption, required by ordinary least squares, that this disturbance term is uncorrelated with all of the independent variables in the equation, including discrimination $D$. Notice, incidentally, that the above formulation presumes all effects to be additive. Missing variables represented in the disturbance term do not interact, statistically, with discrimination or either of the control variables $W$ or $X$. Nor can the dependent variable, inequality $I$, feed back to affect any of the remaining variables. Such a simple model is of course naive in the extreme, and perhaps for this very reason is seldom explicitly formulated. A reader is simply told that the investigator has controlled or made adjustments for several other potential causes of inequality.

What if one of the control variables, say education, is related to discrimination? Certainly this is a reasonable assumption if the discrimination has been taking place over a sufficient period of time that potential black applicants have become discouraged and failed to obtain the necessary educational credentials. If one is able to distinguish between discrimination at several time periods, perhaps a more realistic model would take discrimination at time 1 as affecting education at time 2, which in turn affects *inequalities* at time 3. Such inequalities, of course, may themselves feed back to affect future levels of both education and discrimination. Perhaps it is also the case that, say, black educational levels at time 1 affect employer attitudes and therefore employer discrimination at a somewhat later time. If so, there may be reciprocal causation between education and discrimination. Needless to say, past employer discrimination may have affected the second control variable, say work experience, which may also have been affected by education and past levels of inequality.

Such possibilities mean that the true or more realistic causal model may be much more like that represented in Figure 1.1B than in Figure 1.1A. If so, then the simple residualizing strategy will also suggest misleading interpretations, to say nothing of a rather strange "measure" of employer discrimination. Even in the simple setup where there is a single causal arrow going from discrimination to education, this means that there will be both direct and indirect effects of discrimination on inequality. By controlling for education, these indirect effects will be ignored and some of the effects of discrimination will have been deleted. In what sense, then, can one claim that the resulting measure is an adequate or unbiased measure of actual discrimination?

One must also recognize that whenever inequalities are found, and discrimination by one party inferred on the basis of such inequalities, one is making implicit assumptions to the effect that the behaviors of the second party can safely be ignored. In the example we have been considering, the responses of minority candidates are ignored, or at best weakly controlled by the introduction of one or two minority characteristics. No feedback effects from weaker to stronger parties are allowed. Blacks do not influence whites, applicants have no effects on allocators, children do not impact back on the behaviors of their parents or teachers, delinquents on the court system, and so forth. Indeed, the use of single-equation statistical analysis procedures imposes this very kind of simplifying assumption by requiring the assumption that disturbance terms are uncorrelated with all independent variables in the equation.[1]

Simplifying assumptions must always be made and will be required whenever indirect measurement is needed. But *how* simple must they be, and what if those we use for the sake of convenience are actually far from realistic? Here, the vested interests of the researcher who needs to make such simplifying assumptions are likely to combine with that same researcher's substantive biases as a social scientist. Sociologists, who for the most part take a liberal to radical stance on many social issues, have a particular set of biases that tend to define relatively weak parties as "victims" or as dependent actors whose responses or other behaviors can safely be ignored. Conservatives, however, may take precisely the opposite stance, namely that these same responses and behaviors are what have caused the inequality or other type of social outcome that is being investigated. It is not employer or allocator decisions that have produced the inequalities but failures on the part of the losing candidates! The allocation system has been fair, and what liberals simply assume to be allocator biases are really no more than honest appraisals of true candidate differences.

The methodological problem we face is therefore closely connected with the question of whether or not our interpretations—and measures—will be accepted by those who are unwilling to employ precisely the same simplifying assumptions we wish to use. Perhaps some potential critics can be overwhelmed by a statistical tour de force that successfully hides our implicit assumptions from view, as for example in our measures of discrimination. Indeed, those who share our theoretical assumptions or substantive biases may be convinced by our findings and theoretical arguments, but this of course does not make them valid. Unfortunately as well, there will be many others who, also making simplifying assumptions, will reach very different conclusions from the same set of empirical facts.

What implications are suggested by this single illustrative example? Perhaps the main point to emphasize is that if reality is indeed complex then our assumptions must somehow or another incorporate this complexity if we are ever to reach agreement concerning the adequacy of each other's arguments. If one person makes assumptions A, B, and C, but refuses to accept assumptions D, E, and F, whereas a second makes precisely the opposite set of assumptions, then there can be no agreement *unless* we have collected sufficient data to permit tests of all such assumptions. Studies that simply delete certain information, for example, will then require one to make untestable assumptions about how the missing variables are operating. In order to convince skeptics who do not wish to accept these latter assumptions, we shall then require data concerning the missing variables.

The general implication is that both complexities and disagreements concerning assumptions require larger scale and more complex empirical studies, as well as more complete theoretical models that at least allow for the operation of a more inclusive set of variables than either of the disputing parties, alone, believes is necessary.

## THE PROBLEM OF AGGREGATION BIASES

Theoretical definitions of discrimination typically refer to individual or micro-level decision processes, as for example, when discrimination refers to a bias based on a candidate's race or ethnicity, sex, age, or other "irrelevant" characteristic. In the ideal, one would want to catch the allocator in the act of making such a discriminatory decision and then aggregate a number of similar decisions into a single measure of some kind. Unfortunately, however, we have just noted that such critical information is practically always missing, so that a residualizing operation involving highly imperfect controls is often used to construct such an aggregated measure. Assumptions about the impacts of neglected variables are then required, and among such assumptions will be those pertaining to *how* a candidate pool—which generally provides the denominator for such measures—has been obtained. Were black and white candidates really equally qualified? Was a random device used to determine which whites and which blacks applied for the positions in question? Undoubtedly not. Can self-selection be ruled out? Practically never!

What happens when our theoretical statements and definitions refer to a micro-level process but yet our data are provided on an aggregated basis? How valid are cross-level inferences when our theory and data are on different levels of analysis? Under what conditions is it safe to infer from aggregated data back to micro-level social processes? The literature on this topic is technical in nature and basically pessimistic in terms of the implied outcomes. The bottom line is that it is rarely safe to make such an intellectual leap unless a set of highly restrictive simplifying assumptions can realistically be made. This being the case, the overall implication is that data at the micro level must be collected in order to justify the use of such necessary simplifying assumptions (Hannan, 1971; Langbein and Lichtman, 1978).

The basic conditions necessary for "consistency" across the two levels to hold, so that regression coefficients obtained at the aggregated level can be assumed equivalent to those at the micro level, are: (1) that the equations be linear in format and that the "corresponding" variables at each level play the same roles at both levels, implying the absence of contextual effects in the micro model; (2) that the aggregation or grouping criterion used not be dependent on any of these variables; and (3) that there is near-perfect specification of the macro-level equation, including the absence of measurement errors in any of the independent variables and a disturbance term that is uncorrelated with all such variables. Some of these assumptions are, of course, required by the use of ordinary least squares or other statistical approaches in common use. It is assumptions (1) and (2) concerning the absence of contextual effects and the nature of the grouping criterion that warrant our closer attention in the present context.

Let us first examine the implications of assumption (1). Suppose one has a micro theory involving, say, some individual behavior such as an allocation decision as a dependent variable, and a set of micro-level independent variables that also pertain to that same individual actor. One may aggregate over a number of such allocators and their corresponding individual characteristics, obtaining group means (or proportions) for all such variables. Assumption (1) would break down, however, if there were contextual effects stemming from the characteristics or behaviors of the other allocators in the actor's network. If such other actors, perhaps through their past behaviors, are also influencing the behavior of any given allocator, then the group mean (on either an independent variable $X_i$ or the dependent variable $Y$) also belongs in the micro-level equation. If one now aggregates up and uses only the macro equation, there will be a confounding of at least some of the individual and contextual level causal variables. As Firebaugh (1978) formulates the problem, if the group mean $\overline{X}$ on an independent variable belongs in the equation for the micro dependent variable $Y$, net of the influence of the corresponding micro independent variable $X$, the equations at the two levels will take on a different form, and one cannot safely infer back from the aggregated to the individual-level variable. It will be impossible to separate out the two kinds of causal variables. Thus a simple cross-level analysis, in which micro-level inferences are made on the basis of aggregated data, will lead to unknown biases.

There is an even more serious potential source of bias in using macro data in this fashion, however, and this involves the violation of the second of the above assumptions. Basically, assumption (2) concerning the grouping criterion requires that there be no self-selection (into the aggregated samples) that is based on one or more variables that are dependent on any of the outcome variables being studied. Consider, for example, aggregated test scores for schools or districts that are used to assess the "outputs" of these schools or districts (Bidwell and Kasarda, 1975; Hannan, Freeman, and

Meyer, 1976). The basic theories are about micro-level performances of individual students, and of course, the learning processes that have influenced them. If it were reasonable to assume
random selection into schools or districts and isolation from parental influences during the period of study, then perhaps such
aggregated test scores, as out*comes,* could be used to measure the
true out*puts* of each school of district.

But what if parents, through neighborhood selection or withdrawal to private schools, have jointly affected *both* the school or
district composition and the learning of their own children? Perhaps they have selected a neighborhood precisely *because* of the
local school's reputation for excellence. If so, then a past level of
the supposedly "dependent" variable, namely school outcome
levels, has influenced whether or not particular students are enrolled. And, of course, the children of parents who have so selected
their schools may also be favorably influenced by these same
parents, a fact that is unlikely to be measured by available school
data. The criterion for aggregation, namely the school or district, is
entangled in a complex web of causation, including feedback
effects from "dependent" to supposedly independent variables.

Self-selection is virtually inevitable in most real-world social
processes. If a study were done at the micro or individual level,
using the child as unit of analysis, certain specification errors
would be difficult to avoid. What is usually unrecognized by data
analysts, however, is that whenever there has been aggregation by
a partially dependent variable (here, the child's location in a particular school or district), any such specification errors will usually
be *amplified,* thereby leading to even greater biases than would
have obtained in a micro analysis that did not contain adequate
controls (Hannan and Burstein, 1974; Langbein & Lichtman, 1978).

There may be a few circumstances where measurement errors at
the macro level are less severe than those at the micro level, but in
general we are much more likely to be misled when we must use
data that refer to the wrong level of analysis. If our theories are
about how school children learn, then the child is the proper unit
of analysis (Blalock, 1989a; Hannan et al., 1976). Similarly, if the

theories are about discriminatory decision processes or how persons are assigned to positions, the individual allocator or applicant, as the case may be, is also the proper unit. Highly aggregated data are suspect *unless* the analyst has a well-formulated theory and makes only those assumptions that have been shown by other studies to be highly plausible. If, for example, parents do not select their children's schools by means of neighborhood choices, if children's past performance levels do not affect their later class assignments, or if job applicants do not enter a local competition based on past allocation decisions, then one may safely proceed with the aggregated data.

The researcher's substantive and ideological biases, as well as his or her vested interests in making convenient simplifying assumptions, again are likely to enter the picture. As we have implied, such simplifying assumptions are often made in a perfunctory manner, as for example whenever one uses a regression equation and assumes that (unobserved) disturbance terms are uncorrelated with all independent variables in that equation. It may be highly convenient and also consistent with the analyst's own biases to assume, for example, that black and white applicants have exactly the same distributions of qualifications, or that this is at least true net of their years of formal schooling. As we have already noted, the problem is that those whom the researcher is attempting to convince may make a very different set of assumptions, namely that black applicants' qualifications are weaker than those of the whites. If so, that critic would argue, it should come as no surprise that blacks are less well represented among the winning candidates.

Fortunately, one often has available selected sets of data at the individual level. In the so-called status-attainment literature stimulated by the pioneering study by Blau and Duncan (1967), certain outcome information is usually collected: a person's income at a given time, his or her occupation and educational attainment level, parental characteristics such as father's occupation or mother's education, and perhaps certain information concerning siblings, test scores, school composition, curriculum selected, and so forth.

Survey research methods are usually used in such studies to re-
cover easily recalled pieces of information about the past, such as
a few parental characteristics, first salaries, time in the labor force,
educational degrees, and job histories. Sophisticated event-history
analysis procedures may even be used to tease out the differences
involved whenever sequences may differ from one individual to
the next, or whenever the temporal intervals between such discrete
events may also differ.

What such micro-level studies of attainment processes practically always neglect, however, are the myriad decision processes
that have resulted in these discrete event outcomes. This includes
day-to-day parental neglect or encouragement, teacher behaviors,
peer interaction patterns, and a series of crucial decisions made by
college admissions officers, personnel officers, supervisors, and
family members. Nor will there be any data regarding the actors'
own decisions regarding choices among friends, reactions to parents and teachers, choices among jobs, work habits or gradual
changes in performance, and so forth.

Obviously, such process data are both expensive to collect and
usually almost impossible to obtain by direct observation. Insofar
as important causal mechanisms are omitted from one's micro
analysis, however, this very practical limitation means that we are
very likely to be misled in our interpretations of what is taking
place. As already noted, one must then make a series of simplifying
assumptions regarding the adequacy of the model as it has actually
been specified. Such assumptions are implicit in the single assumption that the disturbance term in one's equation for the dependent
variable is uncorrelated with each of the independent variables
that have been explicitly included.

If one is extremely fortunate, aggregation *may* tend to cancel out
some of the idiosyncratic influences that impact on the separate
individuals involved. What we now know about this aggregation
process, however, is that it is precisely the opposite that is more
likely to occur. Aggregation will amplify any such specification
errors that already exist in the micro model *unless* the aggregating
criterion, which is usually either a territorial (e.g., county) or a

group membership (e.g., classroom or clique) criterion, does not involve self-selection on a dependent variable.

The general implication of all this, as well as our earlier discussion of the discrimination example, is that very complete and well tested micro-level theories are necessary even to make reasonable *measurement* decisions at the more macro level. Before one infers system-level discrimination, for example, one needs just such a micro theory in order to justify whatever simplifying assumptions are necessary to compensate for data gaps at the macro level. If such a micro theory remains implicit, as is often the case in macro analyses, there are almost bound to be confused arguments revolving around one's macro-level interpretations of social processes. Are racial or gender differentials due to discrimination, selective training, ability or motivational differences, or perhaps something else? There will not be any way to resolve such controversies, apart from the use of clever persuasive devices, efforts to cover up or minimize the importance of one's own untested assumptions, or perhaps even resorts to ad hominem attacks on one's opponents. None of these approaches, of course, are likely to lead to cumulative knowledge.

## DATA GAPS, UNTESTABLE ASSUMPTIONS, AND BIASES

Obviously, the more substantial the gaps in one's empirical evidence the greater the number of untested assumptions and intellectual leaps that must be made in making causal inferences about any type of social process. As noted, we are often in a position to measure structural properties, such as income inequalities, whereas the actual processes that have produced such properties must be inferred from much more fragmentary evidence. Where one is studying the past or must rely very heavily on data collected by others, such gaps will practically always be highly selective and uneven. So also, then, will be the plausibility of one's simplifying assumptions concerning the operation of missing variables.

Whenever one is undertaking the study of a poorly understood phenomenon, it obviously makes sense to begin with the variables that are easiest to measure and that are most readily available. Many kinds of potentially interesting causes can thereby be ruled out or at least set aside while stronger empirical relationships are more intensively investigated. In the study of stratification and so-called status attainment, for example, it is advisable to work with large data sets involving substantial numbers of individuals. Given the costs of such research and the likelihood that those who have collected the data will have had interests that only partly overlap those of the investigator, it will usually be necessary to confine one's analysis to rather simplistic objective indicators such as parental schooling, father's occupation, the respondent's highest degree, number of siblings, first job, current occupation, and present income. Where school variables are also considered, there may also be records of grades, scores on standardized exams, and perhaps a few "contextual" variables such as the percentage of blacks in the school, average family incomes, student-faculty ratios, and so forth. Perhaps respondents will also be asked to recall certain major events, such as the divorce of their parents, deaths in the family, residential changes, and type of curriculum in which they were enrolled.

As noted, some such information may be inserted as indicators of contextual effects. Perhaps even the average test scores of one's classmates, local unemployment figures or occupational distributions, or legislative expenditures can also be obtained from various sources. Together, such a list of variables may contain a diverse set of indicators of experience or exposure variables expected to impact on the individual's subsequent attitudes or behaviors. Gaining additional information may indeed be out of the question for any given investigator, especially whenever the numbers of cases is large, crucial records either confidential or missing, and the accuracy of recall very much in doubt.

Whenever such missing data can reasonably be assumed to constitute intervening variables that operate in simple ways between so-called independent variables and their presumed effects, it can also be argued that their collection and inclusion would merely add detail to the analysis or frosting to the cake, in the sense of enabling the investigator to specify more adequately the nature of the mechanisms through which one apparently static variable (say, father's occupation or number of siblings) influenced some response variable, say a student's test performance. Indeed, the absence of such more detailed information gives the analyst a vested interest in making certain kinds of simplifying assumptions, rather than others. Missing intervening variables are assumed to be linearly related to included variables and to involve only additive rather than nonadditive joint effects. Most critically, causal feedback loops involving such unmeasured variables are assumed away. Relatively powerless actors are assumed not to affect more powerful ones, and especially so when the latter's behaviors cannot be measured.

Consider, for example, teacher-student and student-peer interaction patterns. Children's behaviors in the classroom are assumed not to influence those of their teachers, so that earlier performances cannot feed back to affect later ones through teacher responses. Peers impact on any given student, so that it is meaningful to speak as though all associations with average peer scores (say on tests) can be treated as peer *effects*, rather than being due to self-selection processes through which similarly performing peers seek one another out. Nor do parental behaviors continually interact with those of their children or of their children's teachers. A single control for, say, mother's (formal) education is thought to take care of the parental influence factor, instead of viewing parent-child and parent-teacher interaction patterns as involving ongoing processes. If teachers modify their later behaviors partly on the basis of prior experiences with either children or their parents, such modifications are ignored by in effect implicitly assuming them to be negligible. Even the *aggregated* effects of student behaviors over a number of years are also conveniently ignored.

In the present work we shall focus on only one of the several kinds of social processes that are commonly ignored because of existing data gaps, namely what we are referring to as *allocation processes.* What is really critical in the study of such processes is that they practically always involve two- or multiple-party behavior sequences. In particular, the early behaviors of those we shall refer to as allocators (e.g., parents, teachers, or employers) are likely to affect subsequent responses of those who are competing for their favors, with such responses including choices involving self-selection mechanisms that are typically neglected in most empirical analyses. As we have already noted, such self-selection processes, if ignored, can result in substantial biases and therefore highly misleading conclusions whenever one is moving from data concerning macro-level inequalities to inferences about discrimination, or from data that have been aggregated according to a unit into which there has been self-selection (e.g., a school or neighborhood) back down to individual-level behaviors of theoretical interest (e.g., test performances or acts of deviance).

How can we find ways of deliberately overcoming such biases? The only feasible mode of attack appears to be that of formulating reasonably complete theories that contain both those variables that can rather easily be measured and those that, in many studies, will have to remain unmeasured. One may then attempt to extract the implications of causal models that contain a mixture of both kinds of variables, noting the conditions under which the neglect of specific variables—merely because they are difficult to measure—is likely to lead one astray. This may then help to prioritize efforts to bring this latter type of variable into focus.

From the standpoint of those who actually collect such data, this in turn seems to imply a much greater need for exploratory work based on small nonprobability samples in order to find more effective ways of modifying larger scale data collection efforts in the direction of more inclusive sets of variables, measured in different ways and undoubtedly requiring a mixture of data-collecting strategies. In short, our theoretical model-building work needs to keep several steps ahead of our empirical efforts.

The primary purpose of the present study is to provide such a stimulus for reducing the major data gaps that currently hamper our ability to gain a fuller understanding of social differentiation, stratification, and mobility as well as the micro processes that underlie the macro phenomena associated with them.

## COVERAGE AND ORGANIZATION OF THE BOOK

For the most part, we shall assume that both the allocators and those who are competing for positions or other goods being distributed by such allocators are only loosely organized and that major power grabs by segments of the latter are beyond the scope of our discussion. That is, competitors or potential competitors may self-select themselves into or out of applicant pools, and they may react to allocation decisions and attempt to apply pressure on the allocating agents or their principals. There may also be informal alliances between either the allocators or their principals, on the one hand, and certain segments among the competitors, on the other.

We shall not consider issues that are more appropriately discussed in works on power and conflict, however. For example, throughout history there have been powerful segments of the population that have attempted to control allocators by means of force or to replace one set of allocators by another. Whenever a state's armed forces are controlled by mercenaries rather than indigenous elites, for example, these military groups may attempt to gain direct control over such elites. During the third and fourth centuries A.D., Roman emperors found themselves virtually at the mercy of the mercenary armies they supposedly controlled, with the result that rival armies succeeded in overthrowing their emperors and replacing them in rapid succession with those of their own choosing. In virtually all Central and Latin American countries there have been close alliances between landed elites and the armed forces, with the overwhelming majority of the top-rung officers being drawn from elite families.

Whenever such highly organized parties obtain direct control over important allocation processes, a host of factors will come into play in addition to those on which we shall focus in the present work. In effect, one or more of the groups that are supposedly in competition for the goods being distributed are actually serving in a double capacity: as the principals to whom allocators are beholden for their positions, and as one of the groups to which goods are being distributed.

The tack we shall take so as to avoid complications of this nature is to redefine such controlling parties out of the allocative process by subtracting out the share they have taken for themselves from the total pie to be distributed among the remaining competitors. Thus if elites usurp, say, 80% of the cultivatable land, there will remain only 20% to be distributed among peasants and small farmers. From this perspective, then, both the *amount* and the *nature* of the remaining goods to be distributed may be treated as exogenous variables, or at least as predetermined over the short run. In longer term more macro-level accounts of distributive processes it would be necessary to consider how these parameters change over time, partly as a result of feedback processes stemming from aggregated individual or collective responses to the kinds of macro factors that we shall be treating as givens in the present work.

Each of the six substantive chapters that follow will therefore focus on more micro-level decision processes that are, however, influenced by a number of exogenous factors. The actors with whom we shall be concerned are thus autonomous but subject to constraints, only some of which they will be in a position to modify. Chapters 2 and 3 focus primarily on these constraining factors, with Chapter 2 being concerned with the nature or properties of the goods or positions being allocated and how these may impact on allocators' decisions. In Chapter 3 some additional kinds of constraining factors are introduced, particularly those pertaining to the relationships between allocators and several other parties: the principals to whom they are responsible, third parties that may or may not form alliances with allocators or perhaps some of the candidates they are evaluating, and of course these competitors themselves. Chapter 4 shifts the focus to the decision process itself and how this is impacted by allocator characteristics, including the several goals or objectives that motivate their actions.

In Chapters 5 and 6 we shift to a concern with different kinds of candidate pools from which eligible competitors are drawn. Here we add to a focus on the allocators themselves a concern about candidates' decisions in terms of pool entry, preparation by obtaining necessary skills, and the kinds of factors that influence these decisions. Chapter 6 deals more specifically with what are termed sequential pools that feed into one another and that also involve self-selective mechanisms of one kind or another. In Chapter 7 we are concerned with how candidates, particularly losing ones, react to the allocation process and how notions of distributive and procedural justice affect not only these candidates but allocators as well. Finally, in Chapter 8 we close with a very brief discussion of some implications for research priorities and the nature of the missing information we must somehow or another obtain if we are to fill in important gaps in our information about allocation processes as they affect social inequality.

In each of the six substantive chapters we follow a similar format. The first two thirds to three quarters of these chapters contain discursive accounts as well as illustrative examples, where these seem needed to clarify points being made. No effort is made in any of these chapters, however, to deal systematically with particular kinds of allocation processes, such as hiring policies, job promotions, or the allocation of time and energy to school children, clients, or family members. Instead, the arguments are intended to be general in scope, although qualified in terms of the kinds of explanatory variables that are needed to distinguish one type of situation from another. In other words, instead of dealing with concrete instances of allocation processes, one by one, the effort is to construct sufficiently complex models to encompass a wide variety of situations and kinds of allocative processes.

In each of these chapters the final sections represent a more systematic effort to formulate explicit causal models dealing with the ideas presented discursively in the earlier portions of the chapters. With the exception of two delimited models (Models II and IV) referring to specific kinds of processes, the remaining six causal models are rather complex, each containing between 28 and 43 variables. Since these models will most certainly tax the reader's patience, I have used basically the same presentational format in presenting and then briefly discussing each of the models. Variables are separated into three classes: exogenous or (nearly) independent variables, intervening variables, and (nearly) dependent variables. Each variable is then listed and given both a descriptive definition and a shorter label used in the diagram itself. The impacts of first the exogenous and then the intervening variables are then discussed, and finally brief note is taken of those few instances where some of the dependent variables are, themselves, causally interrelated.

This mode of presentation will be discussed in greater detail in the following chapter, but it is important to emphasize at the outset that complex models of this sort can only be legitimately broken apart under very special conditions. Fortunately, in all but one of our models these conditions are nearly met. With a few exceptions in each model, as we shall note, the variables are assumed to form a recursive system involving one-way causation. Such a system permits both the theorist and the data analyst to proceed step by step through the causal system, ultimately arriving at the dependent variables. In terms of data analysis this justifies the separate estimation of the parameters in each equation, with one equation being written for each variable that is taken as dependent on at least one other variable in the causal system. In more complex non-recursive models, as exemplified by Model IV in Chapter 4, it is not only not legitimate to break the equations apart in this manner, but it is also often the case (as in Model IV) that the situation is mathematically intractable without additional assumptions. This fact implies that empirical estimates of the relative impacts of each variable cannot be obtained.

Thus the models contained in the book are in one sense highly complex, but in another overly simplistic. They contain large numbers of variables, which at this stage is necessary in view of the complexity of the real-world processes we are examining. But they do not allow for other kinds of complications, including long-term feedbacks from some of the supposedly dependent variables in each model to the remaining variables in the system. Over the long term, such feedbacks almost certainly take place. Furthermore, certain kinds of aggregated "dependent" variables, such as allocator decisions, have macro-level consequences, as for example those that involve changes in governmental policies or protest-oriented social movements.

Considerations of this sort are simply not treated in the present work, which we have noted as a more micro-level and short-term focus. One of the next steps in the theory-building enterprise, then, is to hook up the kinds of models presented in Chapters 2 through 7 with macro analyses that take many of our own "exogenous" or independent variables as phenomena to be explained in their own right. Our argument, however, is that without benefit of more micro analyses, such macro theories are likely to require so many untested assumptions, and to ignore such huge data gaps, that our intellectual and ideological biases are likely to predominate, resulting in unanswerable theoretical disputes that merely hamper the process of arriving at a cumulative body of knowledge. A premature leap to the macro level, without an adequate understanding of micro processes, is therefore unwise. Thus the primary objective of the present endeavor is to fill in at least a portion of the micro-level picture, where real actors are involved in making decisions that affect one another's outcomes.

## NOTE

1. Such an assumption automatically fails in the case of reciprocal causation between $X$ and $Y$. If $X$ causes $Y$, then the disturbance term in the equation for $Y$ is assumed to be uncorrelated with $X$. But this disturbance term, representing all of the omitted causes of $Y$, will then also be an indirect cause of $X$ through the effects of $Y$. Therefore it will be correlated with $X$, contrary to the required assumption for ordinary least squares. This produces a bias in parameter estimates unless alternative procedures are used. See Namboodiri, Carter, and Blalock (1975).

T W O

# *Properties of Allocated Goods*

We shall be considering a wide variety of allocation situations and types of goods to be allocated among competitors. These include jobs, promotions, wages and salaries, spatial locations, admission to college, grades and academic degrees, home mortgages, the allocator's time and energy, and even negatively valued goods such as prison sentences, failing grades, or job layoffs. One way to handle such a diversity of goods is simply to name them and treat them under separate headings such as jobs, promotions, college admissions, and so forth. Our interest, however, is in formulating a general theory of allocation processes, and therefore it is necessary to raise the level of abstraction and attempt to identify a number of *variables* or dimensions along which allocated goods can be measured.

In the following section we shall list and briefly discuss a number of such dimensions that will be important in our subsequent analysis. After making several remarks about related topics, we shall conclude the chapter with a section presenting the first of several complex causal models representing a formalization of relevant aspects of the allocation process.

## TYPES OF PROPERTIES

### *1. Divisibility*

Some goods such as money, land, and the allocator's time can be divided either equally or unequally among competitors. Others must be awarded on an all-or-nothing basis. Some college applicants are accepted whereas others are rejected. Only a certain number of jobs will be available to an employer to assign, meaning that losers will have to be turned away. We must recognize, however, that to a limited degree allocators will be in a position to "chop up" some of the goods that are at their disposal, so that there may be various gradations of winners and losers. By creating relatively fine distinctions among jobholders, for example, it may be possible to allow for a number of rank levels and therefore competitive opportunities for incumbents to move incrementally from one level to another. Grades may be awarded on an A, B, C, D, or E basis, or they may be located along a continuum ranging from 4.0 to 0.0, thus turning the grading system into what for all practical purposes amounts to a continuous distribution.

Where distinct boundaries must be drawn between those who are to be included and those to be excluded, the problem of the selection of a cutting point becomes especially critical for the allocator. Where numerical quotas have been set, as for example the number of players a professional football team may keep on its roster, accurate measurement capable of making fine distinctions may be especially critical unless a special "limbo" pool of near-winners can be created. Thus colleges or preparatory schools often place selected persons on ranked waiting lists, so that vacant positions can be filled without going through a costly supplemental screening process.

Whenever such persons may also be successful candidates in other competitions, the problem for the allocator is to keep them "lined up" and sufficiently uncommitted to competing organizations so as to enable them to reverse any decisions they may have made to rival allocators. Where the competitive process among allocating units is coordinated and well regulated, certain dates may be designated and made uniform, so that competitors who may have received several favorable responses will have to commit themselves irrevocably if they are to remain eligible for the positions concerned. Needless to say, whenever competition among allocating units becomes severe, there will likely be pressures to bypass such procedures and undercut one's competitors.

### 2. Once-And-For-All Versus Repeated Allocations

Closely related to, but analytically distinct from, the above distinction between continuous versus discrete kinds of goods is the question of whether or not each candidate will receive repeated allocation treatments. In most cases, a student applies once and only once for admission to a given college. Similarly, job candidates ordinarily apply only once to a particular employer. In contrast, teachers allocate time to students and parents to their children on a continuing basis. This means that if one child is shortchanged on a particular occasion there will be later opportunities to correct for any temporary inequities created. Employees may be evaluated annually for promotions, especially if positions have been finely graded into hierarchically arranged levels involving only minor salary differentials. Salary adjustments may be made even more frequently, again providing opportunities to adjust the rewards according to incremental changes in performance.

Whenever there are numerous allocation decisions made at regular intervals, precise measurement of qualifications may be less necessary than is the case if single decisions will result in the dropping of losing candidates from future applicant pools. Problems of encouraging competitor motivation will also depend on whether or not candidates will have a second chance. Those who have lost rather badly may need to be encouraged to drop out from future competitions, whereas those who have come close to winning may be motivated to improve their credentials for the next competitive opportunity. Employees who remain on the job will need to be encouraged to maintain or improve their performance levels in spite of the possibility that they may have become embittered by what they perceive as an unjust decision process. This is in contrast with those losers who will never be seen again and who, presumably, need to be told very little about their relative standing among the losers.

In situations that involve multiple allocation processes produced by a decision to create a large number of finely graded positions, we anticipate that competitors will pass through what we shall later refer to as *sequential pools.* In these situations, all of those who have successfully passed through one pool will become theoretically eligible to compete to join the next higher pool. Only some will succeed, however, and presumably these will remain to compete with those who have more recently been admitted from lower pools. Where there are differential rates of progress among competitors we may anticipate morale problems and, in some instances, a lowering of performance levels. In research universities, for example, some Associate Professors may be passed over for promotion year after year, seeing much younger persons first rising to their own rank and then moving beyond them to Full Professor. Where allocators are also concerned about the job performances of all their employees, they may also find it necessary to promote primarily on the basis of seniority or else find ways of moving the less successful persons into other positions, as for example deanships or other administrative offices.

### 3. Retractability

Can the allocated goods be taken back and therefore be made contingent on the awardee's future behavior? Obviously, if an employee can rather easily be fired for lowered performance or a vassal's land reclaimed whenever his loyalty becomes questionable, the allocator's power over awardees will be increased. We must recognize, however, that there will be many instances where goods are in *theory* capable of being retracted, whereas in actuality it may be prohibitively costly to do so. In academic settings, a faculty member's tenure is virtually never totally guaranteed and may be revoked for a number of reasons. In practice, however, we recognize that the systematic revocation of faculty tenure would likely result not only in the censure of the administration concerned but also in faculty revolt. Therefore, once tenure has been granted, the holder becomes virtually secure in his or her position.

Likewise, there have been numerous instances where emperors or monarchs have found themselves unable to reclaim titles or landholdings awarded to powerful members of the nobility, with the result that positions that were initially granted as contingent privileges for past services become inheritances that are in effect passed along from one generation to the next without the need for more than token approval by the granting agent. Although technically retractable, the property or other goods involved become in actuality owned and totally controlled by the recipient party or its heirs. The real power then resides with the recipient, rather than the initial allocator.

Goods that are genuinely retractable obviously provide the allocator with continued power over recipients, since at any time the latter may be replaced by others whose loyalty or performance levels are more assured. This provides the allocator the opportunity to play each recipient off against the others, especially in those instances where the goods concerned are divisible and reapportioned according to a regular schedule involving relatively frequent allocation decisions. Recipients, in turn, will be motivated to attempt to "lock in" their own benefits, while opening up those of their competitors to future reallocation decisions.

Continued allocations involving goods that, themselves, help to create power resources for the awardees are therefore likely to produce highly unstable situations for the individual allocators and those whom they have selected as awardees. The nature of the system itself, say that of a feudal arrangement involving vassalage, may remain in place, whereas the power distribution among individual players may change rather drastically over the short run. Under such circumstances we would expect a high degree of social conflict to accompany the allocation process.

## 4. *Generalized Value of Allocated Goods*

Some allocated goods may be highly valued by a wide variety of parties precisely because they may be exchanged for a number of other types of goods. In our own society money is one such good. Precisely because dollars may be exchanged for many other goods, an individual's salary (or other monetary compensation) becomes a kind of common denominator by means of which otherwise noncomparable goods can be evaluated. An accountant, a lawyer, and a doctor may all have positions that enable them to earn $100,000 per year, making it possible for outsiders to evaluate their worth and to assign them a comparable social status.

Other types of goods, however, may appeal to a much smaller subset of potential competitors and this in turn may affect both the nature and sizes of applicant pools. Not all of us wish to compete for political office or for positions on the police force. Only a very few scholars may submit articles to a particular specialized journal, just as a highly localized art competition may draw applicants from a very small pool of artists. Some high school graduates may not want to be accepted at the local private college, except possibly as a last resort. We shall later examine possibilities of this sort in a discussion of "hierarchical" pools characterized by the fact that some allocating units may have much more to offer than others.

The point we need to make in the present connection is that the goods being offered may possibly be highly valued by a wide variety of potential competitors, or their appeal may be much more restricted and perhaps of interest only to those who turn out to be losers in other contests. The basic criterion of concern, here, may be assessed in terms of the answer to the question, "What proportion of all potential applicants have sufficiently high utilities for the goods being offered to motivate them to become active competitors in what we shall refer to as the 'explicit' pool of candidates who actually apply as competitors in the allocation decision process?"

### 5. Depletion and Replenishment of Allocated Goods

Allocators often expect to engage in repeated allocations, although not necessarily with the same explicit pools of applicants. Each year, college admissions officers select a new set of entering freshmen because, at the opposite end, a comparable number of other students exit the system either through graduation or dropping out of the program. A certain number of job holders will retire, resign, or be laid off, making continued allocations at the job-entry level necessary. Kings or emperors may wish to have available a sufficient amount of land to reward those who have served them, making it virtually necessary continually to search for new territories to conquer. Mortgage and loan associations obviously require capital with which to make new loans, and so forth.

Given that many types of goods will become depleted through the allocation process, there must therefore be mechanisms developed through which they can be replenished. Yet such replenishment may be problematic in many instances, creating strains and dilemmas for the allocators. Where allocated goods can be retracted and reallocated, such problems may be relatively easily resolved, thereby assuring a continued flow of goods from and then back to the allocators concerned. Where recipients retain such goods, however, or where they are used up in the consumption process, allocating agents face a loss-of-power situation unless such a continued flow can be assured. Ideally, from their perspective, regularity and predictability of replenishment become highly desired characteristics of whatever goods they are in charge of allocating. This is especially the case for allocating agents who are serving at the behest of principals and who, themselves, are in need of job security in the allocating role. Who would want to become an admissions officer at a nearly bankrupt college or work in a personnel office of a similarly situated local industry? What king wants to find himself in the position of running out of land that can be awarded to his army?

### 6. Degree to Which Goods Are Subject to Devaluation

Some goods retain their value, regardless of how many recipients there are, whereas others are only valuable to the degree that they are perceived as scarce. If every high school graduate can gain admissions to a particular college, then obviously being admitted does not constitute a reward for unusual performance. Scarce jobs are not only likely to be accompanied by high salaries, but those who earn them in open competition also gain honor or prestige. The essential feature of the dimension under discussion here is whether or not the value of the goods awarded to successful competitors is a decreasing function of the number of awards being made, relative of course, to the size of the competitive pool.

Allocators can sometimes resolve dilemmas by merely making more awards. Teachers, for example, can increase the proportion of A grades, while simultaneously reducing the numbers of failing students. In the extreme, all students may simply be awarded a "pass" grade, with no distinctions among awardees then being necessary. This of course means that the allocator is making no decisions at all, which may free him or her from facing the consequences of unpopular decisions. Everyone "wins," though at the cost of devaluing the goods being offered. So-called grade inflation is the result, and in the extreme case it also means that those who later attempt to make judgments distinguishing among apparently equal candidates cannot possibly rely on the allocation decisions made at previous stages. The degree received becomes meaningless, provided that those who assess its value are not being deceived by what has occurred. If such allocation nondecisions are in reality taking place, it therefore becomes tempting to cover up or disguise the nature of grading practices. All students are receiving a "quality education," and each is being evaluated in accord with his or her own unique characteristics or, perhaps, rate of "progress." All of the students concerned are deemed worthy of graduation, regardless of their actual performances.

If the allocating agents are given numerical quotas to fill, they will of course not have the opportunity to devalue the goods they allocate, at least in the short run. If it becomes apparent, however, that their procedures result in decisions that are highly arbitrary or that they are selecting among candidates on an almost random basis, the value of such goods may also be deflated, not because there are too many winners but because those who do win are perceived as being no more deserving than are the losers.

Thus it is possible for allocated goods to be devalued both because they are awarded to too high a proportion of candidates and because they are inappropriately awarded. Needless to say, the latter reason will often involve varying perspectives on the quality of the allocation process, with winners perceiving that such procedures have been rigorous and fair and with losers believing precisely the opposite. Of course if the numbers of winners and losers can be kept secret, it may in principle remain possible to maintain the value of the allocated goods even though the proportion of winners is actually rather large.

### 7. Degree to Which Recipients Share Future Power With Allocators

In many instances allocators' and recipients' paths will never cross again. College admissions officers go about next year's selection process without ever meeting this year's entering freshmen. Those who make job hiring decisions may have nothing to do with subsequent job assessments or promotions. Those who lend home mortgages to recipients are unlikely to see them again. Yet kings must deal with the nobility to whom they have awarded large estates, recognizing that these very same recipients may later turn against them. A faculty that makes the effective hiring decisions regarding new members will have to live with their new associates on a day-to-day basis, expecting that some of them may later rise to positions that are superior to their own. The same applies to those who select from among junior executives to fill senior positions in the company.

Whenever allocators expect to have ongoing relationships with recipients, and possibly some of the losing candidates as well, additional considerations are likely to enter the picture. Indeed, allocators may have vested interests in favoring weaker candidates, or at least those who appear to be highly tractable or potentially loyal to themselves. They may even anticipate that some candidates will be willing, in effect, to pay kickbacks in return for the favor they have received in being selected.

Actual role reversals may occur through which former allocators may find themselves the subjects of decisions being made by some of the earlier contestants. Needless to say, allocators under such circumstances may be expected to pay much closer attention to their decision processes, and to obtain more accurate information about each candidate, than in those situations where both recipients and losers will remain in weak power positions relative to those of the allocators. Also, the more vulnerable allocators are, as agents of their principals, the greater their potential concern that certain of the candidates will later be placed in positions where they can influence such principals.

### 8. Whether Goods Are Positively or Negatively Valued

We will most often be dealing with situations in which the goods being allocated are positively valued: jobs, promotions, salary increases, college admissions, mortgage loans, and the like. There will be other situations, however, where allocators are required to make decisions that impact negatively on selected candidates. Judges and juries decide on a defendant's guilt or innocence and, where the verdict is guilty, upon the length and type of sentence. Companies find it necessary to fire or lay off employees. Faculty sometimes even fail their students, and parents may decide which of their children deserve punishment for a given transgression. Whereas such negative allocations may seem to be the exact opposites of those in which positively valued goods are awarded, we must be alert to the possibility that there may be other important differences between the two kinds of situations.

Often, potential candidates for punitive allocation decisions may be legally protected to such a degree that the costs of making such decisions may be prohibitive. It may be very difficult to fire certain classes of employees once they have been hired. If so, getting rid of them may better be accomplished by passing them off to unsuspecting parties, sometimes even in the guise of a promotion. The laws may be such that certain classes of persons are better protected than are others. Affirmative action policies, for example, may make it much easier to fire a white male employee than either a minority or female. Oppositely, those who are in dominant categories, here white males, may find themselves almost immune from negative decisions, either because allocating agents are biased in their favor or because their allies are sufficiently powerful to prevent such actions. Thus the dynamics of making negative allocation decisions may be somewhat different from those where positive goods are being awarded.

In many kinds of negative allocation situations competitors are likely to be in mutual contact with one another and therefore to be organized to protect against what they consider to be the abrogation of their rights or entitlements. Thus there may be union agreements with management concerning seniority rights or procedures that must be followed in the case of layoffs. Faculty are similarly protected by tenure policies that can be violated only at considerable cost to administrators. Farmers may organize against banks that attempt to foreclose on their mortgages. And, as noted, lawsuits may be anticipated in those instances where actions taken appear to be arbitrary or discriminatory against protected categories.

In other situations allocators or their principals may have made considerable investments in those to whom they may later need to apply negative sanctions. In many instances it will be costly to fire or even temporarily lay off certain workers, only to have to train their replacements a short time later. Organizations that gain the reputation of being unreliable, in the sense of having to undo previous commitments to employees, are also apt to find it difficult to attract highly qualified applicants in the future. Also, of course, in some instances there may be personal commitments to the individuals concerned, thereby adding psychic costs in those instances in which punitive actions must be taken.

Anticipating such difficulties, allocators may take certain protective steps during the initial selection stage. They may be especially careful to weed out high risk candidates or those believed to be troublemakers. Often, this will entail selection procedures that tend to favor the status quo and that penalize minorities or others who, once selected, may be in a position to solicit third-party assistance in their favor. Why hire minorities or women if, should they prove unsatisfactory, it will be nearly impossible to let them go without a risk of court action? For many of the same reasons, allocators may institute special trial or probationary periods during which it is clearly understood that candidates may be let go without the necessity of undergoing elaborate procedural safeguards that would add considerably to the costs and risks of taking such negative actions. Similarly, contracts offered to those who have been selected are likely to contain highly specific escape clauses that have the effect of permitting negative allocation decisions under specified conditions such as financial emergencies.

### 9. Degree of Secrecy for Allocation Decisions

Some allocation processes will be open to the public for inspection, as for example when professional football or basketball players are selected in annual drafts or when candidates for promotion are selected from among a pool of well-informed coworkers. Other processes are subject to explicit regulations that, for example, require the taking of standardized examinations. Many others, however, will involve extremely privatized deliberations in which candidates may not even be aware that they are being considered or at least have no idea who their competitors may be. Election to scholarly honorary societies such as the National Academy of Sciences involves a high degree of secrecy. Except under very unusual situations in which confidentiality has been violated, scholars simply learn that they have been selected for membership. It is not until subsequent selections take place that they have any knowledge as to the procedures that have been followed or what kinds of persons play the major allocation roles.

Obviously, whenever a high degree of secrecy can be maintained, the candidates themselves will have little or no power in affecting outcomes. There remains the possibility of insider collusion, however, through which certain members of the allocating group may either bargain with other allocators on behalf of their favorite candidates or secretly leak information to outsiders with the hope of applying indirect pressure. In general we would expect that the larger the number of actual allocating agents there are, and the greater their diversity, the more difficult it will be to maintain highly secretive policies. Therefore it may become critical for allocators to develop a normative climate that simultaneously provides mechanisms for airing internal disputes but that also sanctions those who may be tempted to "go public" by taking their grievances to higher authorities. For this reason we often find that even where meetings of elected or appointed officials are open to the public, allowances are made for executive sessions during which personnel matters are discussed.

### 10. Monopoly Control of Goods and Competition Among Allocators

This dimension is especially relevant whenever candidates might be tempted to apply to multiple allocating organizations (e.g., business firms, colleges, or mortgage lenders), then being in a position to select among those that have made them awards. Often, allocating parties such as colleges can be ranked according to prestige or other desirable criteria, producing a situation that we shall later discuss under the notion of hierarchical pools.

The essential feature of competitive situations among allocators is that allocators cannot be assured that those whom they select will also elect to accept their offers. This of course gives additional bargaining power to some of the competitors. In general, those allocators that find themselves at or near the top of the prestige hierarchy can count on a higher proportion of acceptances than can those near the bottom. They may therefore be more free to select according to whatever criteria they prefer, whereas those in less fortunate positions may need to use gaming criteria to select among alternative strategies. Some, for example, may ignore the top candidates altogether, assuming that they would never accept any offers they might make. Others may simply assume, perhaps incorrectly, that the very best candidates have not elected to apply to them in the first place. If so, their actual competitors may not include any of the really top-ranked organizations. Under circumstances such as these it may be wise for them to collect as much information as possible, as for example the names of other organizations to which the candidates are applying, so that they may improve their selection strategies.

## HONORARY SOCIETIES, SOCIAL ORGANIZATIONS, AND AWARDS

Certain kinds of valued goods do not fit in neatly with any of the above dimensions but nevertheless warrant special mention. In many kinds of settings, individuals are selected for special honors or awards or admitted to high prestige organizations through allocation processes that are rarely subjected to public scrutiny. Sometimes, awardees are not even aware that they are being considered whereas at other times they may have made formal application, as for example for membership in a fraternity or sorority. Allocation decisions in most such instances are only loosely coupled with others, such as those involving job entry or promotions. Yet it is commonly recognized that persons who have been admitted to a prestigious fraternity or civic organization, or who have gained acceptance in an honorary society such as Phi Beta Kappa or the National Academy of Sciences, will have a decided advantage in terms of their work résumés or academic Curriculum Vitae. Those who have been admitted to a prestigious country club or civic organization will also have the advantage of becoming part of a network of influential persons who may later help them with their careers.

Usually in such instances there will be an allocating committee that has been carefully selected so as to emphasize a limited kind of diversity. The committee will be limited in the sense that its membership is likely to consist of high-status and well-informed members of the association concerned, and yet diverse with respect to the composition that is to be represented. In the case of a civic organization, for example, it may consist of persons representing whatever diversity of occupations is desired in the membership. If it is to make an honorary award or to select representatives from different academic fields, then such a committee will be chosen to represent such disciplines. There may indeed be actual quotas for new members from distinct groupings, as is the case with respect to the National Academy of Sciences, or there may be a strong normative system favoring a careful balance of characteristics among those selected. Such a selection committee may have the ultimate say in the selection process, or the entire membership may exercise the right to ratify its slate of candidates and to reject some persons under unusual circumstances. Usually, extreme secrecy is preserved so that outsiders will come to believe that the selection process has been entirely "objective" in nature. Winners are likely to be announced at a public ceremony, thereby emphasizing the prestige of the organization concerned and the honor attached to admission.

There may, however, be attention given by outsiders to the final distribution of winners, and especially to the absence of winners from highly underrepresented categories such as minorities and women. If the organization concerned wishes to retain its standing in the relevant community, it may therefore find it necessary to bend its procedures so that token numbers of underrepresented groups are admitted. Where candidates from such groups also possess what I have elsewhere (Blalock, 1967) referred to as "competitive resources"—meaning that their characteristics are actually such that they would otherwise be highly desirable as members—the initial entry of a few such members may rather rapidly result in a near-equalization of their total representation. If, however, such persons have relatively weak credentials and have been admitted primarily to reduce outside pressures on the organization, we expect them to be admitted in only token numbers. Constant outside surveillance will be needed to build up their representation.

Given that the actual allocation process is likely to remain highly confidential, such surveillance may depend rather heavily on those few minority members who have previously been admitted. From the standpoint of the organization concerned, there may be a considerable strain induced by the dual need to justify its practices to outsiders, while at the same time maintaining the prestige or snob value accruing to its membership. Elite organizations, after all, are supposed to consist of elite members. Otherwise their overall status will suffer. For this reason alone, the allocation process is likely to be shrouded with secrecy and the publicly announced selection criteria glorified. That there might be selection errors can hardly be admitted.

## DISTRIBUTIONAL ALLOCATIONS: THE CASE OF POLITICAL DECISIONS

Whenever the goods or services to be allocated are divisible and repeatedly distributed to a relatively constant set of competitors the situation is somewhat different from those instances where applicant pools involve self-selection mechanisms, where those who expect to lose often drop out of subsequent competitions, and where there are a smaller number of awards being made than there are competitors. Examples of what we shall refer to as *distributional allocation decisions* include the allocation of time or energy to one's own children or a class of students, the allocation of positions and salaries to existing departments within a university, or political allocations distributed among regions of a country or types of communities or neighborhoods. For the sake of specificity, we may confine our remarks to political allocations.

In democratic forms of governments, the allocation procedures conducted by legislative bodies or the executive branches of government are likely to involve extensive bargaining and compromise. Legislative bodies, for example, are typically composed of agents whose responsibility it is to represent and protect the interests of their own local constituents. In effect, the allocating body therefore consists of a kind of committee made up of persons oriented to bargaining on behalf of particular constituents.

As a result, the ultimate allocation package is likely to represent compromises based on the relative power positions of such constituencies, modified by whatever coalitions among them have been able to exert an impact on the ultimate decision package. It may not be so much a consideration of equity that prevails, though this may play some role. The overriding concern among the allocators may be the objective of remaining in office or of being reelected by their constituencies (Downs, 1957). Nevertheless, such a complicated allocation process may possibly result in a rough evening out of the goods and services being provided, if not on each single occasion then perhaps over the longer run. Since power will be unevenly distributed, however, inequities are almost bound to arise.

Another distinctive characteristic of political allocation processes is the fact that the competing recipient and nonrecipient parties will usually remain in place over repeated allocations. This is the case even where recipients are individuals such as social security beneficiaries, veterans, unemployed workers, school children, or most any other category of beneficiaries of such policies. The relative numbers of such recipients may of course alter, thus producing a need for reallocation decisions, but rarely will any given category become so small that it in effect disappears from view.

This fact of an almost constant set of competitors, combined with the necessity of making repeated allocations, means that the allocators concerned will often find it to their collective advantage to think in terms of only incremental changes in policy. Perhaps there may be an allocation formula developed to take care of small changes in the relative sizes of the competing parties, so that per capita allocations remain relatively fixed. Without such formulae or other means of rationalizing incremental changes, the allocators concerned would likely find themselves facing major power struggles over each and every allocation decision. Once army bases have been distributed around the country, for instance, it becomes exceedingly difficult to close one or two without undoing the entire package. Only very minor adjustments are likely to be made.

As may also be true in connection with other kinds of allocation decisions, political reallocations are more easily accomplished in times of overall growth than during periods of decline, since the taking away of a valued good is likely to evoke a stronger reaction than occurs when allocators are in a position to supply increments to all or nearly all parties. Even so, there is apt to be a tendency to allocate both positively and negatively valued goods on a prorated basis, if only to simplify the lives of those who must serve in the allocating role. Thus any preexisting inequities are likely to be perpetuated for considerable periods of time. This is true because, at the time of each specific allocation, the agents concerned are most likely to be placing their own short-term interests and survival ahead of longer term equity considerations.

What is critical is the *source* of the allocating agent's power. Is it electoral votes, a military elite, a landed aristocracy, or multinational corporations? In political situations the allocators, themselves, may be serving as agents for some of the units to which allocated goods are being made. Governments formally headed by leaders whose positions are heavily dependent on the military or huge business enterprises are cases in point. Under such circumstances, it would indeed be surprising if such agents were not strongly biased in favor of their own principals. In order to maintain a smoothly running political system, however, they are also likely to attempt to disguise or cover up both the allocation criteria and processes being employed and also the final distribution of goods to these interested parties. Budgetary secrecy or other manipulative devices are thus likely to be employed to deflate the apparent value of the goods being received by these parties. Ideological arguments, such as the need for national security, are likely to be employed along with such deceptive practices. Those allocating agents who actively challenge such practices are also likely to be severely sanctioned.

As is true in other allocation situations, political allocators must find ways to replenish any resources being distributed. Taxation policies are therefore likely to be closely tied to allocation practices, though sometimes with temporal delays that, as in the present-day United States, may result in substantial budgetary debits or surpluses. If allocators employ a short-term time perspective—as is certainly the case with respect to our own executive and legislative branches of government—problems of resource replenishment may simply be deferred, so that another set of allocating parties may have to wrestle with them at a later point in time. Over the long term, however, replenishment must be accomplished if allocating agents are to retain the loyalty and support of recipient parties. Emperors and kings wishing to repay their soldiers for previous services have typically found it necessary to extract greater and greater surpluses from defeated parties, thereby placing economic strains on the entire system. Such, of course, was the fate of the Roman Empire. Eventually, the goods ran out.

Political allocators are also likely to find themselves actively faced by rivals for their privileged positions, meaning that they must be continually alert and adept at convincing their supporters that they are actually benefiting from their behaviors. As long as there is an increasing supply of goods to be allocated, this task may be relatively simple. Under conditions of resource depletion, however, allocators may find it increasingly necessary to provide disproportionate amounts to the most powerful recipients merely to maintain the status quo for these parties. If so, of course, they run the risk of severely alienating the losing parties, who may form a coalition favoring their replacement. This means that the allocators concerned will have an additional incentive for attempting to assure that a continuing flow of resources comes under their own control. Where the total resource supply is in fact diminishing, this in turn is likely to mean an increasingly repressive regime.

## CAUSAL MODEL I:
## EFFECTS OF PROPERTIES OF ALLOCATED GOODS

Our discussion has thus far been discursive and unsystematic. Given the tentative nature of the entire discussion of allocation processes it may seem premature to attempt to develop causal models of the several processes discussed in this and the remaining chapters. Yet we have implied that such processes are indeed complex, and we have already introduced a number of variables in discussing the several properties of goods to be allocated, along with some of their implications. At this point it is therefore advisable first to list such variables explicitly and then to suggest, via a complex causal diagram, how they are expected to be causally interrelated. We shall do the same at the end of each of the remaining substantive chapters.

The more common approach used in the sociological literature is to state expected direct linkages in propositional form, usually as bivariate hypotheses of the form "the greater the $X$, the greater (or lower) the $Y$." Sometimes causal direction is implied in terms of the sequencing of the two variables, with the independent or causal variable $X$ preceding the dependent variable $Y$. Often, however, the direction of causation is left ambiguous or, perhaps, the implication may be that there is reciprocal causation or feedback between the two variables. Some authors may deliberately beg the issue of causal ordering by merely implying covariation between $X$ and $Y$, but such a practice is not only ambiguous in the many instances where causal influences are really being implied, but it will also emaciate the deductive power of the theory as soon as one attempts to specify indirect linkages (Blalock, 1969; Costner and Leik, 1965). For example if one tries to move from the dual propositions "the greater the $X$, the greater the $Y$," and "the greater the $Y$, the greater the $Z$," it does not necessarily follow that "the greater the $X$, the greater the $Z$." This can be seen if one allows for the possibility that both $X$ and $Z$ positively affect $Y$. If the direction of causation in the second proposition is thus reversed to read, "the greater the $Z$, the greater the $Y$," one immediately sees that there is no implied correlation between the two causal factors $X$ and $Z$. Therefore in tracing out the linkages among variables that are not directly interrelated, one needs to make a series of explicit assumptions regarding the direction of the causal flow.

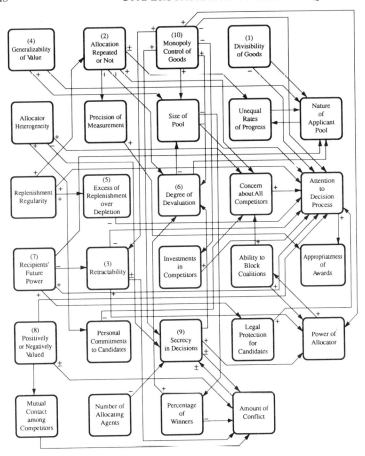

**Figure 2.1.** Model I: Effects of Properties of Allocated Goods

Furthermore, whenever the number of variables becomes large, the number of possible bivariate pairs becomes unmanageable in propositional format. All of the models in subsequent chapters contain more than 30 variables. With 30 variables, there will be (30)(29)/2 = 435 pairings, far too many for readers to be able to follow the argument. One will very quickly lose sight of the forest because of the trees. A causal diagram, even though seemingly complex, is far more compact. If there is assumed to be a "direct" causal connection between any pair of variables, this can be indicated by an arrow, with perhaps a sign attached to indicate whether the impact is assumed to be positive or negative.[1] In the case of simple chains, as for example $X \rightarrow Y \rightarrow Z$, the sign of the linkage between the two end variables can then be determined by noting whether or not the product of the two signs is positive or negative. In more complex setups in which there may be several variables intervening between $X$ and $Z$, one must also allow for the possibility that the sign of their total association may be indeterminate, unless all of the intervening variables operate in the same direction.

For the most part, the models we shall present are nearly recursive in format. In a totally recursive causal model, it is possible to order the variables causally such that there is no feedback (or causal loop) from any "dependent" variable to one of its causes. This makes it possible to order the variables $X_i$ such that there are no effects from any variable with a higher numbered subscript to one with a lower number, and this in turn permits the analyst to proceed, equation by equation, to estimate (by ordinary least squares) each of the coefficients in an equation for a particular dependent variable.

Whenever there is reciprocal causation, either between a pair of variables or perhaps within a larger subset of the total model, the situation becomes more complicated, and it is no longer legitimate to break the model apart, equation by equation. In the model of Figure 2.1, as well as subsequent models to be presented in the remaining chapters, there are a relatively small number of such reciprocally related pairs or short causal loops, but for the most part the reader will note that the variables are causally ordered. This is what we mean by saying that the model is nearly recursive. In instances where reciprocal causation is involved, it is sometimes possible to specify definite lag periods. In other instances, however, the causal flows may either be nearly instantaneous or continuous, so that in estimating the relative magnitudes of the two influences it will be necessary to make use of simultaneous-equa-

tion techniques of the sort commonly employed in the econometrics literature.[2]

In more complex types of simultaneous-equation systems, there
may be an entire set of "endogenous" variables that mutually affect
one another, as well as another set of "exogenous" or predetermined variables assumed to be unaffected by any of the endogenous variables. It is the set of interrelationships among the
endogenous variables that the theorist is attempting to explain in
terms of some combination of the other endogenous variables and
the exogenous factors that are taken as givens by the theorist. The
simple distinction between independent, intervening (or mediat-
ing), and dependent variables thus breaks down, as one allows for
the possibility that some of the supposedly dependent variables
affect the others, and that there may be reciprocal causation among
intervening variables. In the case of the models provided in the
present work, however, we shall make a rough grouping of our
variables into one of three categories: (1) exogenous or (nearly)
independent, (2) intervening, and (3) (nearly) dependent.

It is sometimes assumed that causal modeling can handle only
linear and additive relationships, but this is not the case. For
example, if one postulates nonlinear linkages of the sort that often
occur when a subjective variable $Y$ (say, a utility for money) is
linked to an objective one $X$ (say, income in dollars), one may use
a power function to represent a possible satiation effect (Hamblin,
1971). Also, whenever two or more conditions are expected to be
necessary for a phenomenon to occur, or whenever any one of
several factors will be sufficient, some sort of multiplicative equation may be more appropriate than an additive one (Blalock, 1969).
For the most part, however, our own formulations will assume
linear and additive equation formats unless otherwise specified.
The important point to note is that the causal modeling approach
is far more flexible and capable of handling numerous kinds of
complications than critics often imply. We shall not consider measurement complications, but these too can be built into one's
analysis provided one is willing to postulate an explicit "auxiliary"

measurement theory to account for possible sources of measurement bias (Blalock, 1982; Costner, 1969; Herting, 1985).

## The Exogenous Variables

The model of Figure 2.1 contains 10 exogenous variables that we are presuming to be taken as givens in our micro-level process model. Indeed most, though not all, of the properties of allocated goods under discussion in the present chapter will be assumed exogenous. A macro-oriented theory, or perhaps another micro model involving different kinds of processes, might for example examine the question of why only certain kinds of jobs are being allocated, who has decided how jobs should be carved up, how many are available under what conditions, and so forth. Such a theory would, itself, involve an additional set of exogenous factors that needed to be treated as unexplained or as givens. In this sense, no (testable) theory can ever be considered "complete."

In the econometrics literature, the defining characteristic of an exogenous variable is that it cannot be affected by any of the mutually endogenous variables (Fisher, 1966). If, for example, there were a feedback loop to one or more of the supposedly exogenous variables, such variables, being partially dependent, would have to be considered to belong among the mutually endogenous set. Exogenous variables may, however, be intercorrelated. In a few instances, we will treat certain variables as "nearly exogenous," meaning that they may be partly determined by others among the set of exogenous factors. With these provisos in mind, we move to a listing of the exogenous variables in the model. Titles given in parentheses refer to the labels actually used in the boxes of Figure 2.1.

(1) The generalizability of the values of goods being allocated (Generalizability of Value)

(2) Whether or not the allocation process is repeated (Allocation Repeated or Not)

(3) Does the allocator have monopoly control over the goods being allocated? (Monopoly Control of Goods)

(4) The ease with which goods can be divided by allocator (Divisibility of Goods)

(5) The heterogeneity of allocating agents (Allocator Heterogeneity)

(6) The regularity of replenishment of goods (Replenishment Regularity)

(7) The future power of recipients, vis-à-vis allocators (Recipients' Future Power)

(8) Whether goods are positively or negatively valued by competitors (Positively or Negatively Valued)

(9) The extent of mutual contact among competitors (Mutual Contact Among Competitors)

(10) The number of allocating agents participating in decision (Number of Allocating Agents)

## The Intervening Variables

As noted, some of the variables designated as intervening in Figure 2.1 are reciprocally interrelated causally, so that strictly speaking the model is not totally recursive. As a general rule, intervening variables suggest the causal mechanisms through which exogenous factors impact on the ultimate dependent variables. Needless to say, then, whenever one is attempting to analyze any specific type of allocation process, say the selection among candidates for a set of jobs or offices, it may be possible to treat many of these intervening variables as basically constant. Still others, however, will undoubtedly need to be introduced. The notion of "intervening variable," as well as that of "direct effects" should therefore be considered as relative to the set of variables one has actually included in the model. If in a given model $X \rightarrow Y \rightarrow Z$, the omission of $Y$ from the model would imply that the linkage between $X$ and $Z$ should now be considered as "direct" in the simplified or reduced model. With this in mind, we introduce the following 11 intervening variables.

(1) The degree to which candidates' qualifications can be accurately measured (Precision of Measurement)

(2) The size of the pool of actual applicants (Size of Pool)

(3) The degree to which the rate of replenishment of goods exceeds the depletion rate (Excess of Replenishment Over Depletion)

(4) The degree to which the value of the goods to candidates decreases with the number or percentage of awards (Degree of Devaluation)

(5) The ease with which goods can be retracted from recipients (Retractability)

(6) The extent to which allocators have made prior investments in applicants or competitors (Investments in Competitors)

(7) The ability of allocators to block coalitions among competitors (Ability to Block Coalitions)

(8) The degree to which allocators have made personal commitments to some or all candidates (Personal Commitments to Candidates)

(9) The degree to which allocators can keep deliberative processes and criteria secret from candidates (Secrecy in Decisions)

(10) The legal or other protection provided to losing candidates or from negative decisions (Legal Protection for Candidates)

(11) The percentage of winners among candidates (Percentage of Winners)

## *The Dependent Variables*

Our seven "dependent" variables are also not strictly speaking truly dependent since, in several instances, there are either feedbacks to intervening variables or causal relations postulated among the dependent variables themselves. Therefore they should be considered as "primarily dependent" in that they appear either close to the end or at the very end of causal chains. The list is as follows.

(1) The degree to which there is inequality in the rates of candidates' progress through a sequence of stages, such as job levels (Unequal Rates of Progress)

(2) The degree to which allocators are nearly equally concerned about all competitors (Concern About All Competitors)

(3) The nature of the applicant pool, with dimensions unspecified (Nature of Applicant Pool)

(4) The degree to which allocators pay careful attention to the decision process (Attention to Decision Process)

(5) The degree to which awards or outcomes are deemed appropriate by competitors (Appropriateness of Awards)

(6) The extent to which allocators have power to use discretion in the decision process (Power of Allocator)

(7) The extent or amount of conflict over the resultant decision (Amount of Conflict)


*Discussion of the Model:*
*Effects of the Exogenous Variables*


Our prior discussion of 10 properties of goods being allocated will serve to motivate the following very brief argument specifying the presumed causal linkages among the 28 variables of the model of Figure 2.1. Since not all of these linkages were discussed earlier, however, we shall supplement the earlier discursive account with a few additional comments. For reference, each of the 10 properties already listed is designated by the corresponding number placed at the top center of the appropriate box.

Exogenous variables are located across the top of the figure and down the left-hand column and a short distance along the bottom row. Intervening variables are placed toward the center of the figure, with dependent variables either toward the bottom or at the extreme right side. This means that the majority of arrows are directed from left to right and from top to bottom. Insofar as possible, a similar layout will be used in each of the diagrams in succeeding chapters. We proceed by discussing the effects of the exogenous variables in the order in which they have been listed.

Generalizability of Value is assumed to directly and positively affect the size of the applicant pool, under the assumption that the greater the generalizability of the good, as for example a high-paying and attractive occupation, the larger the number of persons who will be induced to apply for it. Generalizability is assumed to affect the nature of the applicant pool, as well, as for example the average qualifications of applicants and perhaps even their homogeneity. Since the nature of a pool will be multidimensional and will vary according to the kind of position or good being allocated, we cannot assign either a positive or negative sign to the arrow connecting these two variables.

Whether or not the allocation process occurs repeatedly is assumed to affect four variables and to be affected, in turn, by Replenishment Regularity. Repeating an allocation process is assumed, usually, to improve the Precision of Measurement both by increasing the allocator's motivation to improve efficiency (not in the model) and through trial and error. Under many circumstances, which we have not specified, repeated allocations may also increase the extent to which the value of the good is devalued. A prize that is rarely awarded or a position that becomes available only once during a person's career will presumably be more highly valued than one that is offered annually or even more frequently.

When allocations occur repeatedly, and thus when allocators are more likely to be concerned that losing contestants remain in the pool for subsequent contests, the allocator's concern about all competitors is assumed to be increased. But by the same token, when allocations occur regularly, this will tend to result in modifications in rates of progress for different contestants. If allocators consciously favor losers in previous contests, this may reduce rates of inequality. If, however, repeated contests permit superior candidates to move more swiftly up a hierarchical ladder, inequality may be increased. Therefore, we are unable to specify the sign of this particular causal link and have indicated this fact by placing the "±" symbol beside the arrow leading to Unequal Rates of Progress.

Property (10), Monopoly Control of Goods, is postulated to affect seven of the remaining variables directly and is thus a very important exogenous factor in the overall model. Size of Pool is assumed to be positively affected in that, with monopoly control, candidates will have no additional competing pools to enter. Monopoly will also increase the allocator's power but negatively affect the allocator's attentiveness to the decision process because he or she will not need to worry about any competitors capable of taking advantage of the allocator's mistakes. Monopoly control should also make it less necessary for an allocator to invest heavily in members of its candidate pool and should increase the degree to which allocation decisions can be kept secret. Presumably, also, monopoly control should make it easier for allocators to retract goods previously awarded, since recipients will have no place else to turn. Finally, monopoly control is expected to increase Degree of Devaluation because of the lack of competition with other allocators. The assumption, here, is that a large number of competing allocators drives up the value of the award.

Divisibility of Goods, property (1), is assumed to affect directly only the nature of the applicant pool and the allocator's attentiveness to the decision process. In the case of applicant pool composition, some candidates may prefer to enter contests in which there are very few winners and where the prizes at stake are considerable. Others may prefer competitions where there are a large number of graded awards. With respect to allocator attentiveness, if the allocator can divide up the pie almost arbitrarily it makes it possible to offer compensations to near-winners. Perhaps it will also make less of a difference which competitors are the winners and which the losers. In particular, by making nearly equal allocations to all competitors, allocators can relieve themselves of the responsibility for making difficult decisions or having to justify arbitrary distinctions between winners and losers.

Allocator Heterogeneity is taken as a direct cause of three variables. By broadening the set of allocators, let us say into a selection committee, we may generally expect to increase the degree to which there is concern about nearly all of the competitors, rather than some distinct subset among them. At the same time, however, it becomes more difficult to hide from view the nature of the decision process, so that Secrecy in Decisions is reduced. Finally, we expect an increase in the degree to which there is a personal commitment to individual candidates, and especially so to the extent that allocators have been selected to represent the interests of specific sets of competitors, such as women or racial and ethnic minorities.

As already noted, Replenishment Regularity is expected to affect positively the extent to which there is an excess of replenishment over the depletion of goods to be allocated. Although not included in the diagram, regularity of replenishment also reduces the uncertainty under which allocators must operate in settings where the number and nature of future goods or positions impacts on allocators' current decision processes. Replenishment Regularity is also expected to affect positively allocators' attentiveness to the decision process. If there is every expectation that future goods or positions will be available on a regular basis it becomes rational to devote increased energy to developing more effective evaluation tools.

Recipients' Future Power, property (7), is taken as a cause of four variables. There should be a negative effect on Retractability. If recipients gain power as a result of having been given important positions, land, or other relatively permanent positions, it may be difficult for allocators to take back such goods once they have been awarded, thereby helping to sustain the power of such recipients. Needless to say, the expected future power of recipients is expected to have a direct, positive impact on allocators' attention to decision processes, one of the ultimate dependent variables in the model. In particular, allocators can be expected to attempt to select tractable and loyal candidates, in so far as they are able to do so.

Recipients' Future Power is also expected to have a somewhat weaker and perhaps variable effect on Legal Protection for Candidates insofar as powerful groups are in a position to unionize or otherwise organize collectively to help regulate the practices of allocators. Finally their future power may also directly affect the nature of the applicant pool, presumably through self-selection mechanisms. Those who highly value job security or the obtaining of powerful positions would be expected to be overrepresented in the applicant pool.

Property (8), whether or not the goods or positions being allocated are positively or negatively evaluated, is assumed to affect two variables directly, one of which is the amount of conflict expected as a result of the allocation decision. Here it is difficult to predict, in general, the sign of the relationship, and so a ± sign has been inserted into the diagram. Presumably, goods or positions to which very high positive or negative values have been attached will tend to generate higher levels of conflict than those that are valued to a lesser degree in either direction.

Positively or Negatively Valued is also expected to impact on allocators' attentiveness to the decision process, with this effect being increased to the degree that there is mutual contact among competitors. As noted in our earlier discussion, there may be a spurious association between such mutual contact and whether or not goods are positively evaluated, and this possibility is indicated by the double-headed arrow connecting these two exogenous variables. Organized competitors such as company employees may attempt to protect themselves against negative allocations, such as job loss, by instituting a set of rules and regulations specifying criteria to be used by relevant allocators. This possibility has not been included in the diagram, however. Apart from this, Mutual Contact Among Competitors is assumed to affect only Amount of Conflict, through the mechanism of making competitors more aware of their collective stake in the nature of the allocative process. Whether this actually increases or decreases the amount of conflict is left unspecified in the model.

Finally, the number of distinct allocating agents is assumed to have a negative impact on Secrecy in Decisions. Actually, although not included in the model, it is perhaps more reasonable to assume that it is the heterogeneity of the set of allocators, rather than their numbers per se, that has a negative impact on secrecy.

This completes our discussion of the direct impacts of the 10 exogenous variables. We next turn to a consideration of the effects of the intervening variables, both on each other and on our set of ultimate dependent variables.

*Discussion of the Model:*
*Effects of the Intervening Variables*

Precision of Measurement serves as an intervening variable between Allocation Repeated or Not and Appropriateness of Awards, the idea being that repeated allocations should enable allocators to improve their measuring instruments, leading in turn to judgments that the awarding process has led to appropriate decisions.

As noted, Size of Pool is affected by three variables. In turn, it is expected to have a negative impact on the allocator's attentiveness to the decision process. A very large pool, in particular, means that allocators will need to use shortcut devices to weed out the vast majority of candidates. It will obviously also mean a lower percentage of winners, with this in turn increasing the potential for conflict.

The Excess of Replenishment Over Depletion, property (5), is expected to have a negative though probably a rather weak impact on attentiveness to the decision process, under the assumption that allocators will be less concerned about whom they select if they believe that subsequent competitions can help correct for any mistakes they may make. Where new positions are expected to be scarce, they must be more selective. In order to keep the figure as simple as possible we have not inserted certain subjective variables, such as allocator expectations, into the model as additional intervening variables.

Degree of Devaluation, property (6), is affected by four variables, as already noted. In turn, it is expected to have a negative impact on Size of Pool since the positions or goods being offered will become less and less attractive to potential applicants. It is also predicted to impact on the nature of the pool, presumably by lowering the qualifications of those who do elect to enter the pool.

Property (3), Retractability, is postulated to affect three variables. It should have a negative impact on allocators' attentiveness to the decision process since, if positions can later be reassigned, it becomes less critical to make the correct decision in the first place. Retractability should, however, have a positive impact on the allocators' power by giving them the leverage to withdraw positions or goods that have already been awarded, contingent on satisfactory performance by recipients. Finally, Retractability is predicted to affect Amount of Conflict, though with an indeterminate sign. On the one hand, if allocators can retract awards this may result in more compliant beneficiaries. On the other hand, this may also result in increased misunderstandings, mistrust, and rivalries between recipients and their potential replacements.

Investments in Competitors is assumed to affect the single variable Attention to Decision Process, the presumption being that allocators will make careful selections to the degree that they wish to protect their investments. Here we may also anticipate a partly spurious relationship between these two variables. Where it is critical to locate the best possible persons, allocators may be expected *both* to invest in their training and to be more careful in the ultimate selection of winners.

Ability to Block Coalitions is listed as an intervening variable because it is assumed to be reciprocally linked to Power of Allocator. Powerful allocators will in general be in a position to utilize some of their power to block such coalitions, but such blocking actions will in turn reduce the power of potential coalition members and thereby enhance the power of allocators. Allocators' ability to block such coalitions is also expected to have a positive impact on their Concern About All Competitors. Where coalitions are likely to form, allocators must pay special attention to such more powerful groups of competitors, presumably at the expense of the remainder. Personal Commitments to Candidates is likewise expected to have a negative impact on a concern about all candidates, especially whenever the total number of candidates is large. Presumably, it is difficult for allocators to have strong personal commitments to more than a relatively small absolute number of candidates.

Secrecy in Decisions, property (9), is predicted to be reciprocally related to Amount of Conflict, but with indeterminate signs in both directions of the causal flow. Secrecy may in some instances reduce conflict provided that competitors are not highly organized. In contrast, however, the very fact that deliberations are kept secret may increase levels of distrust (not included in model) and thereby increase the probability of conflict. In the opposite direction, a high level of conflict may either increase or decrease allocators' efforts to maintain secrecy. Powerful allocators may succeed in doing so, but weaker ones may recognize the desirability of openness as a conflict-reduction mechanism. Thus the causal mechanisms linking these two variables are anticipated to be complex and conditioned by other variables, only some of which are included in the model. In general, Secrecy of Decisions is also assumed to enhance the power of allocators. In a very different way, secrecy is predicted to reduce the degree of devaluation of awards to the degree that secrecy reinforces the "mystique" that evaluators' judgments are well grounded. In instances where the total number of awards is relatively large, but where individual recipients believe they are actually more scarce, secrecy may also enhance the value of the award by increasing its perceived scarcity value.

Legal Protection for Candidates is expected to affect a single dependent variable, namely Attention to Decision Process. Where allocators are threatened by punitive legal actions, they will not only be more careful in making awards but can be expected to document more completely the nature of the decision process itself. As noted in our earlier discussion, if only some of the candidates are legally protected, this may lead to differential attentiveness as well as biased selection procedures (not included in model.)

Finally, the Percentage of Winners is predicted to have a negative impact on Amount of Conflict, if only that a large percentage of (satisfied) winners implies a lower percentage of (disgruntled) losers. Percentage of Winners is expected to have a positive impact on Degree of Devaluation for rather obvious reasons. Too great a

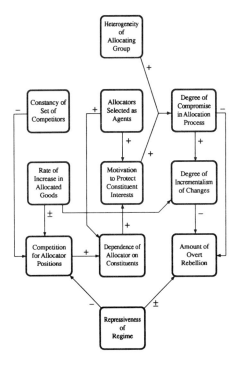

**Figure 2.2.** Model II: Political Allocations

percentage means that the prestige of winning will be reduced, and it may also imply the necessity of splitting the total pie into a large number of pieces.

When we turn to our set of dependent variables we note that most of the causal connections with these variables have already been discussed. It remains to cover the small number of instances where causal connections are postulated among the dependent variables themselves.

Unequal Rates of Progress is assumed to be reciprocally related to the Nature of the Applicant Pool. As we shall later note, there are many situations in which individuals pass through a sequence of pools, with successful candidates from one pool being eligible to enter the next. Where progress through the competitive system has been uneven, this will of course affect the composition of subsequent pools. In the reverse direction, the composition of any given pool—and in particular its heterogeneity—is likely to have an impact on differential rates of progress. Individuals with weaker credentials will be slowed down or stopped as they attempt to move to the next pool. Only some college graduates will be accepted into professional schools.

Concern About All Competitors is primarily dependent in our causal model but is also assumed to affect Attention to Decision Process. Presumably, a high level of concern for all candidates will translate into an increased desire to assure "procedural justice" in the selection process (not included in model), which will in turn lead to greater attentiveness to this process on the part of allocators. Attention to Decision Process, which the reader will note to be one of our most important dependent variables, is expected to have a positive impact on judgments to the effect that awards have been appropriately made.

Finally, as already noted, Power of Allocator is assumed to be reciprocally related to Ability to Block Coalitions, and Amount of Conflict is postulated to be reciprocally related to Secrecy in Decisions.

This completes our necessarily brief discussion of the first of our complex models. Before turning to another set of factors impacting on the allocation decision process, which will occupy our attention in the next chapter, we conclude the present chapter by providing a much simpler supplementary model dealing with the special case of political allocations, which we discussed earlier as an example of what we referred to as distributional allocations.

## CAUSAL MODEL II: POLITICAL ALLOCATIONS

Our brief discussion of distributional allocation systems in which there are repeated allocations to a relatively fixed number of recipients was illustrated with the example of political allocations, say to states, counties or local communities. The model of

Figure 2.2 contains a set of 11 variables rather simply connected in a totally recursive setup. There are 5 exogenous variables, 5 intervening variables, and a single ultimate dependent variable, Amount of Overt Rebellion. Presumably, there will be a set of additional subjective variables, such as satisfaction or dissatisfaction with one's share of the goods being allocated, as well as attempts to remedy the situation short of overt rebellion. This may suggest feedback mechanisms to some of the supposedly exogenous variables, but complications such as these are not taken into consideration in this very simple model.

One of the exogenous factors, the Constancy of Set of Competitors, may not vary across the situations actually being considered, but we must allow for the possibility that certain of the competitors may leave the scene, whereas others may be added. If so, the model postulates that any changes in the operative set will tend to increase the degree of Competition for Allocator Positions.

A second exogenous factor is the Rate of Increase in Allocated Goods. If there is a decrease, instead, this may be represented as a negative change in the rate of increase. The rate of change, in either direction, is assumed to affect the extent to which allocators use an incrementalist strategy in making awards, as represented by the variable labeled Degree of Incrementalness of Changes. The rate of increase (or decrease) in goods to be allocated is also assumed to affect Competition for Allocator Positions. The argument is that whenever substantial changes are anticipated with respect to what or how much is to be allocated, this should intensify competition among constituents to make sure that their own representatives are members of the effective allocating group. We have indicated an indeterminate sign (±) on the arrow connecting these variables to indicate that *either* increases or decreases in the goods to be allocated should tend to increase competition.

Repressiveness of the Regime is inserted into the model to allow for the possibility that nondemocratic or autocratic powerful regimes may be in a position to dampen competition for allocator positions or even to usurp the allocator roles altogether. Repressiveness is also assumed to affect the ultimate dependent variable,

Amount of Overt Rebellion, though with an indeterminate sign. It is sometimes hypothesized that rebellion is most likely in instances where a regime is moderately repressive (Blalock, 1989b; Gurr, 1970; Hibbs, 1973). A regime having an initially very low level of repressiveness is expected to experience an increase in rebelliousness with an increase in repressiveness. In contrast, one that is toward the high end of the repressiveness continuum may actually inhibit rebellions by moving to a position of extreme repression.

The box labeled "Allocators Selected as Agents" refers to the degree to which allocators have been deliberately selected to represent a certain subset of constituents, rather than the population as a whole. This variable is assumed to affect positively Dependence of Allocator on Constituents, the argument being that allocators selected to represent a group of constituents will be more beholden to them and therefore more likely to be motivated to protect their interests, perhaps at the expense of those of the remaining competitors. The difference between "at large" and district or other territorial-based election systems is a case in point.

The final exogenous variable, Heterogeneity of Allocating Group, is assumed to interact, multiplicatively, with the intervening variable Motivation to Protect Constituent Interests in their joint effects on the degree to which compromises will be necessary in the allocation process. This multiplicative, rather than additive, effect is represented in the diagram by arrows joining before they reach the Degree of Compromise box. The idea, here, is that the regression coefficient linking heterogeneity and compromise will, itself, increase the motivation to protect constituent interests. Correspondingly, the coefficient linking motivation to compromise will be an increasing function of heterogeneity. High degrees of heterogeneity and motivation will produce greater effects than in the case of an additive joint effect. By the same token, however, whenever the level of either variable is near zero, the effect of the other will be minimal.

Turning next to the effects of the remaining intervening variables, Competition for Allocator Positions is postulated to have a positive effect on the degree to which allocators are dependent on their respective constituents. The idea is that allocators, say members of Congress, who are seriously challenged by competitors will be subject to greater control by their constituents than those who are in much more safe positions. The Dependence of Allocator on Constituents, in turn, is expected to affect, positively, the motivation to protect such constituents' interests.

Degree of Compromise affects two of the remaining variables. There is assumed to be a positive effect on the degree to which changes are made only incrementally. Compromises, for example, often make it far simpler to increase or decrease the amount of awards on a proportionate basis, rather than seriously examining how the pie has already been sliced. Compromise, however, is expected to have a negative impact on the amount of overt rebellion produced. Finally, the last intervening variable, Degree of Incrementalism, is predicted to have a direct negative impact on the likelihood of rebellion or conflict.

Our summary of the two models provided in the chapter is now completed. In the next chapter we deal with another set of constraining factors as we discuss some of the impacts that other parties have on allocators. The discussions in both this and the following chapter pay only slight attention to subjective variables, however. In particular, allocators as human actors are not depicted as causal agents in their own right. By examining the nature of their diverse objectives in Chapter 4, we shall attempt to correct for this deficiency.

## NOTES

1. The "directness" of a relationship is always relative to the variables that have been included in the model. One can always turn a "direct" relationship into an "indirect" one by inserting an intervening variable between the two variables of concern. Similarly, the removal of an intervening variable may turn an indirect relationship into a direct one (Blalock, 1964).

2. In nonrecursive systems of this sort, there will generally be the further complication of the equation system containing too many unknowns, relative to the

number of pieces of empirical information. This "underidentified" system then becomes mathematically hopeless, meaning that there can be *no* empirical method for estimating the parameters unless further restrictive assumptions are made. See Duncan (1975), Hanushek and Jackson (1977), Johnston (1984), and Namboodiri et al. (1975).

# THREE

# General Factors Influencing Allocation Decisions

Our working assumption is that allocators will in general attempt to allocate as few goods or services as are necessary in order to achieve whatever purposes they have in mind. This presumes that such goods have a scarcity value and that it will ordinarily be to the allocator's advantage to hold back as many of them as feasible in order to retain them for future allocations or as means for influencing or controlling recipients or for motivating non-recipients to participate in future allocation competitions. Yet there will be constraints that operate on all allocators, so that such a tendency to withhold goods will be counterbalanced by a number of other considerations. In our listing of factors that impact on allocation decisions, we shall therefore need to be concerned about such constraints and the variables that affect them.

## CONSTRAINTS ON ALLOCATORS

### 1. Relationships to Principals

In many if not most instances allocating agents will be acting on behalf of principals who may hold power over them, either because the agents are directly under their employ or perhaps because the allocators find themselves under obligation to them. Personnel officers or lending agents do not own the companies or banks on behalf of which they select future employees or make mortgage loans. Teachers who allocate their time to students or who grade their work are responsible to school principals and indirectly to the general public. Politicians who decide how tax dollars are to be distributed are ultimately responsible to the electorate, and so forth.

Principals may differ considerably, however, in terms of the degree to which they specify rigid rules concerning the procedures and criteria to be used by their allocating agents and also the extent to which they closely monitor their decision processes or even the outcomes of these processes. Some allocating agents in effect have a free hand and therefore genuine power in the form of delegated authority. Furthermore, those whom they are evaluating may have very little access to the principals themselves, making it difficult for them to provide feedback concerning such allocators' performances.

One of the basic considerations in this connection is the degree of job security for the allocating agents. Who rewards and punishes them for transgressions, and what parties are in a position to prevent them from employing their own idiosyncratic criteria or making decisions designed to benefit primarily themselves, rather than their principals? Under some circumstances allocating agents may be able to organize to block intrusions on their authority or to inhibit close surveillance of their work. Teachers' unions, for example, may be in a position to insist on strict seniority criteria rather than supervisor evaluations of their performances. Those who apportion their time unfairly among students, show favoritism, or utilize arbitrary or idiosyncratic grading practices may receive exactly the same rewards as those who engage in more evenhanded practices. In effect, they are virtually immune from sanctions by their principals.

In contrast, allocating agents may be placed in weak positions so that they are forced to serve as convenient scapegoats whenever their principals are attacked for unfair practices. They may have been told informally to utilize unofficial screening criteria that favor one group of candidates over others. Minorities and women, for example, may be systematically passed over for promotions or may be discriminated against in the hiring process or perhaps in their applications for bank loans. Yet the allocators' principals may wish to afford themselves the opportunity for deniability in the event that, say, governmental agencies begin to examine their actual practices. If so, it may be simplest to invoke only the officially approved policies and to claim that it is their biased agents who have failed to adhere to these policies.

The absence of close supervision and detailed monitoring will often facilitate the deniability of responsibility on the part of such principals. After the heat has been turned off and a new set of allocating agents has been hired, they may then return to their former unofficial practices. Under such circumstances, the allocating agents themselves may be in a weak power position vis-à-vis both their own principals and any third parties (e.g., governmental agencies) that have not been in a position, themselves, to monitor the interactions between such agents and their principals.

### 2. Relationships to Third Parties

As implied, there will often be third parties involved, sometimes serving as protectors for one or more of the competitor categories but also perhaps having direct interests in the quality or nature of the selection process. In any given instance, allocators may need to estimate the chances that such parties may intervene or question the procedures being used. Such probabilities may depend primarily on the outcome, rather than the decision process itself. Under affirmative action guidelines, for example, those who are making hiring decisions may believe that if they favor women or minorities there will be much less risk of governmental intervention than if the relative frequencies of "protected" categories fall below a certain target figure. Oppositely, they may believe that if they favor white males and hire only token numbers of minority workers they

will receive fewer complaints and perhaps greater future cooperation from those in charge of recipient departments.

One of the critical issues in this respect is the degree to which
disgruntled losing candidates are believed to have direct access to
and influence over powerful third parties. This includes the credibility of such candidates, the extent to which they can provide hard
evidence that they have been targets of discrimination, and the
mechanisms available to third parties for redress. As noted, the
allocating agents may find themselves scapegoated by their own
principals whenever actual policies and unofficial practices are at
variance with those espoused by relevant third parties. They may
therefore be careful to assure that the *outcomes* of their decision
processes meet certain minimal criteria, even where the *procedures*
they have followed may be discriminatory. If so, it will obviously
be to their advantage to withhold as much information as possible
concerning the actual criteria that have been used, as well as the
relative weights that have been attached to them.

Third parties may also form alliances with the allocators, or their
principals, either vis-à-vis all competing candidates or some important segment among them. The aim may be to keep candidates
as tractable as possible so that they do not dare challenge the
decision process. Prior to the Great Depression of the 1930s, the
American government played precisely such a role in protecting
the ability of business enterprises to make almost unimpeded
allocation decisions with respect to the hiring and firing of workers. Anti-union legislation, for example, was instrumental in blocking organized efforts to influence hiring decisions or layoff
practices aimed at reducing effective organization efforts on the
part of employees. Other governmental policies, as for example
those designed to keep unemployment at relatively high levels,
have been used to assure large applicant pools involving unorganized labor markets and a weakened bargaining position of individual competitors. Still other governmental policies have
operated to handicap black candidates by providing them with
inferior educations or by permitting police to break up protest
demonstrations on their behalf.

### 3. Relationships to Competitors in the Allocation Process

Allocators may have nearly identical relationships to all those who are in competition for the goods and services to be allocated. At the one extreme, recipients and nonrecipients alike may have to accept decisions without protest or without any opportunities to influence the allocation process itself, except, of course, by providing evidence of their own individual credentials. For the most part, applicants to colleges and universities simply apply for admission and then await either positive or negative decisions. If the latter, they may merely apply to other schools, eventually being accepted somewhere else. Job applicants may find themselves in similar positions, as may applicants for mortgage loans or food stamps. Such persons, usually unorganized, have virtually no power over the allocating agents, though they may perhaps attempt to ingratiate themselves with them or offer them side payments of one form or another.

In contrast, there may be powerful organizations representing some or all of the competitors. In some instances where there are distinct categories of competitors, such as racial, religious, or ethnic groups, there may be an insistence that members of such groups actually be represented among the allocating agents, as for example members of a decision-making team. Thus blacks or women may be placed on college admissions committees, in effect serving as monitors able to disclose biased procedures to their constituencies. In other instances organizations may be in a position to restrict the allocation criteria used, as for example by insisting that layoffs be in accord with seniority or racial or ethnic quotas. They may also succeed in forcing on the allocator certain automatic criteria, such as fixed increments in annual salaries or regular promotions after a given lapse of time. What this suggests, then, is that there may be power struggles between allocating agents, their principals, and groups representing the interests of competitors.

Some competitors, especially those who have become organized, may distrust allocating agents as being arbitrary and biased or as favoring their own private interests at the expense of equity considerations. Ordinarily, those who find themselves on the losing end of the decision process will have vested interests in distrusting the allocating agents, especially in those instances where their unsuccessful bids would result in threats to their own self-esteem. Rather than accepting the possibility that their own competitive merits were inferior to those of the winners, it would be far more convenient to blame an unfair system or individually biased allocators.

Where allocation decisions become patterned, as for example the disproportionate rejection of minority candidates, the tendency among losers is likely to be that of blaming the system rather than looking more closely into the possibility that their average competitive credentials are inadequate. If blacks do poorly on standardized exams, then these exams must be biased and the allocators who rely on them held accountable for the use of unfair criteria. Perhaps, of course, such blacks may have been poorly trained or less well motivated to do well on the exams. Or the nature of the black and white applicant pools may really be at issue. It could be, for example, that a higher proportion of unqualified blacks than whites have decided to apply. By the same token, however, the applicant pools may have been approximately equally well qualified but racially biased criteria used to the disadvantage of blacks. Given the ambiguities and unknowns involved, we would therefore expect black and white applicants to develop very different working theories as to the nature of the underlying reality that has produced any inequalities in outcomes.

Where competitors are in a position to influence one another prior to entry into the competition itself, some of them may attempt either to place roadblocks in each other's paths or to restrict performance levels so as to equalize the apparent qualifications of the remaining competitors. Thus coworkers may develop and enforce workplace norms so as to sanction overperformers and thereby slow down productivity levels. Students may punish those who "apple-polish" or "brown-nose" their teachers or who otherwise appear too eager to please those in authority. They may also ridicule good performances or those students who insist on conscientiously doing their homework. In sharp contrast to those students who perform well on athletic teams, they may likewise provide very low status to those who display high scholastic aspirations. Ogbu (1978, 1990), for example, notes a tendency for blacks and other "castelike" minorities to define their own peers as being "white" if they adhere too closely to their teachers' expectations. This is in spite of the fact that they and their parents may also give lip service to wanting to perform well and to enter occupations that require college or professional degrees.

Finally, there may be some circumstances under which competitors may later be in a position to turn the tables on the allocating agents, either by becoming allocators themselves or by being able to sanction those allocators from whom they believe they have not received fair treatment. The most obvious case in point is the ability of voters to remove from office those politicians whose policies they do not like. In effect, politicians make allocations or distributions to different categories of recipients and then must anticipate the subsequent decisions of the latter at the time of the next campaign. Where elections are frequent and expected to be close, it is no wonder that political decisions usually involve very short-term considerations that are as noncontroversial as possible. Those allocation criteria that are addressed to long-run objectives or require unpopular decisions are likely to receive low priority. Politically popular slogans that involve low risks and few costs are then likely to be used to disguise more immediate considerations of greater value to the allocators' own interests. The notions of quality education, safety nets, equal opportunity, and national security have the motherhood-and-apple-pie quality that serves such a purpose, since they are unlikely to alienate substantial numbers of voters.

### 4. Amounts of Discretion and Monitoring

In this and the remaining sections we may be much more brief, since we have already alluded to the relevant causal factors in our previous discussion. As noted, allocators may be monitored by both their own principals and at least some of those who are in the competition for awards. In general, the more extensive and close the monitoring, the less the power of decision making that actually remains in the hands of the allocating agents. Discretion depends upon other factors as well, however. Where the criteria for selection are clearcut and objective, and therefore where allocation formulas may be utilized, discretion will be necessary only in those instances where competitors' qualifications are nearly equal.

Implied in this, as well, is the degree of homogeneity among such competitors. If there are substantial differences in their obvious credentials there will generally be less room and necessity for supplementary allocator judgments. Where candidates' past performances or other characteristics are nearly identical, however, the kinds of supplementary information needed may, in effect, provide allocators with the opportunity to rely on subjective criteria such as "personality," "reliability," "potential," interest in the position, or "compatibility" with future associates. Monitoring will also be made much more difficult.

### 5. Time and Knowledge Constraints

Allocators may be forced to make a large number of decisions within a very brief period of time, as for example when applicants to college or graduate and professional schools are being considered. If so, they will also have very little opportunity to collect additional information, even in those instances where it would otherwise be desirable to do so. Some information is relatively easy to obtain, whereas other kinds require considerable effort and may also be perceived as unreliable at best. Furthermore, the nature of the performance expectations for winning competitors may be such that really detailed information is not needed. If, for example, persons are being hired for routine work and if they can rather easily be replaced should their performances prove unsatisfactory, it may be most efficient to hire on the basis of extremely superficial information and then to weed out poor performers at a later time. Therefore the *need* for careful screening may be slight.

There may be other situations in which allocators may genuinely wish to obtain more complete information but lack the resources necessary to do so. Candidates may also falsify their credentials, letters of recommendation may be inflated, or their prior performances may have involved tasks or settings that were very dissimilar to those that will be expected. The marginal value of increased information in all such situations may be insufficient to warrant the added costs of validating existing information or constructing expensive testing procedures to obtain more reliable evidence. In all settings, then, the information upon which allocators must rely will be imperfect. The degree of faith they have in such evidence may also vary across evaluators, suggesting that some may rely more than others on supplementary information or subjective judgments.

### 6. Multidimensionality of Task Criteria

If allocators are selecting among candidates for simple tasks, it may be relatively easy to develop evaluation criteria that are basically unidimensional. This means that such candidates can be unambiguously ranked and then a cutoff point determined so that those who perform in the top X% will be selected. Contrast this situation with one in which the required tasks are multidimensional. This will generally mean that candidates can be only partially ordered. A first candidate may be superior to a second with respect to tasks A and C, whereas the second may be superior with respect to tasks B and D. If so, the allocator will then need to develop weights and some sort of numerical scoring system to produce an unambiguous ordering.

Since such weights and scoring systems are also likely to be perceived as arbitrary and therefore subject to dispute, there will not only need to be greater monitoring of the allocator's decision process but also a greater likelihood that the resultant outcome can be legitimately challenged. Thus an additional structural factor, the nature of the task and setting for which candidates are being screened, will ordinarily impact on the allocation process and be a possible source increasing the likelihood of allocator bias. Some allocators, for example, may tend to favor those performance dimensions that result in a higher percentage of their own group's being selected in preference to members of other categories.

### 7. Size and Composition of Applicant Pool

Allocating agents are often placed in ambivalence producing situations. On the one hand, they would like to have a large and reasonably diverse set of candidates from whom to choose. On the other hand, the larger the numbers involved the greater the effort that must be made to select among them. Preliminary screening criteria, such as the possession of an educational degree, may make it possible to eliminate many candidates in a kind of first cut. Whenever such simple criteria are only very imperfect predictors of candidates' true potential or their expected contributions to the organization concerned, however, the errors made in using these selection criteria may be considerable.[1] Thus the costs entailed will be a function of the nature of the applicant pool.

As we shall later discuss, the explicit applicant pool will usually constitute a nonrandom sample of those who are actually qualified, and an even smaller subset of those who, with additional training, might have obtained such qualifications. Either the allocating agents themselves or another set of agents employed by the principals may need to be concerned with tapping such larger, more inclusive pools. To do so may be costly, however.

Thus it may be advantageous to delegate this responsibility to others. From the standpoint of private enterprise, for example, our public school system and our colleges and universities may perform this function at public expense. To the degree that it also imparts to potential candidates the kind of intellectual orientation, belief system, and willingness to accept negative decisions on the part of future employers, the educational system will also facilitate the entire selection process and thereby help to provide a steady supply of suitably motivated and properly tractable candidates. It is no wonder, then, that both in our own and in socialist systems of government we typically find a partnership between those who prepare candidates for selection and those who ultimately choose among them (Bowles and Gintis, 1976).

### 8. Costs of Incorrect Decisions

Sometimes it will be obvious when allocators have made poor decisions. This will be especially likely whenever the losing candidates remain around and can easily be compared with those who have been selected, as for example is often the case whenever a few persons have been selected for promotions whereas the remainder continue to perform their previous roles. This is in contrast with, say, decisions made by college admissions officers. Faculty may be aware that incoming students are poorly prepared, but since they have no way of comparing them with those who have been rejected, they are more likely to place the blame on those who have trained the entire pool of candidates, rather than on those who have selected among them. We have also noted that there will be other situations in which selectees who subsequently perform poorly can be let go at minimal cost. Moreover, performance levels may be so uniform that the selection process itself is of little importance.

In all of these kinds of situations we would expect that, regardless of the officially designated criteria in use, allocators will be tempted to reduce their own costs by substituting or emphasizing criteria that are simplest to employ and least likely to cause trouble for themselves. If certain kinds of candidates are thought to be unlikely to protest decisions being made, they may also find themselves effectively eliminated from competition in favor of those who threaten to apply sanctions to allocating agents. From the standpoint of the principals concerned, almost any individuals selected by their agents will be perceived as equally satisfactory, so the less the trouble and the cheaper the allocation costs involved, the better the net outcome for the allocators themselves and the less likely that the allocation process will be closely monitored.

### 9. Normative Factors and Equity Considerations

As we shall discuss in some detail in Chapter 7, equity concerns may be important factors to allocators as well as to the candidates themselves. There may be a concern for both outcome and procedural equity. By the latter we refer to the fairness of the actual decision process, as well as the degree to which allocation criteria and their true weights have been accurately conveyed to all concerned and have been satisfactorily justified to them. Outcome equity is difficult to evaluate in individual decisions, but in the aggregate often refers to the frequency distributions of successful and unsuccessful candidates. In both types of equity considerations, there will be substantial room for disagreement and debate. If a smaller proportion of blacks than whites have been selected, does this in itself constitute a bias or were the initial pool distributions different with respect to desired or desirable characteristics? Should candidate A of category I be favored over candidate B of category II simply because, in the past, a disproportionate percentage of IIs have been selected? If so, this may correct for outcome inequities at the expense of procedural equities.

As we shall see in connection with our subsequent discussion of equity problems, there is very likely to be considerable disagreement as to just what kinds of factors should be considered as constituting a candidate's inputs or investments. How important is past service and seniority or an individual's loyalty? Is prior training considered important primarily because it will be directly useful on a job or because it serves as a predictor of motivation, work habits, or consistency of behavior? Social psychologists generally argue that individuals are self-serving with respect to their preferences among such criteria, tending to overvalue their own investments (and capabilities) and devaluing those of their rivals. If so, then we may anticipate that losers will rather readily find ways of perceiving the allocation process or outcome as having been unjust, whereas winners will have the opposite perspective.

What is critical, of course, is how different kinds of parties will *act* in an allocation situation and how equity considerations may become involved in group mobilization efforts. Blacks, other minorities, and women may or may not have been treated equitably in a particular allocation process, but if they perceive the situation to have been inequitable and if they are also in a position to convince third parties (such as governmental agencies) that they have been unfairly treated, then they may also apply pressure on either the allocating agents or their principals. Or if the latter expect that only white males will react to unfavorable decisions, they may be tempted to bias their decisions in their favor, using selected equity principles to bolster their own positions. Ideological factors will also come into play in such situations. Those criteria that have in the past been commonly accepted as being at the core of equitable decision making may remain so unless actively challenged.

Allocators will themselves develop internalized equity standards, sometimes but not always rationalized in accord with what they recognize to be to their own advantage. Some may adhere strictly to the stated rules, thereby risking the possibility of being fired or otherwise sanctioned by their peers. Those who disagree in fundamental ways with practices of such peers or the policies of their superiors may decide either to go public or to resign their positions, thereby encouraging a self-selection process that results in a closer fit between allocators' individual preferences and the policies they are being asked to implement. In many situations, then, it is reasonable to take allocator turnover as an endogenous variable affected by equity concerns, among other factors.

## SITUATIONS INVOLVING
## OPEN COMPETITION AMONG ALLOCATORS

Another set of factors likely to influence allocation decisions involves relationships with competing organizations. We shall later deal with situations where there are hierarchically arranged organizations in which those near the top have considerably more appeal to applicants than those at the bottom, meaning that whenever a given candidate is selected by several competing organizations a choice is likely to be made favoring those with the highest status. In the present section we shall deal with situations in which competing organizations are more nearly equal in stature, but where each finds it necessary to pay very careful attention to its selection procedures because of the fact that performances among candidates are both highly variable and also crucial to the welfare of the organization concerned.

Situations will obviously vary with respect to the degree to which finding the best qualified candidates is really important to allocators and their principals. We have already noted that in some instances, as for example routinized jobs for which performance levels are relatively uniform and for which the supply of potential candidates is far greater than the demand, unsatisfactory performers can be rather easily replaced by those who are motivated to remain on the job and perform satisfactorily at the standard level. A similar situation holds in all those instances where the costs of on-the-job training are relatively low. Contrast such situations with those in a much more highly competitive occupation in which performance levels vary considerably and contribute in major ways to the success of the enterprise. The case of professional sports immediately comes to mind.

In professional baseball, for example, once the racial barriers to the entry of blacks in the Major Leagues was broken when Jackie Robinson joined the Brooklyn Dodgers in 1947, there was an almost immediate rush to hire other blacks, who had previously been confined to playing in special "Negro" leagues. Blacks have subsequently become overrepresented in those professional sports, especially football and basketball, in which there was in effect an oversupply of minority talent. Why did this occur so rapidly in the case of professional sports, whereas the admission of blacks to other professions has been much more on a token basis? What are the structural factors that influenced these selection procedures and that favored relatively "objective" allocation criteria?

In the first place, performance differences are not only highly variable but they are also very visible to the general public, as well as those who are making recruiting decisions. Sophisticated numerical measures of offensive performance levels, especially, have been developed and are also very familiar to the sports public—such things as batting averages, home runs, runs batted in, and slugging averages. In other sports, offensive players are rated according to yards gained, passes completed, points scored, percentage of free throws made, and so forth. Pitchers are scored according to won and lost records, earned run averages, and strikeouts. Even defensive players are evaluated in terms of blocked shots, quarterback sacks, or tackles made.

Players' performances are also highly critical to team outcomes, as evaluated by won and lost records and attendance levels. In some occupations, one's coworkers have a vested interest in controlling an individual's outputs, so that all members have nearly identical performance records. Not only would this be extremely difficult in the case of professional sports, where behaviors are highly visible, but it is usually the case that the overwhelming majority of one's teammates share the collective goal of winning games. They may feel envious of the top performers, but they will also be ambivalent because such persons also contribute disproportionately to winning efforts, to say nothing of gate receipts. Rarely do we find other instances in which individual performances stand out in such an obvious way, and where there are so many observers in a position to assess the adequacy of recruiters' decisions. In a sense, the public represents the agent's principal and is often in a position to exert a major influence in determining whether or not a coach or manager remains in the job.

Nor are future competitors in a position to impact on any given candidate's socialization or skill level. In such a heavily competitive occupation each individual must repeatedly enter into competition not only with teammates but numerous other nearly anonymous candidates who may at any point be recruited from other teams or brought up from the minor leagues (in the case of baseball). This is in sharp contrast with occupations where entry is tightly controlled through apprenticeship programs or by admissions officers in professional schools. There are usually successive pools through which a given individual passes—grade school or little league teams, junior high and high school sports, collegiate athletics, and then professional leagues. Given the fact that there are a huge and very diverse number of pool entry points at each stage (e.g., a wide variety of college football teams), it is virtually impossible for future competitors to erect barriers to any one individual, or even a class of individuals, provided that the larger setting in which they are embedded defines all such candidates as eligible. If one team were to turn down highly skilled black athletes, another would pick them up and thereby have a distinct competitive advantage. Since the overriding goal is to win games, and since highly variable performances are perceived as having a truly major impact on these outcomes, the numerous competitors for any given position find themselves in a very weak power position, apart from controlling their own individual performance levels.

Thus the combination of highly variable performance levels, accurate and public measurement devices, and readily apparent connections between individual performances and highly valued team outcomes all result in a high degree of competition, carefully scrutinized, among allocators (recruiting agents). This in turn implies that most if not all such persons will develop a high utility or preference for selecting the very best players, regardless of their own personal biases. In effect, this says that their overall utilities for biased procedures will be small by comparison and that the actual biases introduced into the selection process will be minimal. Where such biases tend to be shared, as for example a reluctance to utilize black quarterbacks, whenever a breakthrough occurs and the first such black actually performs well, we are also likely to witness a rapid decrease in the operational biases of team coaches or managers. The costs of a failure to utilize the best personnel will be too great.

## CONTROLLING THE COMPETITORS

As we have noted, allocators will be faced with a series of restraining factors and will generally be motivated to retain as much autonomy as possible in connection with their decision processes. Since some of these constraints will be brought about by the actions of the competitors themselves, allocators will therefore usually have an interest in controlling or influencing the behaviors of at least those competitors who are expected to "make trouble" or otherwise adversely impact on the allocators' autonomy. How can this be accomplished? Obviously, much will depend upon the relative power positions of the allocating agents and various categories of competitors.

Competitors' beliefs about and satisfaction with the allocation process will almost certainly affect their future behaviors, including their willingness to engage in subsequent competitions. Normative factors, such as the notions of distributive and procedural justice will come into play in this connection, but we shall postpone their consideration until Chapter 7. To the extent that allocators can influence such norms or commonly held beliefs about the allocation process, we may expect them to do so. This includes presenting an accounting—whether accurate or not—of the procedures being used, the criteria employed, and a justification of statistical outcomes where these have been made public.

This need to supply limited information may, of course, be somewhat incompatible with allocators' wishes to retain as much autonomy as possible, as well as providing occupational security for themselves. We therefore expect them to try to convince other relevant parties that they possess special expertise and necessarily confidential information and that they have set aside any personal biases in favor of professional norms of fairness. The need to justify their actions will depend, however, on their own power vis-à-vis those who may be motivated to challenge the decision-making process. To the degree that there already exists a well-established set of norms and understandings concerning the legitimacy of the allocation process, the burden of proof will then be placed on those who wish to challenge outcomes, rather than on those who have made the allocation decisions.

The most common type of problem allocators may be expected to face is that of either convincing the losers that the process has been fair or of preventing or inhibiting them from engaging in organizing protest. Piven and Cloward (1971), for example, suggest that welfare agencies serve an effective control function by keeping clients both dependent on future allocations and mutually isolated from one another, so that they will be basically unwilling and unable to challenge the overall system. These authors also note a dual process in operation. At the same time that the bottom strata of, say, blacks are being kept dependent and mutually isolated, their potential allies among middle-class blacks may have been coopted by the system. Potential troublemakers are thus effectively immobilized, to the advantage of both the allocating agents and their principals (the general public).

Allocators will in general be likely to attempt to break up or at least weaken any coalitions that may exist among potential competitors. In many situations, of course, applicant pools will consist of isolated individuals, but, for example, where promotions or pay increases among employees are to be allocated, competitors may have already organized into labor unions or professional organizations that attempt to regulate the allocation process. As we shall note in Chapter 6, such organizations may sometimes be in a position to control the recruitment process through apprenticeship programs or examinations that have the effect of sharply limiting the numbers of potential candidates. Where company unions can be set up as alternatives it may be possible for allocators to meet certain tangible demands without surrendering control of the essential processes that determine how much and to whom the benefits are to go. University administrators, for example, are often willing to work with faculty senate leaders while opposing the notion that faculty should be given legislative authority to set up their own bargaining agents or labor unions.

In instances where there are important groups of competitors that cannot be easily controlled and that have perhaps allied themselves with powerful third parties, allocators may ease their own situations by employing policies that secretly favor these more powerful groups. In effect, this means that there will be sufficient numbers of winners among such categories that there will be only dampened opposition to the allocators' decision criteria. This amounts to the allocators' either actually splitting the competing group into several portions or taking advantage of preexisting cleavages in such a way as to minimize their own difficulties. Split labor markets, as noted by Bonacich (1972), are a case in point. This kind of mechanism not only produces biased outcomes, but it also feeds a self-perpetuating process in those instances where some members of the successful competitors themselves later become allocators. The powerful are thus able to perpetuate their own power, while at the same time maintaining a smooth-running system as long as the losing categories remain sufficiently unorganized or mutually unaware of what is taking place. To the extent that allocators can hide from view their true decision criteria and convince the public that the process has been entirely fair, such a biased procedure can remain in place for a very long period of time.

Recipients or winners in any given allocation process may also need to be controlled if they are to be placed in positions enabling them to make future demands. Sometimes allocators may be able, in effect, to exploit the losing candidates, provided that the latter can be called back and encouraged to engage in future competitions. For example, a large pool of losing candidates may serve as an effective brake on wage demands if the selected candidates can be threatened with replacement in the event that they do not prove sufficiently tractable. In this connection, it may be convenient to make the winners believe that they were actually "given a break" in comparison with others having nearly equivalent qualifications. They may then become convinced that there are plenty of others awaiting the opportunity to take their place should their performances prove unsatisfactory in any way. Therefore it may be to the allocators' advantage to have a sufficiently large pool of original candidates so that the threat of replacement becomes a realistic one. In response, once they have been hired, successful candidates may eagerly join labor unions or support protective measures such as the kinds of tenure rules that exist in practically all American colleges and universities.

Allocators will obviously be in the strongest position vis-à-vis losers whenever the latter essentially drop out of the picture and are not interested in challenging the system. Sometimes, however, they will remain on the scene and be in a position to threaten trouble or at least to punish the allocators' principals. Those employees who are continually passed over for promotions or pay increases may become disgruntled and even engage in sabotage. Of special concern to allocators will be those who, although other-

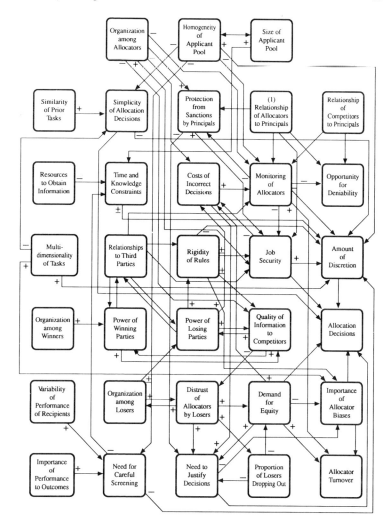

**Figure 3.1.** Model III: Factors Influencing Allocation Decisions

wise qualified, have been passed over because of a fear that they might become too powerful. Kings may bypass their own offspring or other close relatives for powerful positions precisely because they would pose too great a threat to the throne. Eunuchs were favored by many Chinese rulers primarily because, lacking heirs, they were believed to be more trustworthy than blood relatives or members of the nobility.

More generally, losers may play a kind of threat game, as this notion is discussed in the game theory literature (Kelley and Thibaut, 1978). In such game situations, one party controls the allocation process, but the other remains in a position to affect the payoff distribution so that *both* parties lose unless the allocator produces a more equitable payoff distribution. Terrorist cells, or what I have elsewhere (Blalock, 1989b) discussed under the notion of "conflict groups," often play precisely this kind of role. The objective of the losing parties is to influence the allocator by taking the risk of a conflict in which both parties inflict sufficient damage on the other that the stronger one (here the allocator) becomes willing to modify the process. Isolated individual losers are rarely in a position to accomplish this purpose, but organized ones may often succeed in doing so. Anticipating such an outcome, allocators may therefore be influenced to employ more equitable procedures or take other means to make sure that outcomes do not unduly penalize such a potentially disruptive kind of party.

## CAUSAL MODEL III:
## FACTORS INFLUENCING ALLOCATION DECISIONS

The general model used to systematize the prior discussion is presented in Figure 3.1 and contains 11 exogenous variables given across the top and down the left-hand column, 17 intervening variables appearing toward the center of the figure, and 5 dependent variables represented by boxes in the right-hand column. There are in all 33 variables in this nearly recursive model. As before, we begin by listing each of the variables and then turn first to a brief discussion of the direct causal linkages with each of the exogenous variables and then to a similar discussion of the assumed effects of the intervening variables.

## The Exogenous Variables

The following exogenous variables are listed in the order they appear, first across the top of Figure 3.1 and then down the left-hand column.

(1) The degree to which allocators are themselves organized (Organization Among Allocators)

(2) The homogeneity and composition of the applicant pool (Homogeneity of Applicant Pool)

(3) The size of the applicant pool (Size of Applicant Pool)

(4) The nature of the relationship between allocators and their principals (Relationship of Allocators to Principals)

(5) The nature of relationships between sets of competitors and these same principals (Relationship of Competitors to Principals)

(6) The similarity of prior tasks performed by competitors to those expected of them (Similarity of Prior Tasks)

(7) The degree to which allocators have the necessary resources to obtain adequate information about competitors (Resources to Obtain Information)

(8) The degree to which expected tasks are complex and multidimensional (Multidimensionality of Tasks)

(9) The degree to which winning candidates are organized, either prior or subsequent to the decision (Organization Among Winners)

(10) The degree to which performance levels of winning candidates can be expected to vary (Variability of Performances of Recipients)

(11) The importance of recipients' future performance to the outcomes for the organization (Importance of Performance to Outcomes)

## The Intervening Variables

Intervening variables are listed according to their order in the diagram, beginning at the top and moving from left to right and then downward.

(1)  The degree of simplicity in making the allocation decisions (Simplicity of Allocation Decisions)

(2)  The degree to which allocators are protected from sanctions by their principals (Protection From Sanctions by Principals)

(3)  The degree to which allocators are constrained by time and knowledge limitations (Time and Knowledge Constraints)

(4)  The costliness to allocators of incorrect decisions (Costs of Incorrect Decisions)

(5)  The extent to which allocators are monitored by either their principals or groups of competitors (Monitoring of Allocators)

(6)  Allocators' and competitors' relationships to third parties (Relationships to Third Parties)

(7)  The degree to which rules applying to allocation procedures are rigid and enforced (Rigidity of Rules)

(8)  The degree of job security provided to allocators (Job Security)

(9)  The degree to which winners or recipients have power over allocators (Power of Winning Parties)

(10)  The degree to which losing parties have power over allocators (Power of Losing Parties)

(11)  The amount and quality of information provided by allocators to competitors (Quality of information to Competitors)

(12)  The degree to which losing competitors are organized to challenge the decision (Organization Among Losers)

(13)  The amount of distrust of allocators by losing parties (Distrust of Allocators by Losers)

(14)  The extent of the demand for equitable decisions placed upon allocators (Demand for Equity)

(15)  The degree to which there is a need for allocators to use care in selecting among competitors (Need for Careful Screening)

(16)  The degree to which there are demands on allocators to justify their decisions (Need to Justify Decisions)

(17)  The proportion of losing candidates who drop out of subsequent competitions (Proportion of Losers Dropping Out)

## The Dependent Variables

Finally, we list the five dependent variables given in the final column of Figure 3.1.

(1) The opportunity provided principals to deny responsibility for or knowledge about allocation decisions (Opportunity for Deniability)
(2) The amount of discretion provided to allocators in the decision process (Amount of Discretion)
(3) The actual allocation decisions made by allocators (Allocation Decisions)
(4) The degree to which allocator biases are important in the decision process (Importance of Allocator Biases)
(5) The rate of turnover among allocators (Allocator Turnover)

## Discussion of the Model: Effects of Exogenous Variables

Organization Among Allocators is one of the most important of the exogenous variables, with postulated direct effects on five other variables. It is assumed to have a rather obvious direct effect on the Job Security of allocators, and especially so whenever seniority or other labor union type policies have resulted from the organizational power of such allocators. It is also presumed to have a negative impact on the quality of information that allocators provide to competitors, again because of the increased strength of such allocators and their reduced accountability. Protection From Sanctions by Principals is also assumed to be positively impacted by this exogenous variable, whereas the Monitoring of Allocators is expected to be reduced. Finally, there should be reduced costs to allocators whenever they make incorrect decisions.

Homogeneity of Applicant Pool is also an important exogenous variable, which is taken to be spuriously related to the pool's size, if only because it seems likely that a very large pool will often mean that a diversity of persons have applied. Homogeneity is assumed to have a positive effect on Amount of Discretion because whenever applicants appear very similar, and have nearly equal qualifications, selection among them will likely entail subjective judgmental criteria idiosyncratic to each allocator. Whenever pool members are nearly alike, there should also be less need for principals to pay close attention to the selection process, and therefore less Monitoring of Allocators. Homogeneity should reduce Simplicity of Allocation Decisions, however, since there will be relatively few clearcut or obvious differences in competitors' qualifications, making it necessary to search for other distinguishing qualifications. Finally, homogeneity should reduce the Need for Careful Screening among applicants, since it should make relatively little difference which ones are ultimately selected. Size of Applicant Pool, as a separate exogenous factor, is assumed to affect only one other variable, namely Time and Knowledge Constraints. Other things being equal, a large pool means less time devoted to the scrutiny of each applicant.

The relationship of allocators to their principals is assumed to affect four variables directly, though with unspecified signs since this particular exogenous factor is presumed to be multidimensional. It is expected to affect allocators' protection from sanctions, the monitoring of allocators, principals' opportunities for deniability, and the job security of allocators. The fifth exogenous factor, Relationship of Competitors to Principals will also, in general, be multidimensional and is assumed to affect both Monitoring of Allocators and Principals' Opportunities for Deniability. Where one is studying the power that competitors have over principals, this suggests that deniability opportunities will be reduced but monitoring increased.

All but one of the remaining exogenous variables are postulated to affect only a single variable. The similarity of the prior tasks that candidates have performed to those that they will later be expected to perform is anticipated to simplify the allocators' decision process, and especially so to the degree that such earlier performances have been observed or are highly visible to others. Resources to Obtain Information is expected to have a rather obvious negative impact on Time and Knowledge Constraints. Multidimensionality of Tasks is also expected to have a negative effect on the simplicity of allocation decisions by requiring allocators to assign differential weights to such tasks and to collect more information from each of the competitors. This same exogenous variable is predicted to have a positive impact on Importance of Allocator Biases and on the dependent variable Amount of Discretion.

Organization Among Winners is anticipated to increase the power of such parties, both in terms of the direct impact on the decision process itself and also their power after it has been made. Highly organized winners may also gain power not only over the allocators but their principals as well, thereby serving to perpetuate the advantage similar candidates may have in future competitions. Finally, the two exogenous factors, Variability of Performance of Recipients and Importance of Performance to Outcomes, are expected to have positive impacts on Need for Careful Screening, as our illustrative example of professional sports suggests. Allocators' utilities for making correct decisions should be increased to the degree that differential performances really make an impact in terms of the relevant organization's competitive position or level of success.

## Discussion of the Model: Effects of Intervening Variables

In discussing the 17 intervening variables we shall proceed from left to right and then downward. It will be seen that a number of these variables play important roles in the model, being linked to large numbers of others as both their causes and their effects. We shall discuss only the effects of each variable, however, since its causes will be covered in the treatment of the other variables, some of which are exogenous and the remainder intervening. As was true for the previous model, a few of the intervening variables are linked to each other through mechanisms involving reciprocal causation, meaning that the overall model is not completely recursive.

Simplicity of Allocation Decisions is assumed to affect two variables, the allocation decisions (or outcomes) themselves and the amount of discretion afforded to the allocator. In the latter instance the effect is assumed to be in the negative direction, with a high degree of simplicity implying that allocators can make rather routine decisions that do not require a whole lot of time or the use of subjective judgments. Protection From Sanctions by Principals also affects two variables. High degrees of protection should mean less of a need to justify decisions and increased job security.

Time and Knowledge Constraints is assumed to affect Amount of Discretion, though with an ambiguous sign. On the one hand, considerable constraints may mean that allocators are forced to rely heavily on highly subjective judgments and therefore will increase their discretion. On the other hand, lowered constraints may make it possible to collect large amounts of information that then must be weighted or evaluated according to criteria that may leave a lot to the allocators' personal judgments. Thus the direction of the sign in this instance may depend on the operation of numerous variables not contained in the model.

The costs of incorrect decisions are predicted to have a positive impact on monitoring to the extent that principals wish to assure themselves that the best possible candidates are being selected. For much the same reason, the greater the (expected) costs, the greater the need for allocators to justify their decisions to their principals, and possibly also to losing candidates as well. Thus this particular intervening variable is also assumed to affect two other variables in the model.

Monitoring of Allocators plays a central role in the model, being affected by six variables and a cause of five others. It is expected to impact negatively on principals' opportunity for deniability, at least in settings in which outsiders are well aware of the close monitoring and are in a position to hold such principals responsible for the outcomes. Monitoring is also assumed to increase allocator turnover rates to the degree that monitors are critical of allocator practices or have different value priorities than the allocators themselves. Extensive and close monitoring is also predicted to reduce allocator discretion and job security, for rather obvious reasons, though again all the more so to the degree that principals and allocators have divergent interests. Finally, monitoring is expected to have a negative impact on allocators' protection from sanctions. Closely monitored allocators will be in a poor position to cover up their mistakes or disagreements with their principals.

The rather general factor titled Relationships to Third Parties is expected to be reciprocally related to both the power of winning parties and to that of the losers. Given the multidimensionality of this factor, however, the signs of impacts in either direction cannot be specified. Relationships to Third Parties is also predicted to impact on the extent to which allocators are monitored by their principals and the rigidity of the rules imposed upon such allocators. The idea is that important and powerful third parties will be in a position to insist on tight controls over allocators, should they wish to do so. Presumably, the extent that they actually do so will depend upon prior allocator decisions as well as reactions by winning, and especially losing, candidates.

Rigidity of Rules is assumed to affect four variables. It is expected to have a negative impact on the amount of allocator discretion and the importance of allocator biases, under the assumption that clearcut and well enforced rules are ordinarily designed to delimit discretion and, in most instances, to assure equitable or fair decision processes. Rigidity is also assumed to affect allocator job security, though the sign of this relationship will depend upon the nature of such rules and the "fit" between such rules and allocator preferences, capabilities, and actual practices. In some instances where the fit is poor, rigidity may actually reduce job security, though in most instances we would expect rule rigidity to enhance job security by routinizing the decision process. Finally, we predict that rule rigidity will affect the quality of information provided to competitors. Where the rules are public, rigidity should improve the information flow. In contrast, where the rules are known only to the allocators and their principals the rigidity of such secret rules may instead reduce information flow. For this reason we have used the sign ± in both these latter instances to indicate that the signs of these two relationships can be either positive or negative.

Job Security is postulated to affect three variables. Lowered job security should increase the costs of incorrect decisions unless, of course, the relevant principals actually prefer them to be incorrect—a highly unlikely possibility. Job security considerations should also impact on allocators' ultimate decisions, presumably in the direction of making them more conservative and risk aversive. Finally, the greater the job security the greater the allocator's actual discretion, for much the same reason. Secure allocators may be expected to go out on a limb more frequently than those whose positions are very much in doubt. This may also permit them to give more free rein to their own biases, but we have not drawn in an arrow to the Importance of Allocator Biases box under the assumption that this particular relationship will ordinarily be rather weak.

Power of Winning Parties is assumed to affect (and be affected by) Relationships to Third Parties. It is presumed that a powerful type of candidate, for example, will be in a position to influence third parties and that, conversely, third parties may act to enhance the power of such candidates. Power of Losing Parties is similarly expected to be related to Relationships to Third Parties. An arrow has also been drawn from losing party power to rule rigidity under the assumption that aggrieved but powerful losers will be in a position to insist on there being a definite and enforced set of regulations that allocators must follow. Powerful losing parties are also expected to be in a position to increase the costs to allocators of incorrect decisions, thereby in turn indirectly affecting allocators' needs to justify such decisions. Finally, Power of Winning Parties and Power of Losing Parties are assumed to be reciprocally related, positively, to the quality of information provided to competitors.

Quality of information provided to competitors, as just noted, is expected to affect the power of losing parties by providing them with a weapon with which to challenge the allocation process. It is also assumed, generally, to have a negative impact on losers' distrust of allocators by opening up the decision process to their inspection, thereby reducing suspicion. This assumes, of course, that losers *believe* that the information they have been provided is actually correct and that they agree with the allocation criteria being used. Finally, the quality of information provided is also expected to enhance the power of the winning parties, as well.

Organization Among Losers is presumed to affect, positively, the power of losing parties and to have positive reciprocal causal effects on losers' distrust of allocators. On the one hand, distrust is expected to enhance organization. On the other, an organized group of losers will be in a better position to influence otherwise isolated losers by sowing the seeds of distrust among them. Additionally, allocator distrust is expected to place additional demands upon them to justify their decisions. Distrust should also increase demands for equity and fairness in the allocation process, although in the case of those losing competitors having weaker qualifications it may also result in demands for quotas or equalized percentages, regardless of candidates' objective qualifications or prior investments. Finally, a high degree of distrust is expected to result in increases in the proportions of losing candidates who drop out of subsequent competitions.

Demand for Equity is expected to increase the need for allocators to justify their decisions and to reduce the importance of allocator biases. Since the demand for equity may also affect the ultimate decision itself, an additional arrow has been drawn to the box titled Allocator Decisions. Equity demands should also increase allocator turnover, especially in those situations where allocator biases have been considerable and where allocators highly value substantial discretion in the decision-making process. Although not noted in the diagram, a combination of high equity demands and high turnover is expected to result in a self-selection process favoring those allocators whose own preferences are compatible with such equity demands. Finally, equity demands should also increase the costs to allocators of incorrect decisions unless, of course, such decisions inadvertently happen to result in increased rather than decreased equity. Our assumption is that, in general, incorrect decisions are also more likely to be inequitable.

The Need for Careful Screening among candidates is expected to reduce the amount of allocator discretion under the assumption that such a need will result in the use of criteria that more effectively discriminate between qualified and unqualified candidates and that more fine-grained evaluation tools will be developed. Such a need for careful screening should also reduce time and knowledge constraints to the degree that allocators and their principals find it desirable to set aside more time for the evaluation process and that they allocate additional resources to improve the quality and amount of information obtained from each applicant.

Need to Justify Decisions is assumed to affect these decisions themselves, if only to increase the care with which they are made and to eliminate selection criteria that are difficult to justify. Such a need is also predicted to reduce the importance of allocator biases for much the same reason. Finally, the Proportion of Losers Dropping Out is expected to have a negative impact on demands for equity and the need to justify decisions, under the assumption that those disgruntled losers who decide to drop out will not exercise much pressure on either the allocating agents or their principals.

Turning to our list of dependent variables we see that, for three of the five, namely Opportunity for Deniability, Allocator Decisions, and Allocator Turnover, there are only incoming arrows that have already been discussed. The remaining two "dependent" variables might have been classed as "intervening," but since they are assumed to affect only other dependent variables we have elected to refer to them as dependent. In the case of Amount of Discretion we have drawn in an arrow to Allocator Decisions for obvious reasons. Finally, Importance of Allocator Biases is assumed to affect both Allocator Decisions and Allocator Turnover. Presumably, those allocators who prefer to let their own biases color their decision making will elect to leave their positions (or may be fired) in situations in which such biases are not permitted to play important roles in the final decision. As suggested earlier, this may in turn result in self-selection processes that provide a closer fit between allocator preferences and the nature of decisions they are expected to make.

This completes our discussion of Figure 3.1. In the following chapter we shall take a closer look at the allocators themselves, the nature of their subjective states, and how these impact on the decision process itself. Ideally, the causal model we shall develop in Chapter 4 should be combined with both that in Chapter 2 and the present model to provide a giant model of the allocation decision process. Each of our separate models is sufficiently complex, however, that the reader's patience would be unduly taxed by any attempt to combine them. So we shall proceed as though each is distinct.

## NOTE

1. Economists use the term *statistical discrimination* to refer to instances where, say, employers favor whites over blacks, or men over women, on the basis of the probability that the former will perform better, on average, than the latter. That is, they save the costs involved in obtaining detailed information about individual candidates by relying on average statistics. It is in this sense that the discrimination involved is referred to as "statistical." Although they did not use this specific term, students of race relations made basically the same arguments long before this specific term came into usage. See Aigner and Cain (1977), Arrow (1973), Lundberg and Startz (1983), and Thurow (1975).

# Allocator Decision Processes

Allocators come in different sizes and shapes. Many are agents who have been hired by their principals to play highly specific roles as college admissions officers, members of personnel departments, intake personnel who screen applicants for eligibility in social programs, bank officers who are authorized to make mortgage loan decisions, or teachers who allocate grades to their students. In some instances a principal and an agent may be one and the same person, or the interests of principals and agents may almost exactly coincide. Often, however, it becomes necessary to consider allocating agents as distinct actors, whose interests and personal agenda may differ in important ways from those of the principals on behalf of whom they are supposedly acting.

Agents may be hired for relatively brief time periods and may be primarily concerned with making decisions that, in the short term, enable them to remain in office. Politicians are notorious for their pork-barrel, coalition-forming practices that are designed to appeal to the immediate interests of their constituents or sponsors, rather than long-term collective benefits. In many countries those responsible for collecting taxes or administering local justice are almost expected to accept bribes in return for looking the other way or favoring those who are willing and able to provide them with side payments. Having taken quick profits, they may then move on to other offices. University administrators often make allocation decisions based on immediate pressures from their state legislatures or influential regents, rather than in terms of the long-term interests of their faculties or student bodies. Admissions officers may be given secret instructions or hidden quotas, as for example to admit the children of wealthy alumni or students with unusual athletic prowess. If they do not, their jobs may be at stake.

In order to analyze allocator decision processes more generally it is important to attempt to specify a set of possible allocator goals that, on the one hand, are general enough to encompass a wide variety of possible allocation processes and, on the other, sufficiently specific to suggest hypotheses regarding the conditions under which allocation decisions will take one particular direction rather than another. Our basic assumption is that all actors, including allocators, will have multiple goals and that under most circumstances no single goal will so dominate the others that compromises and dilemmas will not play important roles in the decision process.

Given multiple goals, we shall also assume a modified or bounded rationality on the part of the allocator, with a crude sort of satisficing process at work through which the allocator attempts to attain a high (though not necessarily maximum) level of his or her subjective expected utility (March and Simon, 1958). That is, an allocator considers a range of alternatives and selects that course of action that offers the greatest chance of providing a high level of benefits. If the allocator has, say, $k$ distinct goals $G_i$ to which different (subjective) utilities $U_i$ have been attached, that allocator is assumed to associate with each of the courses of action being considered a given probability $p_i$ of achieving the goal $G_i$ by employing that means or course of action.

It will obviously be impossible for any allocator to consider all possible courses of action, especially given that most allocation decisions must be made during a relatively brief period of time that does not permit a thorough search outside of the actor's repertoire of reasonable alternatives (Tilly, 1979). Also, the subjective probabilities $p_i$ attached to each alternative course of action will have to depend partly on the allocator's prior experiences with similar candidates, and partly on whatever working theory the allocator may have regarding at least the short-term consequences of the specific decision. In particular, it can be expected that in most settings allocators will be especially careful to avoid highly visible mistakes that might result in their being fired or otherwise severely sanctioned. In other words, they may be more concerned about minimizing their maximum losses than in taking undue risks, unless of course they have been specifically instructed to do so.

Let us next discuss a number of different types of allocator goals so as to provide more succinct meaning to some of these very general points.

## ALLOCATOR GOALS

### 1. To Select the Best Qualified Candidates

Presumably, in nearly all allocation decision processes an important goal will be the most obvious one, namely to select rationally so as to maximize one's chances of choosing the best qualified candidates. Although qualifications will obviously vary and be more or less clearly defined or measured, at least the official policy is likely to be that of using fair or just means of selecting the best candidates. Perhaps this will entail evaluations of past performances, say as an employee or as a candidate who has been successful in highly similar settings (e.g., as a football player). If so, the task may be relatively straightforward, and it may also be easy to evaluate the allocator's performance.

Especially in those situations in which the expected future performances are only tangentially related to previous ones, considerably more discretion may have to be given to the allocator, with obvious implications for the operation of possible biases influenced by the allocator's other objectives. In some instances there are additional opportunities for biased outcome distributions that cannot be directly attributed to the allocators themselves. In the traditional Chinese examination system, for example, it was extremely difficult for those without the necessary leisure time to devote years of study to master a very difficult written language and to memorize the Confucian classics so as to do well on such examinations, regardless of how honestly they were evaluated. Therefore, as expected, sons and relatives of the wealthy had a decided advantage in such a competitive arena. Similarly, it is claimed that standardized examinations such as the SAT or GRE exams tend to favor whites over blacks, perhaps because of cultural biases in the exams themselves or because of differentials in practice opportunities and exam-taking skills. Whether or not such biases should be attributed to the allocating agents, themselves, or to their principals who decide upon policy matters will, of course, vary according to the situation.

As implied in the previous chapter, even in cases where a universalistic official goal is predominant and procedures are carefully rationalized, it will ordinarily be deemed necessary to protect allocators by assuring that at least some of the relevant information available to them is kept secret from the contestants themselves. Often this is justified in terms of the need to keep each individual's performance level confidential, if only to avoid embarrassment to those who may have lost out in the competition. Usually, however, there will be certain discretionary criteria that allocators may use, especially in those instances where it is necessary to break ties among nearly equal contestants. Or the weights used in arriving at a single ranking of candidates may be either kept completely confidential or glossed over by vague references to "balanced" criteria or taking "individual characteristics" into consideration. Such secrecy may or may not be reasonable from the standpoints of the candidates themselves, depending on the degree to which the allocator's other objectives interfere with this first type of objective or for other reasons tend to bias the selection process.

### 2. To Motivate or Create Loyalty to the Organization Among Candidates

Especially in those instances where candidates have been drawn from a pool of individuals whose continued loyalty is needed, it is often desirable for competitors to believe that their own past performance and loyalty are being rewarded. For example if an opening occurs for a new supervisor, it becomes critical not only to select the most deserving candidate but to retain the loyalty and motivation of the losing ones. This will of course complicate the allocator's decision process. Among other things, competitors may have worked closely with one another, so that they are reasonably well aware of each other's qualifications and previous performance record. They may also have watched some of their rivals feign loyalty, take credit for work done by others, or otherwise attempt to use illegitimate means to exaggerate their qualifications. If the loyalty of losing candidates is to be retained, there will usually have to be some sort of feedback process through which the allocator communicates that such losers came close to winning or that their competitors had unusual characteristics of which they were unaware.

### 3. To Retain Power for the Allocator's Own Group

Although perhaps unlikely to be openly admitted, a third objective of allocating agents may be that of assuring that top positions and ultimate power be retained by members of their own group or category. On the personal level, one recognizes out-and-out favoritism, or nepotism, in those instances where allocators consistently reserve positions for close friends or relatives. Political leaders often reward cronies or major campaign contributors with important positions in government, and dictators may place their own immediate family members in powerful positions. Such policies of course involve simple exchange mechanisms by which favors are returned to those who have shown past support. But they often go beyond this to helping assure allocators that persons having similar characteristics, values, or objectives will occupy important positions so as to provide them future support.

At a less personal level, allocators may decide or be specifically instructed to bias the selection process in favor of persons considered to be similar to themselves (or their principals) with respect to race or ethnicity, gender, age, political orientation, or any other characteristic they deem relevant. In our own society, such biased allocation procedures are considered illegitimate, though they have been implicitly understood to exist in many instances. "No blacks need apply!" Biasing techniques may be explicit, where this is permitted, or they may be put into effect through the use of screening criteria that are highly correlated with the characteristics of concern—standardized tests that favor white candidates, performance criteria that favor males, and so forth.

Unless such biases are publically admitted, it may be exceedingly difficult to determine in any given instance whether or not they have been a genuine factor in affecting the ultimate decision. This is especially true in instances where legitimate screening criteria are correlated with those characteristics thought to be the source of biased procedures. Should a screening criterion, such as test performance, be thrown out merely because all categories of persons do not do equally well on the average? How high must the correlation be between test scores and actual performance on the true criterion (e.g., subsequent job performance) in order to justify the test's use as a legitimate screening criterion? Should police applicants be required to jump over six-foot fences or pass a specific paper-and-pencil examination? The point to be made is that if there are allocator objectives that involve deliberate biases, it may be exceedingly difficult to demonstrate this fact by merely looking at the selection criteria they have used.

### 4. To Avoid Sanctions by Competitors

As previously discussed, certain of the candidates among whom the allocator is selecting may not be powerless individuals and may exert pressures on their own behalf. Their agents or those who have taken it upon themselves to protect their interests may be in a position to apply sanctions to the allocators if outcomes are not to their liking. Prior to the 1960s, white candidates were often favored over blacks, partly because of allocators fears that the hiring of black workers or the acceptance of black students would result in their own job loss or even more severe life-threatening penalties. Once governmental affirmative action programs had been put into place, however, there was at least a credible claim that the situation had been reversed. If too many white males were hired, the allocator might be required to justify his or her decisions. A business firm or university could be taken to court or threatened with a loss of governmental contracts or funding.

We have already argued that it is important to assess the relative power positions of the allocators or their principals, on the one hand, and different kinds of applicants, on the other. We anticipate that weak allocators will tend to have especially high subjective probabilities that their decisions will result in negative sanctions unless they are biased in a certain direction. Perhaps the biases so generated will tend to operate in the opposite direction from any allocator biases favoring their own category. Then again, however, they may operate in the same direction, as was often the case with respect to minority hiring prior to affirmative action programs. Allocators who, as agents, may be undercut by their principals in instances where scapegoats must be located will be in especially vulnerable positions. They may receive signals that the principal prefers a biased allocation procedure that favors the in-group, whereas if such biases are actually detected and challenged, it may be the allocating agent, rather than the principal, who pays the penalty. In contrast with the biasing goal discussed in the previous section, however, this sort of "negative" influence, involving a threat, will also typically require continued surveillance. We would expect that it is far less likely to be incorporated into the allocators' own value preference hierarchies than is the type of bias that favors their own group.

### 5. To Satisfy Other Allocators or One's Superiors

Many allocators will find themselves embedded in networks of other allocators, who may serve to reinforce normative practices relevant to the decision process. Realtors, for example, may adhere to informal practices that effectively block the showing of certain homes in white neighborhoods to black families. If there are multiple allocators operating out of the same department, they will rather naturally discuss cases and develop informal norms or standards that supplement the officially recognized ones. This is especially likely whenever considerable discretion is placed in allocators' hands. It is also likely where the officially endorsed criteria are either vague or difficult to operationalize, or whenever their application results in large numbers of ties that must be broken through the use of supplementary criteria such as performance in a job interview or assessments of "personality," "compatibility" with future work associates, or interest displayed in the job.

The allocators' immediate supervisors or other representatives of the principal may also exert a biasing influence, especially if close surveillance is being exercised. Where such superiors send out mixed signals, the allocator concerned may be in an especially vulnerable position requiring extreme caution and perhaps a tendency to lean over backwards not to favor candidates who might prove controversial. For example the officially stated criteria may be somewhat inconsistent with criteria the allocator understands are the real ones to be used, but yet the principals concerned may be operating in such a way as to provide themselves the opportunity for deniability should the decision be challenged. The allocating agent may then be caught in the middle.

### 6. To Ensure Private Gain

We note the obvious possibility that allocators' objectives may include private gain in the form of side payments, bribes, campaign contributions, and so forth. Where allocators are poorly paid it may even be expected by their principals that potential recipients will supplement allocators' incomes in such a way, in much the same fashion that waiters are tipped by customers. Applicants in competition with one another may of course be differentially aware of what is taking place, and some may be in a better position than others to provide sufficient side payments to bias the selection process in their own favor. Still others may refuse to play the game or, if they are aware of what is going on, may never enter the competitive pool in the first place. Clearly, if this type of allocator goal is sufficiently strong, and if allocators are provided with a great deal of discretion without being closely monitored, the system is wide open to abuse.

Whenever certain types of applicants are in a more favorable position than others to provide bribes and other kinds of side payments, such applicants will also have a vested interest in maintaining a corrupt system. They are then likely to form a coalition with the allocating agents and perhaps also select themselves into the pool of potential future allocators, thus helping to reinforce and perpetuate the corrupt and corrupting system. Unless others are willing and able to break up the pattern by careful monitoring and the insistence on the rigid application of more objective criteria, the "spoils system" may remain in place for a considerable period of time. Indeed, our own Civil Service system involving standardized exams, evaluated blindly, was developed precisely to counteract practices of overt favoritism in the awarding of government jobs.

### 7. To Assure Equity or Fair Play[1]

Finally, allocators may have incorporated societal norms regarding equity principles and have a high utility for equity. If so, there is considerable evidence in the experimental literature on equity that the allocator will attempt not only to use these principles in the allocation process itself but also to restore equity in the event that an inequitable decision has been made in the past. Affirmative action procedures were designed with such a restorative objective in mind. If allocators with high utilities for equity have the opportunity to make repeated allocation decisions involving exactly the same individuals (say, in deciding on annual pay raises), they may be expected to use such opportunities to redress any perceived wrongs that have been done in the past. Where they are making repeated decisions involving similar candidates, they may also be expected to balance out a decision that is adverse to a given group by one that is more favorable to it. Needless to say, such subsequent decisions, although favorable to underrepresented *categories*, may be inequitable to some of the *individuals* involved. Allocators who have considerable concerns for equity may find themselves engaged in difficult juggling acts trying to satisfy their own internalized demands in such instances.

Equity theorists also note that inequitable decisions may be made "psychologically equitable" by means of cognitive distortions of various kinds. Here, rationalizations involving vaguely defined criteria may rather easily be invoked. An allocator who has compensated for previous patterns by favoring, say, a black job applicant over a slightly more qualified white may do so on the grounds that the former applicant had greater "potential" or filled a "need" in the department into which he or she was being placed. In contrast, minority candidates may be systematically passed over on the grounds that anticipated outcomes would be unfavorable because other employees would not accept them or cooperate with them to increase work productivity.

If one accepts the relatively simple equity formula that inputs be proportional to outcomes, it still remains possible to juggle the notion of a candidate's inputs to include almost anything one wishes. Indeed, equity theorists also point to the self-serving tendency of allocators in all those instances where persons are permitted to allocate rewards to themselves. They may do so, for example, by simply emphasizing those inputs or investments that favor themselves over other candidates. We may assume much the same self-serving propensities on the part of third-party allocators, especially in those instances where there is room for considerable discretion in the choice of criteria or the weights to be attached to such criteria. Thus even in those instances where there is a major concern that equity principles be followed, there is also considerable room for slippage in their actual application.

## TIME PERSPECTIVES
## OF ALLOCATORS AND MODEL IV

Allocating agents are often placed in situations that virtually force them to make decisions based on very short-term considerations. They may or may not be in a position, later on, to make compensatory allocations, nor may they even be motivated to do so. Parents, for example, may be continually faced with the actions of a problem child who, for whatever reasons, demands their immediate attention. Thus they may allocate virtually all of their time and energy to that child at the expense of other siblings. Whether they then later compensate those other children may depend on whether or not the problem child continues to demand their attention. Of course in many instances we would anticipate a continued process of differential demands accompanied by a catering to these demands that, over the long run, has important and negative consequences for the child's competitors. A similar phenomenon may take place in the classroom, where slow learners and troublemakers may usurp virtually all of the teacher's time, day after day.

In such instances the allocator is in effect attempting to reduce the immediate strains produced by a select subset of competitors, often without adequate regard for their own long-term interests or other equity considerations. If the allocating agents, themselves, are either serving on a temporary basis or perceive themselves to be making decisions that may, at some later time, be compensated for by another set of allocators, such short-term considerations may come to predominate. Teachers are often placed in such settings, for example. Either they may be primarily concerned with getting through the day as smoothly as possible, under trying circumstances, or they may persuade themselves that other teachers will somehow correct for their own inequitable allocations of time and energy. Perhaps they may believe that those students who do not cause problems really do not need as much assistance. Where pressures exist to improve the performance levels of the slowest students, so that they may be passed along to the next higher level, and where their supervisors are primarily concerned that the students not "make trouble" for themselves, such short-term considerations can be expected to predominate.

University officials are often faced with annual or biennial budgetary processes imposed by state legislatures and are therefore likely to make allocation decisions based on political considerations, as for example the need to please troublesome lawmakers, influential alumni, or trustees. They may also make expedient decisions favoring those faculty who bargain for higher salaries by threatening to resign. In addition, there are at times troublesome departments that need to be "corrected" by providing them with additional funds to hire new faculty with distinguished reputations. Those units that do an effective job without complaining may be penalized in the process.

My own observations of such decision-making processes lead to the conclusion that, under the circumstances, there are strong tendencies for allocators to think only in terms of the short run by deliberately refusing to examine long-term drifts or trends in say, differential salary levels, student-faculty ratios, or faculty quality in general areas such as the Humanities.[2] There is also a tendency to hide allocation criteria from the view of departmental chairs or representatives of faculty senates, often under the guise of the need for confidentiality. Where there is "consultation" with the faculty or lower level administrators, the very real need to meet legislative deadlines provides a convenient opportunity to rush through allocation decisions without providing such other interested parties with sufficient time to collect their own information or even to digest that which they have been given. The rushed atmosphere in such situations is then often followed by a lull, during which no real discussion or consideration of long-term trends ever takes place. Then there is again another hurry-up period and short-term decision process, sometimes exacerbated by unanticipated legislative policies or changes in the economic climate. Equity concerns are placed on the back burner.

Short-term thinking and the minimization of allocator effort also often lead to what has been termed "disjointed incrementalism" that fails to restore equity imbalances (Braybrooke and Lindblom, 1963). If, for example, there are at any given time substantial salary inequities arising as a result of "market" considerations, the path of least resistance may still be to ignore the problem and to adjust salaries by applying a constant multiplier to every unit, say a 5% salary increase. Similarly, if new positions become available or must be taken away, it is simplest for allocators to prorate such benefits or costs among units, rather than examining their current levels in relation, say, to student-faculty ratios or faculty performance. It is generally much easier to justify across-the-board incremental allocations than it is to face up to equity concerns, which will of course be defined somewhat differently by each recipient unit. In effect, it is the allocator's own convenience that becomes the operative allocation criterion.

Cynicism and a sense of helplessness is likely to be one long-term result of such processes, but it will in general be difficult to pin the responsibility on the allocators themselves. In the case of faculty, for example, those who recognize that faculty salaries are set primarily by the market will become tempted to seek outside offers even when they have no real intention of leaving. Others, reluctant to follow this strategy, will reduce their loyalty or perhaps even lower their own performance levels or seek additional sources of financial compensation.

Where it is possible to pass inequities down the line to other recipient parties, a compensatory mechanism may in effect restore equity at the expense of these other parties. Social science departments, for example, typically find themselves understaffed relative to science departments and some of the humanities (e.g., small foreign language departments). Faculty in understaffed departments may not be overworked, however, if they merely accept such an equitable allocation system and compensate by teaching extremely large lecture courses in which objective examinations and short papers replace more intensive contacts and more frequent feedback opportunities for their students. Or unqualified teaching assistants may be given heavy responsibilities incommensurate either with their salaries or experience.

Thus the effort to restore equity at one level results in an inequitable allocation process at another. The long-term consequences of such processes may be hidden from view of university administrators and ignored by the faculty, who are often much more concerned with their own short-term welfare. Since it is often exceedingly difficult to assess long-term consequences, and since the causal chains that produce them are also likely to be highly com-

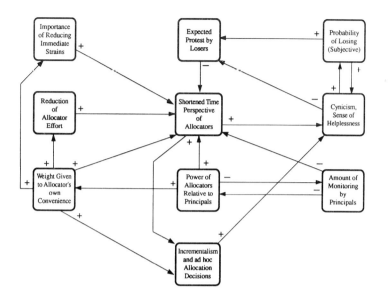

**Figure 4.1.** Model IV: Time Perspectives of Allocators

plex and subject to varying interpretations, all parties concerned may continue to think primarily in terms of the short term and their own immediate welfare.

## A Nonrecursive Causal Model

As a supplement to the more inclusive and largely recursive model discussed at the end of the chapter, we can provide a much simpler model containing 10 variables and diagrammed in Figure 4.1. Notice that the model cannot be described in terms of exogenous, intervening, and dependent variables since each variable has both causes and consequences. This can readily be seen by noting that every box has both arrows that enter it and others that lead to another variable. If data were available for each variable, it would therefore not be legitimate to break the system apart, equation by equation. Ordinary least squares (or any other single-equation approach) would lead to biased estimates. Even more important, this particular system is underidentified, meaning that none of its coefficients could be estimated without adding to the model. This would require either the specification of discrete lag periods, and data at the appropriate intervals, or an additional set of truly exogenous variables to which none of the 10 variables in the system had any feedback effects (Hanushek and Jackson, 1977; Johnston, 1984; Namboodiri et al., 1975).

We may nevertheless examine the model. Beginning at the top left and working across and then downward, the model implies that the importance of reducing immediate strains on allocators operates to shorten the time perspectives of such allocators but is itself a function of the weight the allocator gives to his or her own convenience. The degree to which there is an expected protest by losers, however, is predicted to increase the time perspectives of allocators, while itself being affected by Cynicism and Sense of Helplessness among competitors and by their subjective probabilities of losing. This latter variable, which appears in the top right-hand corner, is assumed to be reciprocally and positively related to cynicism. Those who become cynical about the process are predicted to increase their pessimism, whereas those who are already pessimistic about their chances are anticipated to increase their levels of cynicism.

Moving to the second row in the figure, Reduction of Allocator Effort is presumed to reduce the time perspectives of allocators, under the assumption that the easy way out is usually that of making a set of adjustments to immediate pressures or short-term changes. Reduction in Allocator Effort, in turn, is taken as an effect of Weight Given to Allocator's Own Convenience.

Shortened Time Perspective of Allocators is nearly a dependent variable, except that it is assumed to affect cynicism and is therefore involved in the four-variable feedback loop appearing at the top right-hand corner of the figure. Shortened time perspectives are also postulated to affect incrementalism and allocators' tendencies to make ad hoc decisions. Other causes of shortened time perspectives, all coming from the variables in the third row of the figure, are Weight Given to Allocator's Own Convenience, Power of Allocators Relative to Principals, and Amount of Monitoring by Principals. The cynicism variable appearing in the final column is taken as an effect of incrementalism, presumably with a temporal delay that might be built into a more dynamic model specifying time lags.

Turning to the third row, and considering only the linkages not yet discussed, the model implies that the more powerful allocators are relative to their principals, the greater the weight they will tend to give to their own convenience, with this variable in turn increasing tendencies toward incrementalism and ad hoc decision making. Power of Allocators Relative to Principals is also assumed to be in a positive feedback loop (involving two negative signs, however) with Amount of Monitoring by Principals. The greater the allocators' power, the less the monitoring, if only because allocators will be in a stronger position to prevent such monitoring or to permit only very token monitoring efforts. In return, the less the monitoring and therefore information flowing back to principals, the less real power they will be able to exert over their allocating agents.

Finally, when we reach the bottom row we find that the 10th variable in the model, Incrementalism and Ad Hoc Allocator Decisions, has already been discussed. It is assumed to be affected positively by two variables, shortened allocator time perspectives and the weights they give to their own convenience. Incrementalism, in turn, is predicted to affect the amount of cynicism among recipient parties.

## DEVIANT OR CORRUPT ALLOCATOR PRACTICES

Noting that allocators practically always have their own private interests and agenda, which may depart considerably from the objectives of their principals and from those that have been officially recognized, we must examine the ways in which these private interests impact upon the allocative decision process. It is also likely that there will be two normative systems impacting on the allocators, the one for public consumption and the other for insiders. The latter may also be widely recognized and supported by the public, even where it remains only implicit. "Everyone" may know that bribery is rampant and considered as one of the perquisites of the allocator role. If one wants to enter the competition, he or she must be prepared to play the game as it has been defined by the allocators themselves.

In American politics it is well recognized that so-called pork-barreling and log-rolling will take place. Otherwise, any given legislator will be unable to accomplish the objective of providing goods to a narrowly defined constituency—and thus will not be reelected. Admissions officers at private colleges may know that they are expected to favor unusually gifted athletes or the children of wealthy or powerful alumni. Contracting officials in many third-world countries routinely expect side payments if they are to agree to sign contracts with European or American business firms. Those Pentagon officials who are in charge of awarding contracts to selected bidders are frequently drawn from the ranks of these same companies or else they expect to join them on retirement from government service. So supposedly secret information is conveniently leaked to favored bidders. Allocators may sometimes be expected to set informal quotas on certain types of students through the imposition of supposedly neutral criteria, such as the desirability of having a geographically or culturally diverse student body.

The principals on behalf of whom the allocators are operating may or may not be fully aware of such devious practices though, as discussed in Chapter 3, in many instances they may elect to look the other way or to make only very informal hints if they prefer such practices to continue. This permits them the luxury of deniability and the opportunity to scapegoat individual allocators should the practice be publically exposed. Where deviant practices are common knowledge, it is also often convenient to engage in ritual firings of allocators found guilty of the most flagrant transgressions, if only to preserve the cover for the remainder.

Such practices simultaneously remind allocators that they need to remain careful to cover their tracks or to preserve the illusion that officially sanctioned practices are being strictly followed. Even the U.S. Congress has been known on rare occasions to sanction its own most deviant members, should their practices gain too much notoriety. Through such cleansing rituals the public then satisfies itself that the system is working well, even when considerable corruption remains. The temptation to look the other way will be especially great if the costs of genuine reform are considerable.

We recognize, as well, that the recruitment of future allocators is likely to be influenced by their knowledge and expectations concerning the role. If corruption and allocator deviousness become prevalent, one would expect that honest allocators will be difficult to find, whereas those who are not especially concerned about the norm of adhering to the rules of fair play will be attracted to any situation in which they will in effect receive side payments for taking advantage of the existing system. Honest allocators may find the dilemmas involved too costly and may gradually be replaced by those who are more capable of resolving them in accord with their own private interests. If allocators have the opportunity to select their own successors, say through nepotism, it may be very difficult to modify the system in fundamental ways.

One of the keys in this connection is the ability of both principals and representatives of potential candidates to monitor the actual ongoing allocation process. Where the allocating group consists of a team of persons who form a selections committee, it may be possible, for example, for minorities or other underrepresented categories to gain representation on such a committee, thereby inhibiting at least some of the more overt biases of the other members. Likewise, under some circumstances it may be possible to insist that the data on which allocation decisions have been made be opened to the inspection of the public or a neutral third party. In the political arena there may be watchdog groups such as Common Cause, the League of Women Voters, or members of the press that insist on opening up the allocation decision process to public scrutiny.

Often, however, allocation procedures may remain biased or corrupted for long periods of time, so much so that they are merely taken for granted as "the way the system works." Myrdal (1972), for example, noted the practice among what he referred to as "soft" democracies in South Asia of relying much less on rigid regulations or taxation policies that admit no exceptions than on those that permit considerable discretion on the part of relevant officials. Such a system is wide open to corruption, especially whenever such officials are carelessly monitored and poorly paid. The acceptance of bribes may be so widespread that it becomes almost hopeless, and costly, to replace existing officials with more honest ones. The system becomes institutionalized and rationalized as either inevitable or harmless.

Under such circumstances applicant pools may likewise be affected to the extent that certain classes of potential candidates will simply rule themselves out, recognizing that their chances of winning would be too slight to warrant the effort. Or they may not be in a financial position to offer sufficiently attractive bribes to the allocating officials. Cynicism may become rampant, and even those charged with the responsibility of monitoring the system may be bought off or met with total noncooperation. The dividing line between bribery and graft, on the one hand, and legitimate gift-giving, on the other, may also become blurred. In Japan, during 1988 and 1989, there were several political scandals involving just such blurred standards. At what point does the acceptance of a substantial gift by a political figure simply constitute a polite form of behavior, and at what point an instance of bribery? Such practices have also reached the highest levels of American politics, including the Presidency itself.

There is another kind of dependency that may arise whenever the allocating agents have greater power and can convince recipients that they have been favored over those equally qualified. In such instances the effort is to build up a set of arrangements through which recipients feel obligated or indebted to the allocators, with the expectation being that they will later return the favor. Indeed, certain features of this kind of situation were evidenced in feudal attachments of vassals to their lords. Having received the favor of being placed in charge of a large landed estate, the vassal was in turn expected to demonstrate loyalty in the form of military support when needed. Presumably, an allocator who can retain actual control over the goods or land being supplied to those who have been selected will also ensure such subsequent loyalty with a much higher probability than one who lacks the power to withdraw the favor. Many kings and members of the nobility discovered to their regret that recipients' loyalties were highly conditional, especially in those instances where their vassals were able to pass along titles and landed estates to their heirs.

Corrupted systems frequently become recognized by interest groups that do not benefit from them. Whenever there is a very diffuse responsibility for reform efforts, however, as is the case with respect to current American electoral procedures, it may simply mean that there are many complaints but few coordinated efforts to correct widely known abuses. In other instances, there may be organized efforts to change the system that are counterbalanced by approximately equally strong movements in the opposite direction.

Major social cleavages may exist but result in inaction primarily because the status quo seems more satisfactory than any other alternative that could possibly achieve united support. Dominant groups may, for example, be only subconsciously aware that an allocation process is biased in their favor but may be forced to rally behind it in the event of a serious minority challenge. Should such a challenge actually be successful, say as a result of court action, the dominant group may find other more subtle ways to maintain a biased selection procedure that has been suitably modified to delete the specific practices that have been successfully challenged, while substituting others that are on the surface not overtly discriminatory. Jewish quotas may, for example, be replaced by residential quotas, as actually occurred in the 1940s and 1950s in connection with admissions to elite New England colleges and universities.

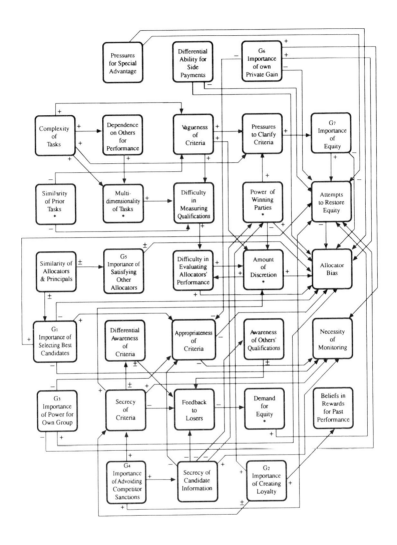

**Figure 4.2.** Model V: Allocator Decision Processes

In all such instances, the probability of reforming the system is likely to depend on the relative resources of beneficiaries as compared with those who stand to lose more than they gain from existing practices. One factor that favors the status quo is the likelihood that successful competitors under a corrupt system are more likely to be able (and willing) to afford to offer bribes or other forms of side payments. Those who consistently lose, in contrast, must usually depend upon alliances with third parties, such as an impartial court system. If such third parties can also be bought off by the coalition of corrupt officials and affluent applicants, there literally may be no place to turn. Unless a very high degree of cynicism develops within the elite—as apparently occurred in France prior to the revolution of 1789—the system may remain essentially in place for a very long period of time. There may be superficial efforts at monitoring, combined with a convenient ignorance that affords deniability on the part of those at the top. But the costs of instituting substantial system change may simply be too great.

## CAUSAL MODEL V:
## ALLOCATOR DECISION PROCESSES

In Figure 4.2, containing 31 variables, the 11 exogenous variables appear across the top, down the left-hand column, and across the bottom row. Dependent variables are again placed in the last column, with intervening variables being toward the center of the diagram. Since our discussion in the present chapter basically involves a continuation of Chapter 3, there are several variables common to both models. These variables are designated by asterisks appearing at the bottom of the appropriate boxes and are also starred in the listing of variables below. Since they have already been described, they are simply given the titles (in parentheses) used in Chapter 3. We proceed with a listing of the variables.

## The Exogenous Variables

Again, the exogenous variables are listed as they appear in the figure, beginning with the top row, then down the first column, and finally across the bottom row.

(1) The pressures applied by groups of competitors for special advantages (Pressures for Special Advantage)
(2) The differential abilities or willingness of competitors to make side payments to allocators (Differential Ability for Side Payments)
(3) Goal 6 of allocators, to ensure their own private gain (Importance of Own Private Gain)
(4) The complexity of tasks associated with the position (Complexity of Tasks)
(5) *(Similarity of Prior Tasks)
(6) The similarity of interests between allocators and their principals (Similarity of Allocators and Principals)
(7) Goal 1, the importance to allocators of selecting the best candidates (Importance of Selecting Best Candidates)
(8) Goal 3, the importance to allocators of retaining power for their own group (Importance of Power for Own Group)
(9) Goal 4, the importance to allocators of avoiding negative sanctions by competitors (Importance of Avoiding Competitor Sanctions)
(10) The degree of secrecy in supplying information about qualifications of candidates (Secrecy of Candidate Information)
(11) Goal 2, the importance to allocators of creating loyalty and motivation among competitors (Importance of Creating Loyalty)

## The Intervening Variables

We proceed from left to right and then downward.

(1) The degree to which recipients' later performance will depend on cooperation of others (Dependence on Others for Performance)
(2) The degree to which performance criteria are vaguely defined (Vagueness of Criteria)

(3) The degree to which there are pressures on allocators to clarify the criteria they use (Pressures to Clarify Criteria)

(4) Goal 7, the degree to which equity or distributive justice considerations are important to allocators (Importance of Equity)

(5) *(Multidimensionality of Tasks)

(6) The degree of difficulty allocators have in measuring competitors' qualifications (Difficulty in Measuring Qualifications)

(7) *(Power of Winning Parties)

(8) Goal 5, the importance allocators attach to satisfying other allocators or principals (Importance of Satisfying Other Allocators)

(9) The degree of difficulty others have in evaluating allocators' performance (Difficulty in Evaluating Allocators' Performance)

(10) *(Amount of Discretion)

(11) The degree to which competitors are differentially aware of allocators' true criteria (Differential Awareness of Criteria)

(12) The degree to which allocators' criteria are evaluated by others as being appropriate (Appropriateness of Criteria)

(13) The degree to which competitors are aware of each others' qualifications (Awareness of Others' Qualifications)

(14) The degree to which allocators' actual criteria are kept secret from competitors (Secrecy of Criteria)

(15) The adequacy of feedback to losers concerning the true reasons for allocators' decisions (Feedback to Losers)

(16) *(Demand for Equity)

## The Dependent Variables

Finally, we list the four dependent variables, proceeding downward in the last column.

(1) The degree to which allocators actually attempt to restore equity (Attempts to Restore Equity)

(2) The amount of allocator bias in the actual decision made (Allocator Bias)

(3) The degree to which principals or competitors find it necessary to monitor allocators (Necessity of Monitoring)

(4) The degree to which competitors believe rewards are based on past performance or loyalty (Beliefs in Rewards for Past Performance)

*Discussion of the Model: Effects of Exogenous Variables*

The seven goals of allocators discussed toward the beginning of the chapter are identified at the tops of their respective boxes by the symbols $G_1, G_2, \ldots G_7$. Five of the seven are taken as exogenous and therefore are discussed in the present section. We begin by examining the assumed effects of the three exogenous variables appearing across the top row of the figure.

Pressures for Special Advantage and Differential Ability for Side Payments are each expected to affect negatively the dependent variable Attempts to Restore Equity and to increase Amount of Allocator Bias. Both of these exogenous variables are expected to amplify any preexisting allocator subjective biases, thereby reducing allocators' tendencies to restore equity but increasing the actual biases in their final decisions.

Goal 6, Importance of Own Private Gain, is predicted to have negative impacts on Appropriateness of Criteria and Attempts to Restore Equity. It is also expected to have positive effects on Necessity of Monitoring and on Amount of Allocator Bias. The assumption is that allocators who place a high premium on private gain cannot be trusted and will tend to make biased allocation decisions in line with their own vested interests. To the degree that this is anticipated by others, the perceived necessity of close monitoring will also increase.

Complexity of Tasks is predicted to have positive effects on four variables. If recipients are expected to perform complex tasks it should be difficult to come up with simple, clearcut criteria for evaluating their qualifications. Therefore the effects on Vagueness of Criteria and Multidimensionality of Tasks should be positive. If expected tasks are complex, there should also be added pressures placed on allocators to clarify their criteria, including the relative weights used in arriving at a decision. It is also assumed that complex tasks will generally involve greater dependencies of recipients on others, such as coworkers, in their subsequent environments.

Similarity of Prior Tasks is expected to have negative impacts on two variables, Vagueness of Criteria and Difficulty in Measuring Qualifications. Where candidates have already performed tasks that are very similar to those being expected, one may rather simply translate their prior performances into expected ones, as for example occurs when college athletes are being evaluated for professional teams. Where their earlier performances involve very different skills, however, evaluation not only becomes more difficult but new and presumably less clear-cut criteria may need to be invoked.

Similarity of Allocators to Principals is presumed to affect two variables, although with indeterminate signs represented by the ± sign. It should affect the first goal, that of selecting the best candidates, positively if the principals also share this goal (as seems likely) but negatively in those instances where the principals also wish to select specific categories of candidates. Similarity is also expected to reinforce the fifth goal, Importance of Satisfying Other Allocators, whenever these others also share the goals of their principals. If, however, other allocators do not share common goals with such principals, the allocator under consideration will be placed in a dilemma, finding it difficult to satisfy both sets of others by the same actions.

Importance of Selecting Best Candidates, the first goal, is predicted to have negative impacts on Necessity of Monitoring and positive effects on Attempts to Restore Equity. In the former instance the assumption, of course, is that potential monitors actually share the desire to locate the most deserving candidates, and in the second it is that the cause of equity is served if such candidates are located. Similarly, the importance of this goal is expected to have a positive effect on Appropriateness of Criteria and a negative one on Allocator Bias.

The third goal, Importance of Power for Own Group, is predicted to have a negative impact on Appropriateness of Criteria and on Attempts to Restore Equity, but a positive one on Allocator

Bias. This obviously assumes that the allocator's own group is not actually the most deserving one. Goal 4, Importance of Avoiding Competitor Sanctions, is assumed to have positive effects on the two secrecy variables: Secrecy of Criteria and Secrecy of Candidate Information. It is also postulated to have a positive impact on Attempts to Restore Equity, under the assumption that competitors actually prefer equitable decisions and are therefore less likely to sanction allocators whenever they perceive them to have occurred.

Secrecy of Candidate Information is predicted to impact negatively on four variables: Appropriateness of Criteria, Feedback to Losers, Awareness of Others' Qualifications, and Power of Winning Parties. In general, then, one would expect allocators to prefer to keep each candidate's qualifications secret from his or her competitors. It is also predicted, however, that the greater the secrecy the greater the need for monitoring the allocation process, a possibility that would generally work against allocators' own interests. Not considered in the model, incidentally, is the possibility that allocators may actually provide candidates with *false* information about their rivals' qualifications. Perhaps by successfully doing so they may also obviate demands for information through monitoring.

Our final exogenous variable, the second goal, Importance of Creating Loyalty, is the only variable in the model assumed to affect the dependent variable, Beliefs in Rewards for Past Performance, which we argued may be highly important in instances where candidates' services are desired even after they have lost in any given competition. Importance of Creating Loyalty is expected to impact positively on Power of Winning Parties to the extent that there is a strong need to maintain such loyalty and therefore a willingness on the part of allocators to pay a certain price for such loyalty. Importance of Creating Loyalty is also predicted to affect Secrecy of Criteria, though with an indeterminate sign that is likely to depend on allocators' expectations as to whether or not the actual criteria used will meet with the approval of competitors. Of course, they may be preferred by some classes of competitors but not others, in which case allocators may attempt to provide differential information to such parties.

This completes our discussion of the effects of exogenous variables. We turn next to a consideration of the impacts of the intervening variables, some of which play key roles in the model. We proceed across each row, beginning with the second.

## Discussion of the Model: Effects of Intervening Variables

Dependence on Others for Performance is assumed to affect positively only Multidimensionality of Tasks, the presumption being that task interdependence requires interpersonal skills and willingness to cooperate and coordinate activities, over and above any purely technical skills involved. Vagueness of Criteria is assumed to affect three other variables, all positively. It is expected to increase Difficulty in Measuring Qualifications for rather obvious reasons. But it should also affect Pressures to Clarify Criteria, assuming of course that competitors and/or principals are aware of such a vagueness and do not wish to permit undue discretion on the part of allocators. Such allocator discretion is also assumed to be affected by the vagueness factor.

Pressures to Clarify Criteria, in turn, is presumed to affect, positively, the seventh goal, Importance of Equity. The assumption here is that this particular goal is likely to be enhanced to the degree that allocators are held accountable for their decisions. Importance of Equity is itself assumed to have a positive effect on Attempts to Restore Equity and a negative impact on Allocator Bias.

Multidimensionality of Tasks, which we encountered in Model III, is rather naturally expected to impact positively on Difficulty in Measuring Qualifications, which in turn is predicted to increase Difficulty in Evaluating Allocators' Performance. Thus there is presumed to be a rather simple causal chain running from task complexity, through multidimensionality and difficulty in measuring qualifications, to difficulty in evaluating the allocators themselves.

Power of Winning Parties, which also appeared in Model III, is assumed to affect three variables. The first is Pressure to Clarify Criteria. Of course if nearly all members of a given category or group of persons turn out to be winners, they may possibly rest satisfied with the decision, but the assumption here is that any powerful group of competitors will be in a position to insist on allocator accountability and that they will be sufficiently in doubt regarding the outcome that they will exercise such power. By the same token, powerful winning parties will also be able to reduce allocators' discretion, a variable that also appeared in Model III. Finally, Power of Winning Parties is expected to increase Allocator Bias, assuming of course that there are also less powerful categories of competitors who cannot exercise a similar kind of pressure.

The fifth type of allocator goal, Importance of Satisfying Other Allocators, is also expected to affect Allocator Bias, but with an indeterminate sign depending on the stances taken by these other allocators. Where they, too, are acting in a biased manner, then any allocator who values their support will tend to display a similar bias. If, however, they are acting in an equitable fashion, such an allocator will also be expected to exercise minimal bias.

Difficulty in Evaluating Allocators' Performance is expected to be reciprocally related, positively in both directions, to Amount of Discretion. If allocators' judgments cannot be easily evaluated, this will presumably permit them greater discretion, and especially so to the degree that outsiders find it necessary to respect their expertise. In the opposite direction, a high degree of discretion means that allocators may utilize criteria that are mysterious or nebulous to such outsiders, making evaluation all the more problematic. Difficulties experienced in evaluating allocators' performance is also predicted to increase allocator biases, assuming of course that strains toward bias are present. In effect, allocators will be given a relatively free hand in making decisions. Amount of Discretion, which also appeared in Model III, is also expected to impact positively on allocator bias.

Differential Awareness of Criteria is predicted to affect Feedback to Losers, although with an indeterminate sign. On the one hand, such a differential may result in the further withholding of accurate information to such losers. If, however, the losers have sufficient power as well as the suspicion that they lack information provided to others, they may demand more accurate feedback.

Appropriateness of Criteria is presumed to reduce Necessity of Monitoring, assuming of course that those who might otherwise be suspicious of allocators' judgments will be mollified if they judge the criteria being used to be appropriate and the allocators qualified to employ such criteria accurately. Appropriateness is also expected to reduce Allocator Bias, under the assumption that allocators are actually using and giving substantial weights to such appropriate criteria.

Awareness of Others' Qualifications is predicted to affect a single variable, Feedback to Losers, though with an indeterminate sign. If allocators know or believe losing candidates already possess such information, they may have to be more candid about the total package of criteria. One can imagine situations, however, in which differential or even incorrect information may interfere with the communication process between allocators and losers, and especially so when this results in a high degree of mistrust among the latter parties.

Secrecy of Criteria is likewise assumed to have an indeterminate effect on Differential Awareness of Criteria. Total secrecy may reduce any differentials between winning and losing candidates, but partial secrecy may actually increase such differentials. Secrecy is also assumed to reduce the adequacy of feedback for rather obvious reasons. Finally, secrecy is anticipated to increase both Necessity of Monitoring and Amount of Discretion.

Feedback to Losers is assumed to affect a single variable, Demand for Equity. It is presumed that the less adequate the feedback to losing parties, the more suspicious they will be and the greater will be their demands for equity. Finally, Demand for Equity, which also appeared in Model III, is expected to have a positive effect on allocator attempts to restore equity, the more so to the degree that the allocators concerned place a high value on the importance of achieving equity.

*A Note on the Dependent*
*Variables and Their Implications*

There is only a single direct causal relationship among our four
dependent variables, namely a postulated negative impact of Attempts to Restore Equity on Allocator Bias. It should be noted that
all of our dependent variables deal either with decision bias itself,
or the need to correct for possible biases in the allocation process.
It is of course conceivable that the many postulated direct and
indirect causes of bias may cancel one another out in any given
application of the model. It should be noted, however, that the
predominant biasing factors tend to favor relatively powerful competitors at the expense of weaker ones, and parties that are similar
to the allocators over those that are different. Therefore whenever
there are many other decisions being made by similar allocators,
as for example in hiring situations, one may anticipate a cumulative impact resulting in gross inequalities among different categories of competitors.

Our models have thus far dealt primarily only with the allocators
as actors. We have also assumed that competitors come, ready
made, to the attention of such allocators. In the remaining chapters
the focus of attention will shift more to questions of how a particular set of candidates did or did not happen to appear in lists of
competitors, how such candidates pass from one pool to another,
and how they evaluate allocation decisions in terms of distributive
and procedural justice criteria. We begin, in Chapter 5, with a
discussion of several different kinds of candidate pools and the
factors that affect whether or not given potential candidates actually enter the explicit pools being considered by the allocators of
concern.

# NOTES

1. Considerations of equity and distributive justice will be discussed in detail in Chapter 7, where references will also be provided. Here we merely take note of a concern for equity as one of the possible goals of allocators.

2. March and Olsen (1976), interestingly enough, introduce their notion of "garbage can" decision making with reference to university administrators. This phrase seems to be an especially apt one in connection with the processes with which we are presently concerned.

# Eligibility Pools

In this and the following chapter we shall be concerned with the nature of the pools from which competing candidates are selected, as well as the processes by which individuals self-select themselves into or out of such pools. Thus, for the most part, our focus will be on the behaviors of the competitors themselves and only secondarily on the allocators. We begin with the assumption that allocators merely select from among some list of candidates, although of course their past choices may have indirectly affected the composition of such eligibility pools. In a sense, then, there is a kind of two-party model being employed. Individuals elect to enter or exit certain pools, allocators select from among candidates remaining in such pools, and then winning and losing candidates react to these decisions, perhaps by challenging the outcomes or withdrawing from future competitions.

Whenever one is attempting to assess success rates among two or more categories of competitors or is constructing a measure of inequality as an indirect indicator of discriminatory behavior on the part of relevant allocators, it is necessary to provide a denominator for each of the categories of interest. Numerators will presumably be readily available, being the numbers of successful candidates from each category. Perhaps a company has hired 200 whites and only 20 blacks. Perhaps one university has a student body composed of 85% whites, 10% Asian-Americans, and 5% blacks and Hispanics. But suppose we do not know how many from each category actually applied for admission, and among these how many met minimum eligibility requirements.

In the absence of additional information, a naive assumption is that one may rather simply use the relative numbers of some local population base as an appropriate denominator. If 10% of the local population is black, then unbiased selection procedures should yield approximately that same percentage in all competitive arenas: those hired by company X, the proportion of fire and police officers, those admitted to the nearby university, or those who succeed in making the high school football team. The implicit assumption being made, of course, is that whatever distribution of talents, performances, and personality characteristics exists within an applicant pool, this distribution is completely unrelated to those characteristics being examined: race or ethnicity, age, sex, prior training, and so forth. The completely naive assumption is likely to be rejected in obvious instances, as for example the expectation that there should be roughly equal numbers of boys and girls on the football team. But it is much more likely to be accepted uncritically in the case of an applicant's educational credentials. A high school degree is a high school degree, regardless of the school's location within the city or its local reputation.

The focus of attention in the present chapter is basically on the nature of the applicant pools from which successful and unsuccessful candidates are drawn. It is certainly unrealistic to assume random entry into such pools except in extremely simple situations in which competitors have no choice in the matter. Under what conditions, however, is it legitimate to assume that qualifications of pool members are essentially randomly distributed, so that they are totally uncorrelated with ascribed characteristics? If one makes such a simplified assumption—as is commonly done in quantitative studies of discrimination—what kinds of biases are likely to result?

As we noted in the introductory chapter, if one studies returns to education as an indicator of employer discrimination, and if one measures "education" as "years of formal schooling completed," then one is in effect ignoring quality of education or is assuming that schooling quality is randomly distributed across schools and the applicants from these schools. Yet, if in another context one claims that, in fact, black students receive poorer quality schooling than their white counterparts, how can one at the same time justify such an assumption? Are the analyst's biases behind such an assumption, or is he or she merely being careless in the uncritical use of measures with presumably well-known biases? In short, are the denominators being used the proper ones, given reasonable assumptions about applicant pools?

In order to discuss such questions it is necessary to make a number of distinctions among different types of pools and then to discuss the nature of the processes involved whenever some persons become selected into these pools whereas others are not. If one does not wish to make the extreme assumption of pool homogeneity on all characteristics relevant to an allocation process, then it becomes critical to examine the nature of these pools and the pool entry processes. To this we now turn.


## EXPLICIT, QUALIFIED, AND POTENTIAL POOLS[1]

By *explicit pools* we shall mean the set of individuals who actually appear on the list of candidates who are being evaluated in the allocation process. Such a list may have been purged of obviously unqualified applicants, as for example those who do not possess a high school degree, a required number of years of work experience, or other minimum or maximum qualifications that have been clearly designated in advance. In the case of a hiring situation, the explicit pool would consist of those eligible persons who have actually taken the trouble to make official application for the position in question. Similarly, in the case of candidates for medical school or college entrance, the pool would consist only of those who had filed applications prior to the specified deadline.

Clearly, there may be a number of otherwise eligible candidates who fail to appear within the explicit pool, perhaps through their own choice, because they were unaware of the competition, or because their applications were inappropriately disqualified. Some such qualified persons may live inconveniently far away, though with suitable inducements they might have been encouraged to relocate or to endure somewhat inconvenient travel arrangements. Others might have made application but failed to do so because they believed, correctly or incorrectly, that their chances of selection were exceedingly small or that, if selected, they would be placed in an uncomfortable setting. Still others may have been influenced by friends or family to look for other alternatives, perhaps those in which they would be able to retain closer contacts with congenial affiliates.

There is thus likely to be a *qualified pool,* consisting of the explicit pool *plus* those who would have been eligible but, for whatever reasons, did not make formal application or did not appear on the actual list of applicants for the positions of concern. In most instances it will be unrealistic to assume that members of the explicit pool are randomly selected from the more inclusive qualified pool, in which case empirical evidence will be required to pinpoint the nature of self-selective mechanisms through which explicit pool members' names actually appeared on the list of applicants being considered. In principle, however, if "true" qualifications can be accurately measured, it will be unnecessary to impose a set of causal or theoretical assumptions in order to ascertain the more inclusive qualified pool membership. Once a search has been made for such a membership list, studies may then be conducted to compare the characteristics of those who did and did not make application to appear in the explicit pool. Such information may then be used to evaluate alternative theories concerning whatever selective processes are assumed to have been at work.

There is, however, a still more inclusive sort of pool, which we shall refer to as the *potential pool.* We recognize that there is likely to be an even larger set of individuals who, with suitable additional training or experience, might readily gain the necessary qualifications to enter the qualified and explicit pools. Here we encounter much more elusive problems, however, as "potential" is not only a vague term, but one that may be used selectively by different parties to modify pool boundaries in various ways. One might claim, for example, that there are many local blacks who have the potential for college or a skilled labor position but who were discouraged from obtaining the necessary training. Perhaps some dropped out of high school because they perceived a lack of employment opportunities in the region. They may not have pursued a technical degree in college because they believed that careers in medicine or engineering were closed to them. If so, and with suitable encouragement, they might have developed their potential sufficiently to become eligible for inclusion in the qualified pool. But then again, perhaps not.

In asking whether or not certain classes of individuals belong in such a vaguely defined potential pool, one needs a causal theory concerning the mechanisms by which qualifications are obtained. Especially in instances where prolonged training would have been required, a host of causal factors may have to be introduced, only some of which could reasonably be attributable to the allocation agents or their surrogates. Perhaps a set of overtly discriminatory practices during an earlier decade may have discouraged black youth from completing school. It might even be the case that teachers, school advisers, and local community members may have conveyed the message that there were virtually no opportunities for black or female scientists or doctors. Even though the current situation may no longer justify such beliefs, there would of course be considerable temporal lags involved. A generation of school children socialized to believe these "facts," which may have been accurate at the time they were in grade school, may then be totally unprepared to take advantage of opportunities that have suddenly developed. If so, one could claim that they belong in the potential pool, even though they currently lack the necessary qualifications.

The problem is, of course, that the actual processes at work will not have been this simple. Some of those with the potential may simply have been lazy. Or their interests may have been steered by success stories of another nature, say into aspiring to a career in professional sports. They may have joined nonacademically oriented peer groups, partly because of a lack of alternatives but also because of the inherently interesting activities involved. They may have performed poorly on standardized exams, partly because of poor motivation but also partly because of a genuine lack of abilities or disciplined training. Our theoretical problem is that of pinning down, much more carefully than in the case of qualified pools, the precise causal mechanisms through which persons with the "true" potential for qualified pool entry have failed to achieve these necessary qualifications. The biases of the analyst are especially critical, here, because of the high proportion of unmeasured variables and lack of available data over a prolonged time span.

## SEQUENTIAL POOLS

In examining pool entry mechanisms it will often be necessary to take into account the fact that individuals may pass through a series of stages which, at each point, may determine pool entry at later stages. Children are passed along year-to-year from one grade to the next, with at least the theoretical possibility that they may be required to repeat or, at later ages, be permitted to drop out of the qualified pool for entry into subsequent pools. Still later, they will elect whether or not they wish to enter the labor pool, military service, marriage, or perhaps the pool of unemployed.

A defining characteristic of the ideal-type sequential pool setup is not only that pools are entered in a definite temporal sequence but also that a *necessary* requirement for pool entry at a given level is that one have passed through each of the prior ones. Thus in order to be admitted to college, one must have completed high school. To enter medical school, one must have graduated from college, and in order to practice medicine one must have completed medical school requirements. Whereas satisfactory performance in prior pools constitutes a necessary condition for entry into subsequent ones, however, it is not also *sufficient*. Not all high school graduates will be admitted to college, nor may they even take actions to enter the explicit pools from which college applicants are selected. Given that each successive pool becomes more and more restrictive, and given that there will be a lack of homogeneity among those who have passed through a particular pool, it then follows that some sort of selectivity mechanism will be operative.

"Eligibility" is a word that usually connotes that someone has met a set of minimum qualifications, say as a high school graduate, but that ultimate selection into the next higher level is by no means guaranteed. Many social science researchers, however, impose very simple homogeneity assumptions because of a lack of data. Candidates declared eligible are presumed to be nearly identical with respect to qualifications. Less restrictively, it may be assumed that the necessary *and* sufficient criteria are completely uncorrelated with those status characteristics they, as researchers, are examining. If there are assumed to be ability differences among high school graduates, these are assumed to be uncorrelated with race, sex, or some other characteristic.

Such rather strong assumptions, which are often only implicit, are then used to justify the use of total pool figures as denominators in the fractions used to assess allocator biases. If there are 100 minority and 400 white high school graduates who apply for admission to a given college, then the expected minority percentage among admitted candidates is taken to be 20%. Such a figure may be modified by taking into account a few more attributes, such as high school grades, but similar homogeneity or independence assumptions must then be made in order to arrive at an "appropriate" denominator. Among all high school graduates with at least a 3.0 grade point average (GPA), the distribution of "true qualifications" is assumed to be unrelated to race or sex. The fact that some high schools may be much easier than others, or that courses upon which each student's GPA has been calculated may not have been equally demanding, may be ignored by making the implicit assumption that these factors are also uncorrelated with the ascribed characteristics being examined.

Whenever there are sequential pools, the problem of assigning responsibility for discriminatory allocations becomes especially difficult unless one rather simply assumes that allocators at all lower levels are under the control of those at higher ones. Suppose, for example, that one blames the membership in a professional society, say the American Sociological Association, for the low percentage of minorities in its leadership roles. Only 3% of such leaders may be minority members. Suppose, however, that its membership as a whole consists of only 2% minority owing to a "pipeline" problem stemming from a scarcity of minority applicants to doctoral programs. This very small percentage, in turn, may possibly be blamed on college and university faculty, or perhaps admissions officers, who in turn fault the K-12 system. If it can credibly be argued that it is the sociology *faculty* who are responsible for such small numbers, with these faculty, in turn, being responsible for the policies developed by their professional society, then perhaps any "discrimination" in the latter organization may be attributed to its "gatekeepers" among the faculty.

Again, the problem may be treated as that of finding the appropriate denominator to use in providing a proportion of minorities below which a claim of "discrimination" should be made. Is it the number of minority *members*, the number of minority Ph.D.s or persons in the "qualified" pool, or perhaps even the number of minority students who graduate from college or are thought to constitute a potential pool of applicants? Unless one is willing to assume absolutely no responsibility for pool entry to the minority members themselves, then the responsibility of one set of allocators is necessarily only partial. Some, indeed, may have admitted "underqualified" applicants at one level, only to discover that the performances of such persons were in fact marginal. Others may have actively discouraged all but those with nearly impeccable credentials, in which case it will be probable that those accepted will "overperform" in comparison with nonminority members. Should a relatively poor average performance in the first instance be blamed on the system or on a highly favorable initial allocation involving a high percentage of "at risk" candidates?

The general point is that *some* simplifying assumptions will inevitably be required to assess self-selective mechanisms involved in moving from a prior pool to a later one unless, of course, persons are automatically passed along, or unless a random device is used to choose among successful and unsuccessful candidates at the next and subsequent levels. The assumptions made by allocating agents are likely to differ from those of the critic or data analyst, given the peculiar combinations of biases each may have. The best one can hope for, then, is that such assumptions, as well as the actual allocation criteria that have been used, can be brought into the open where they may be examined for their implications.

Unfortunately, however, it is often the case that all parties will have vested interests in keeping their own underlying assumptions implicit and hidden from view. The social scientist, of course, is provided with scientific normative criteria that supposedly operate to uncover such hidden assumptions, but in fact they usually fail to do so. Perhaps even worse, if one accepts the myth that all such assumptions are being laid bare when in fact they are not, it may be even more difficult, and costly, to bring such assumptions into the open. As noted, one such assumption underlying much of the "returns to education" literature, is that *quality* of education may safely be ignored in relating years of formal schooling to whatever outcome variable one is examining.

The above considerations imply a need for rather complex causal theories specifying the nature of selective mechanisms and biases that may be operative in determining which kinds of individuals, among those who have successfully passed through any one level, are selected into the next. We also see, by implication, that even the notion of a qualified pool is much more elusive than one might think unless one is willing to assume that the "true" qualifications (e.g., a high school "education") coincide with those that have been measured or recorded (e.g., a high school diploma). Obviously, then, it will be even more difficult to pinpoint the actual boundaries of a potential pool in those instances where only a rather small proportion of those who have passed through a given pool are realistically eligible for the next.

# HIERARCHICAL POOLS

By the expression *hierarchical pools* we shall refer to situations in which any given individual may become a member of several different but overlapping pools, either simultaneously or sequentially, and where these pools are ranked in some fashion. For example, a student may simultaneously apply to three different colleges, A, B, and C, that are ranked according to desirability or prestige such that A>B>C. Similarly, a job applicant may apply for three different jobs also ordered in the same way. Some applicants, however, may have applied to only two of these schools or jobs, whereas still others may have applied to four or five. Thus pool memberships will be overlapping, both in the sense that several contain many of the same applicants but also in that any given applicant may belong to a variety of pools, the number of which varies according to the application strategy of the individual.

Thus in the hierarchical setup under present consideration, the overlapping pools are not "nested," as implied in the sequential pool situation. Since positions in one college or business firm are defined as more desirable than those in another, we *are* assuming (in the ideal-type situation) a hierarchy of *preferences* that is the same for each applicant. We shall assume that if three organizations are uniformly ranked in the order A>B>C, then if an applicant is accepted by all three, he or she will in turn accept A; if accepted by only B and C, the preference will be for B, and so forth. We therefore introduce the complication that, with multiple hierarchical pools, the applicant will decide not only which pools to enter but also which offers to accept if more than one organization replies favorably.

If one looks only at the *results* of such selection processes, rather than the offers made that are either accepted or refused, it is very easy to obtain highly misleading measures of allocator biases or discriminatory behaviors. Suppose, for example, that all three organizations are bidding highly for minority candidates and that a given such person is accepted by all three organizations. If he or she then accepts A, this implies that there will be an after-the-fact removal of candidacy from both B and C. Since such an individual will not appear on either of the latter organization's rolls, however, the numerator will have been reduced by one, unless it is based on "offers made," whereas the denominator will be unaffected. Exactly the same patterns of *offers* on the part of allocators in A, B, and C will therefore result in the most favorable percentages in A and the least favorable ones in C. The latter organization will, of course, achieve a lower percentage of successful offers (i.e., those that are actually accepted by their candidates), simply because its *real* pool contains only those persons who were also unacceptable by both A and B.

This particular kind of problem may of course be handled, provided one has the actual data on multiple pool entries, the preference rankings that applicants have made, and a detailed record of the offers made that have been declined. Even in such a favorable case, however, there could be additional subtleties involved, as for example the possibility that allocators in the least favored organization C actually anticipate refusals among its top candidates and concentrate, instead, on the bottom half. The problem is, of course, that such data are rarely available unless applicants have been asked to list the other organizations to which they are applying, along with their preference rankings among them. Even so, would it be realistic to assume honest candidate responses to such supposedly irrelevant inquiries? Probably not.

What all of this implies, then, is that high prestige organizations can be presumed to "look good" in terms of their achieving allocation objectives. If there is, for example, a relatively small pool of minority candidates for which all organizations are bidding, the top ranked ones will be in a position to "cream" from the elite applicants and therefore appear to have the least discriminatory policies if only the final results are tabulated.

If all organizations are using strictly universalistic criteria but different cutoff points, the resulting distributions may be just the reverse, however. If say, black performances on standardized tests are on the average below those of whites, and if organization A is able to use a higher cutoff point than B or C, then relatively fewer minority applicants will be accepted by A. Whether or not such results are deemed based on "discriminatory" behaviors on the part of the allocators in A will then depend on the judgment as to whether the test scores being used were themselves biased against the minority or merely unbiased estimates of their actual performance potential. Once again, the assumptions used by the several parties involved become crucial in assessing the degree of discrimination or biased allocation decisions.

## STRUCTURES OF SEQUENTIAL
## AND HIERARCHICAL POOLS

Assuming that there are distinct sets of allocators for each of several sequential or hierarchical pools, it may make a substantial difference whether or not the pools of either type are very much smaller than the lowest ones. Consider, for example, the sequential

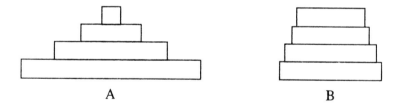

A          B

**Figure 5.1.** Sequential Pool Pyramids Involving Different Relative Sizes

pool setups represented by Figures 5.1A and 5.1B or the hierarchical (and partlyoverlapping) pools depicted in Figures 5.2A and 5.2B. In the first of both sets of pairings, the top pools are very much smaller in size than the lower ones, yielding a pyramidal structure.

**Figures 5.2.** Hierarchical Pool Pyramids Involving Different Relative Sizes

In the second sets, by contrast, the pools are of approximately the same size. These relative sizes may be affected by demographic factors such as the age and sex compositions of the different pools, by rates of pool entry and exit, by the relative attractiveness or the incentives provided to successful candidates, or perhaps by absolute or relative growth rates in the demands for new members at each level.

Suppose we are concerned with sequential pools and are taking the perspective of the allocators in the ultimate or highest pool. In Figure 5.1A there will be a much larger eligible pool of candidates from which to select. Indeed, in Figure 5.1B there may be very few surplus candidates from whom to select, meaning that allocators may have little real choice other than to weed out the very bottom tier of graduates from the prior level. Although their task may thereby be made much simpler, the quality of selectees may be much lower than would be the case represented by Figure 5.1A. This would be true, however, only if we assumed essentially the same exit requirements from the next lower pool. If virtually all members of that pool were automatically graduated regardless of their qualifications or performances, then the selectivity afforded at the next higher level would be more apparent than real. It is to the interest of allocators at the top level, then, to have a relatively large but yet well-qualified pool at the next lower level. The same will obviously apply at all prior levels, though allocators at these levels may perhaps have weaker vested interests in having large pools from which to select.

There may be circumstances, however, in which too large a pool may create problems, as for example when there are so many losers at a given stage that there is substantial social discontent. Should this be the case, it may be necessary for allocators or their principals to locate alternative opportunities for such losers or perhaps to create realistic opportunities for them to compete in subsequent contests in which they have an experience advantage over more recent contestants. In the ideal, then, the rational allocator will attempt to estimate some optimal percentage of winners and losers and then try to maintain the applicant pool at approximately the right size. Where training is prolonged, however, and where the organization's future growth is difficult to predict, this may be a very difficult task indeed. From the standpoint of allocators at any given level in sequential pool setups, it may be helpful to have available a set of competing organizations with somewhat lower prestige, so that those candidates who fail to be selected in a given competition can be syphoned off into other hierarchical pools as a safety-valve mechanism. If the supply of applicants subsequently falls too far, the organization concerned can always modify its selection standards downward. If there are not enough high-quality candidates for Harvard, it can always tap into the pools of lesser institutions.

As implied, the shape of the sequential pool structure will often be a function of processes that are beyond the allocator's immediate control, such things as the changing age structure of the local population or the proportion of persons at each level who wish to continue in the competition for top positions. Knowing this, allocators and their principals are likely to attempt to control those processes that are more amenable to manipulation. Often this means placing sympathetic persons in positions of influence over these processes: state legislators, school superintendents or principals, deans of business schools, and so forth. Enrollment policies at state universities and community colleges, for example, can be affected by legislative budgets, as can priorities concerning the training of different kinds of students. The less predictable or the more variable are the factors beyond allocators' immediate control, the more we would expect them to make indirect attempts to influence allocation decisions at prior levels.

In the case of hierarchical pools the situation is somewhat different. In Figure 5.2A the pools at the top of the status hierarchy are very much smaller than are those nearer the bottom, whereas in Figure 5.2B the relative sizes are much more equal. In both kinds of situations organization A has the advantage in that it can select from a substantial pool, leaving its rejects to move downward in the hierarchy. Lower level pool allocators are therefore at the mercy of policies and structural developments taking place near the top. Should organization A decide to expand, it will attract a relatively large proportion of applicants who would have previously entered organization B, and so forth down the line. There is a sense, then, in which lower level organizations will prefer highly elitist policies among their superior competitors, provided that this also means a higher proportion of rejected candidates at those levels. If the total pool of candidates, say high school graduates, is reduced owing to demographic changes, it is quite possible that those organizations near the very bottom will run out of applicants. If they cannot dip still further downward, they may find it necessary to drop out of the competition altogether, either by literally closing down or drastically altering their functions.

Such organizations, then, will have the strongest incentives to develop policies ensuring a continued flow of applicants. Whether, as nonelite organizations, they also will have *power* to do so is another question. State-supported but lesser quality institutions of higher education may sometimes be located in densely populated areas, providing them with the necessary political clout to pass legislation favoring themselves at the expense of the more elite colleges. Thus in many states we witness a kind of leveling tendency among public institutions that does not have a counterpart among private colleges.

Faced with recruitment problems both public and private colleges may attempt to modify ideological systems by decrying the "elitism" and "snobbishness" of their more successful rivals or by playing down the value of "traditional" forms of education as compared with experimental programs of different types. Such efforts, of course, involve attempts to modify the relative standings of the institutions in a hierarchical pool, or at least to break off a segment of the potential pool so as to create a different ranking system within which their own relative position is improved. Local business colleges, for example, may attempt to convince older adults that liberal arts educations are far less practical than those they are able to provide at lower cost and greater convenience.

At the social system level, which we are unfortunately not able to examine in the present work, there will therefore be a number of strains resulting from the changing relationships among and within organizations placed in different positions with respect to applicant pools. Allocating agents or their principals may have to cope with the larger problem of assuring adequate pool sizes and compositions, often in a competitive, zero-sum game situation vis-à-vis similar organizations. Sometimes the pool applicants will be beneficiaries of such competitive processes, as for example when the total number of potentially qualified applicants falls to low levels. When this occurs, even applicants with very marginal qualifications may find themselves being bid for by lower ranked organizations in hierarchical pools or being pushed into higher level pools in a sequential setup. If there are not enough high school graduates, standards may be lowered and special remedial programs instituted at the next higher level. There are therefore many implications of allocation processes that need to be studied at the macro level.

## POOL ENTRY AND WITHDRAWAL PROCESSES

Competitors rarely if ever enter pools as a result of random processes but are selected into them by a variety of mechanisms. Furthermore, pool entry processes may involve prolonged periods of socialization, so that a variety of agents may impact on these processes at different stages. Potential competitors may also make a series of decisions which, ultimately, will help determine whether or not they enter the final stage, at which candidates are selected from some explicit pool by a final set of allocating agents. Given

253467890123456789201

the variety of processes that may in general be operating, what can be said more specifically about them? Our task in the present section will be that of outlining the nature of certain kinds of rather typical mechanisms. We can then present the first of two causal models that focus specifically on eligibility pools and the processes by which individuals sort themselves into and out of such pools and the nature of the decision processes that allocators may use.

From the standpoint of pool entry processes there will obviously be a number of costs to potential competitors in terms of time and money, including costs of preliminary training or general education, with a number of possible distractions along the way. Many such costs will occur long before actual pool entry occurs, at which earlier times the advantages and disadvantages of alternative pools will be neither salient to the individuals involved nor at all easy to predict. Young children may *say* that they wish to be doctors, nurses, police officers, or cowboys but can hardly be expected to link their chances of ultimate success to the learning of proper grammar, the mastery of arithmetic, or the study of science. The social scientist wishing to study the relative impacts of different socializing agents during this prolonged process would have an almost impossible task, and so simplifying assumptions must inevitably be made. Many factors will be either neglected altogether or treated as involving a form of conspiracy among elite members of "the system."

Later on, there will also be a number of more easily identified costs of entering the ultimate explicit pool, namely those of making formal application, waiting in line, or possibly changing one's residence. There will in addition be anticipated costs should the applicant succeed, as for example travel costs to work, costs associated with having to associate with persons who are believed to be unfriendly or uncooperative, or giving up old work associates. There will be "sunk costs" associated with one's former position, with these being expected to increase with time, so that the anticipated costs of entering a new pool will be greater the longer one has remained in the prior situation.

Potential candidates must also be in a position to learn about openings in a timely fashion and must therefore be tied in with the appropriate informal networks that facilitate pool entry (Granovetter, 1974). Even in instances where entry mechanisms are well known and publicized, as for example the possibility of applying to a local community college, actual entry may be encouraged or discouraged by peers or by those officials with whom potential candidates make initial inquiries. Where officials seem unfriendly, have obviously different behavioral or cultural mannerisms, or send out disheartening signals, pool entry may be discouraged. Complicated application forms, inconvenient inquiry locations, or a lack of familiarity with persons who have previously and successfully applied may also inhibit pool entry. Whether or not the ultimate allocators are aware of or even partly responsible for blocking mechanisms such as these may be difficult to determine empirically, given the opportunity for deniability of responsibility and the subtleties that are often involved. Even so, factors such as these are in principle much easier to identify and correct than those that surround the potential pool applicants in their own local environments. Both may be important in affecting the relative numbers of persons who actually elect to follow through at the application stage of the process.

Closely related to the previously discussed set of factors are the perceived policies of the allocators. "They wouldn't have hired me anyway, so why waste my time applying!" Such perceptions will be a joint function of actual prior allocation outcomes, possible recent changes in such outcomes, officially announced policies (e.g., affirmative action), and the prior experiences of potential pool candidates and their friends and other members of their support networks. Teachers may directly discourage all but the most outstanding of their minority students from applying to the local university or to specific employers having reputations for discriminating against similar persons. Oppositely, they may overencourage students with marginal records under the assumption that past policies have been drastically reversed. Here we are dealing with subjective factors that may or may not be based on an accurate perception of current realities. The assignment of responsibility for influencing such subjective factors will in general be exceedingly difficult and is likely to be heavily influenced by the biases of the social scientist, the allocator, the social critic, or even the potential pool applicants themselves.

There may also be a number of personality characteristics of potential pool applicants that have developed over a long period of time, including such things as self-esteem, general optimism-pessimism, fate-control, the extent to which fear of failure dominates hope for success, risk aversiveness, the degree to which the individual feels responsible to others for support and assistance, and so forth. Obviously, any list of factors that will be most relevant in a given instance will depend upon both the setting involved and the nature of the pool the candidate is considering. Given the relatively low explanatory power *at the individual level* of many of these kinds of personality characteristics, there is a tendency to neglect their overall importance. At the *aggregate level*, however, whenever a given category of persons differs from some other category on one or more of these characteristics, it remains possible that relative *rates* of entry may be impacted, just as birth rates may vary by ethnic group even though predictions at the individual level will be only very weakly associated with categorical group membership.[2]

Finally, as a distinct kind of personality trait, it may be helpful to single out the time perspectives of the actors concerned. Some persons think primarily in terms of the present or the short-term future, whereas others are more inclined to defer gratifications, plan for careers, or work methodically toward more distant objectives. Since in many instances successful competition requires the cumulation of resources and a record of prior successes, those with longer time perspectives may have a considerable advantage in view of the allocators' selection criteria. In a few instances a candidate's time orientation may come out explicitly in a private interview situation or may be inferred on the basis of other information available only to the allocator. In other instances there may be a paper trail of publicly recognized accomplishments or failures that becomes an important ingredient in the allocation decision process. Certainly, it cannot be assumed that it is only the very recent past that provides useful information to allocators, although the degree to which the time factor is discounted and only the recent past evaluated is likely to be a matter of judgment that varies across allocators.

## A Note on Withdrawal Processes

The kinds of allocation processes we are considering are competitive, from which it follows that there will inevitably be losers. Those who consistently find themselves in such positions, or who for whatever reasons anticipate that the costs and likelihood of failure far outweigh the expected benefits of success, will be tempted to withdraw altogether from such competitive processes. This will of course remove them from the explicit pool of concern and probably also from the qualified and potential pools for subsequent competitions.

There can be any number of reasons for this kind of withdrawal behavior. Since there will always be costs attached to competing, including those involved in gaining the necessary minimum credentials, the path of least resistance may be that of passivity. This is especially so if there is a sufficiently rewarding support system available to those who withdraw or perhaps a group of peers who have elected to make the same response. Such persons may reinforce one another and develop a set of defense mechanisms that justify the withdrawal behavior. "The system is working against us!" "The job won't pay enough to make ends meet." "I'd prefer to stay at home and have children or help my parents." "Why be a sucker and work at McDonald's when I can earn much more dealing in drugs?" "School was too boring, anyway." "Why go to college when there are no good jobs at the other end?" Many such explanations are commonly cited in news accounts of ghetto youth, and we may presume that similar ones can be and are easily developed by other categories of dropouts from the competitive race.

From the limited perspective of the allocator, such dropouts merely eliminate a high percentage of expected losers, so that if the explicit pool is large and diverse enough, there is little or no real cost involved and, perhaps, a vested interest in encouraging such self-selecting mechanisms to continue. A large percentage of losers among the explicit pool could mean extensive disgruntlement and perhaps even an active challenging of the allocation process. Those who drop down to a lower pool or entirely out of the competitive system altogether, however, become the responsibility of someone else.

High status organizations that rank near the top of most candidates' hierarchical pools will generally have an abundance of candidates from whom to select. It is the lower status ones, and their allocating agents, who must be most concerned about reduced pools. Thus during periods in which there are relatively small numbers of high school graduates applying to colleges, it is the weaker institutions whose survival is really at stake that must dip down to persuade hesitant applicants that they indeed should consider enrolling. These weaker institutions, of course, usually have much less power in the overall allocation system than do their more prestigious counterparts, and therefore there may be little overall effort to take remedial steps to increase the total pool.

In many Third World countries there is indeed an oversupply of highly educated persons relative to the usually small number of governmental positions that really require specialized training. Such a setup can create a politically dangerous situation, with the losers among the educated elite constituting a vanguard and leadership for opposition movements. In such instances, the situation might be far more stable if the primary losers were much more disproportionately at the bottom end. Early withdrawal, say from an educational system, will from this standpoint be perceived by the elites as far less dangerous and less costly than the overencouragement of intensive competition for a relatively small number of high-level positions.

Gerhard Lenski (1966) has noted that in virtually all societies between the levels of simple hunting and gathering bands and modern industrial societies, there have been large numbers of expendables or outcasts. Such excess persons are likely to be produced, quite literally, as a result of inadequate birth control techniques and will constitute a substantial downwardly mobile population that is basically redundant to the economy. Sidney Willhelm (1971) has made a similar argument in connection with blacks in the American economy. His thesis is that reductions in the need for cheap, unskilled, and distasteful labor will lead to the ghettoization and redundancy of blacks, much in the same way that American Indians have been placed in reservations or permitted to join the ranks of the urban unemployed. In all such instances, as in the case of thousands of homeless persons in America, the general population is likely to become almost totally indifferent to their fate.

In our own society, complete indifference is likely to be masked by a set of contradictory beliefs and inconsistent social policies. On the one hand, there are efforts to maintain the belief that anyone who really tries will inevitably succeed, as did Horatio Alger and the *Little Engine That Could*. This American credo, however, is counterbalanced by what Gunnar Myrdal (1944) referred to as a pattern of "convenient ignorance." Welfare policies are similarly inconsistent. Just enough is provided to maintain the myth that every really needy person has a "safety net" preventing the fall into the abyss of extreme poverty. Yet far too little real support is provided to those who may be genuinely interested in pulling themselves out of the dependency pool through their own efforts. Thus the American public is getting approximately what it wants: a set of programs that help to relieve guilt and inhibit mass discontent, while at the same time being minimally costly, at least in terms of short-term considerations. Long-term costs, of course, can always be put off for others to pay. Meanwhile, those who elect to drop out of the competitive arena find that their own short-term

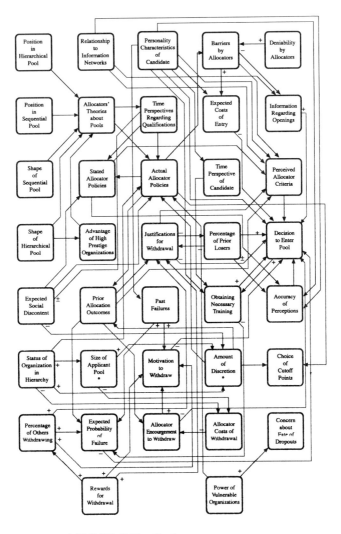

**Figure 5.3.** Model VI: Eligibility Pools

benefits are greater than the expected costs of reentering what is, to them, a threatening world in which they fully expect to remain the losers.

## CAUSAL MODEL VI: ELIGIBILITY POOLS

The 37-variable model of Figure 5.3 represents the first of two general models elaborating on predicted relationships among variables pertaining to the different types of pools discussed in the first portion of the chapter. The second of the two models will be presented in Chapter 6, which in effect constitutes a continuation of the present discussion. In Figure 5.3 there are 13 exogenous variables, given across the top, down the left column, and in the very bottom row. There are also 19 intervening variables, some of which play key roles, distributed throughout the interior of the diagram. The 5 dependent variables are again placed in the final column.

### *The Exogenous Variables*

The exogenous variables are once more numbered in accord with their position in the diagram, beginning with the top row, then moving down the first column, and ending with the two variables in the bottom row.

(1) The status position of the organization in a hierarchical pool (Position in Hierarchical Pool)
(2) The relationship of a potential candidate to information networks (Relationship to Information Networks)
(3) The various relevant personality characteristics of a potential candidate (Personality Characteristics of Candidate)
(4) The real and perceived barriers placed by allocators on a potential candidate (Barriers by Allocators)
(5) The degree to which allocators are able to deny responsibility for decisions in prior pools (Deniability by Allocators)
(6) The position of allocator's organization in a sequential pool setup (Position in Sequential Pool)
(7) The shape of a sequential pool pyramid (Shape of Sequential Pool)

(8) The shape of a hierarchical pool pyramid (Shape of Hierarchical Pool)

(9) The degree to which allocators expect a high degree of social discontent resulting from decisions (Expected Social Discontent)

(10) The relative status position of allocator's organization in a hierarchical pool (Status of Organization in Hierarchy)

(11) The percentage of similar persons who have withdrawn from previous competitions (Percentage of Others Withdrawing)

(12) The rewards expected by a potential candidate for withdrawing from competition (Rewards for Withdrawal)

(13) The power positions of organizations most vulnerable to candidates' withdrawal (Power of Vulnerable Organizations).

## The Intervening Variables

The 19 intervening variables are listed in order, moving from left to right and then downward. The 2 such variables already encountered in previous models are again preceded by an asterisk, with shortened titles in parentheses.

(1) The allocators' working theories about the composition of explicit and prior pools (Allocators' Theories About Pools)

(2) Allocators' time perspectives regarding attainment of candidates' qualifications (Time Perspectives Regarding Qualifications)

(3) The expected costs to a potential candidate of entry into an explicit pool or of winning competition (Expected Costs of Entry)

(4) Quantity and quality of information regarding openings available to a potential candidate (Information Regarding Openings)

(5) The officially stated allocator policies and criteria (Stated Allocator Policies)

(6) The actual allocator policies and criteria (Actual Allocator Policies)

(7) The time perspective of a potential candidate (Time Perspective of Candidate)

(8) The advantages of high prestige organizations relative to lower prestige ones in a hierarchical pool (Advantage of High Prestige Organizations)

(9)  The extensiveness of justifications or rationalizations for the withdrawal of a potential candidate (Justifications for Withdrawal)

(10)  The percentage of prior losers remaining in an explicit pool (Percentage of Prior Losers)

(11)  The actual outcomes of prior allocation decisions (Prior Allocation Outcomes)

(12)  The number of past failures of a potential candidate (Past Failures)

(13)  The degree to which a potential candidate has obtained the necessary training for pool entry (Obtaining Necessary Training)

(14)  *(Size of Applicant Pool)

(15)  The degree to which a potential candidate is motivated to withdraw from competition (Motivation to Withdraw)

(16)  *(Amount of Discretion)

(17)  The degree to which a potential candidate expects to fail in the competition (Expected Probability of Failure)

(18)  The degree to which a potential candidate is actually encouraged to withdraw by allocator (Allocator Encouragement to Withdraw)

(19)  Actual or expected costs to allocator if a potential candidate withdraws from competition (Allocator Costs of Withdrawal)


## The Dependent Variables

The five dependent variables are again listed in the order of their appearance in the final column.

(1)  The allocators' selection criteria, as perceived by a potential candidate (Perceived Allocator Criteria)

(2)  A potential candidate's actual decision to enter the explicit pool (Decision to Enter Pool)

(3)  The degree to which a potential candidate's perceptions are accurate (Accuracy of Perceptions)

(4)  The allocator's choice of cutoff points in a dichotomous decision (Choice of Cutoff Points)

(5)  The degree to which allocator is actually concerned about the fate of dropouts from competition (Concern About Fate of Dropouts)

*Discussion of the Model: Effects of*
*the Exogenous Variables*

As already noted, the model for this chapter has a dual focus on both the allocators who belong to organizations situated in different locations in either a sequential or hierarchical pool setup and also a hypothetical potential candidate for such a pool. Therefore, some of the variables in the model pertain to structural characteristics relating to the pool setup and others to the potential candidate who may or may not elect to enter the explicit pool being considered by the allocators of concern. We begin with the top left-hand corner of the figure, first working across, then downward and finally across the bottom row.

Position in Hierarchical Pool is assumed to affect the relevant allocator's working theories concerning the causes and nature of a candidate's background, but since the latter factor will undoubtedly be multidimensional, no signs can be attached to this arrow. Relationship to Information Networks of course refers to a specific candidate and is presumed to affect three variables: the amount of information the candidate receives about openings, the perceived allocator criteria for selection, and the accuracy of the candidate's perceptions. It is difficult to attach signs to these linkages, however, as much will depend upon the adequacy of whatever networks the candidate is using.

Personality Characteristics of Candidate represents almost a residual category of factors, the exact nature of which will depend upon the kind of allocation process being considered. Such personality factors may also affect other variables in the model, depending on the circumstances, but singled out are those thought to be generally most closely linked to the individual characteristics of potential candidates. These are Accuracy of Perceptions, Past Failures, Perceived Allocator Criteria, Obtaining Necessary Training, Expected Costs of Entry, Decision to Enter Pool, and Time Perspective of Candidate.

Barriers by Allocators are predicted, for rather obvious reasons, to have positive effects on Expected Costs of Entry to the degree that potential candidates are actually aware of such barriers and take them into consideration in their deliberations. Such barriers are also expected to impact negatively on Information Regarding Openings, under the assumption that some such barriers will involve the deliberate withholding of accurate information about possible openings. Barriers are also anticipated to affect Perceived Allocator Criteria. Deniability by Allocators is presumed to affect (positively) only the single factor, Barriers by Allocators, though it should also affect allocators' vulnerability to third parties and competitor pressures, factors that are not included in this particular model for reasons of simplicity.

The exogenous factors Position in Sequential Pool, Shape of Sequential Pool, and Shape of Hierarchical Pool are, like the first exogenous variable mentioned, expected to affect Allocators' Theories About Pools, and specifically how allocators in other organizations make their decisions and what implications these have for the composition of the explicit pool they, themselves, are considering. Additionally, the shape of a hierarchical pool is expected to affect the intervening variable, Advantage of High Prestige Organizations.

Expected Social Discontent is predicted to affect four variables, one of which of course is the actual allocator policy and another the officially stated policy. Expected discontent is also a presumed cause of reduced allocator discretion and is anticipated to affect the time perspective of the allocator. Although, in general, we would predict expected discontent to shorten the allocator's time perspective so as to handle immediate pressures, there may be special circumstances under which expected discontent may increase the allocator's time perspective so as to reduce the harmful effects of delayed responses. For this reason the "±" symbol has been used to represent an indeterminate sign for this particular linkage.

Status of Organization in Hierarchy is expected to increase the size of the applicant pool, under the assumption that more persons will want to apply for positions in high status organizations. We can imagine, however, a few situations under which an extreme elitist reputation may actually frighten away large numbers of applicants. The status of the organization should have a negative effect on allocators' expected costs of withdrawals from the total pool of applicants in that it will be primarily the low status organizations that need to fear a substantial total pool shrinkage. Status of Organization should also have a direct effect on allocators' actual policies and a positive effect on allocator discretion. Allocators in high status organizations are expected to have greater discretion than those near the bottom, who may have little choice other than to take whatever they can get.

Percentage of Others Withdrawing is predicted to have a positive effect on an individual's own motivation to withdraw from candidacy, as well as increasing that person's expected probability of failure. It will also be expected to increase the degree to which the candidate has a tendency to resort to justifications for withdrawing from competition. In all three instances, we are getting at the impact of peer experiences on a given candidate's expectations and behaviors. By the same token, Rewards for Withdrawal is expected to have a positive impact on Percentage of Others Withdrawing, the individual's motivation to withdraw, and the emphasis placed on providing justifications for dropping out.

The final exogenous variable in the model, Power of Vulnerable Organizations, refers to the amount of power possessed by those organizations near the bottom of a hierarchical setup. This variable is expected to impact directly on the actual policies of the allocators in such organizations, and perhaps also on those in more prestigious organizations. It is also predicted to have a positive effect on allocators' concern about the fate of those who may drop out of the overall competition. Such persons, it is assumed, will be disproportionately represented among the restricted pools of the lowest status organizations. To the degree that such organizations are also powerful, they may be in a position to insist that stronger efforts be made to keep such potential dropouts within their explicit pools.

*Discussion of the Model: Effects of the Intervening Variables*

In indicating the assumed effects of the 19 intervening variables, we again proceed by moving from left to right across each row, beginning with the second row in the figure.

Allocators' working theories about the composition of pools are assumed to affect Actual Allocator Policies and also Time Perspectives Regarding Qualifications. In the latter instance the presumption is that allocators will make differing assumptions regarding how several kinds of candidates have prepared themselves, how prolonged their training has been, the extent to which they have been assisted or actually provided with differential advantages, and so forth. Here such things as allocator prejudices, prior experiences with similar candidates, and popular folk images will come into play. In particular, allocators may assume that certain types of candidates are either more or less well qualified than are others, depending on the nature of the theories to which they subscribe. Allocators' time perspectives, in turn, are assumed to affect both their actual and their stated policies. In particular, they may rely relatively more heavily on immediate performance criteria than on reports of past performances.

Expected Costs of Entry on the part of the individual candidate are predicted to affect, negatively, that person's decision to enter the relevant pool. It will be recalled that such expected costs are functions of both personality factors and barriers that have been raised by allocators, with such barriers in turn being affected by the allocators' actual policies. Information Regarding Openings is also expected to affect the decision to enter the pool in question, with such information also being a function of allocator barriers, as previously noted.

Stated Allocator Policies are rather naturally assumed to affect Perceived Allocator Criteria, and therefore indirectly the candidate's decision to enter the pool. Stated policies are also assumed to affect the candidate's accuracy of perceptions, especially whenever the candidate is able to compare such stated policies with information received from his or her network connections. We assume, however, that allocators' actual policies are unknown to candidates and therefore may have only indirect effects, through stated policies, on both their accuracy of perceptions and subsequent decisions. Actual Allocator Policies, however, are assumed to affect Prior Allocation Outcomes, under the assumption that such actual policies have not undergone any changes in the interim. Actual policies, as already suggested, are also assumed to affect allocator barriers and allocator choices of cutoff points in instances where dichotomous decisions are being made.

The time perspectives of candidates, as noted, will undoubtedly be affected by a number of personality characteristics. In the model, this intervening variable is assumed to affect the single variable Obtaining Necessary Training, the presumption being that such training will require prior planning and a reasonably extended period of time before any tangible payoffs can be expected.

Advantage of High Prestige Organizations is predicted to affect allocators' theories about the nature of their effective or real pools, in contrast with the explicit pools with which they are dealing. Where high prestige organizations have a distinct advantage, as for example where they clearly stand out from the others, allocators from lower ranked organizations may very well ignore all applicants expected to be accepted by such organizations.

The nature and extent of a potential candidate's justifications for withdrawal will rather obviously negatively affect his or her decision to actually enter the explicit pool of concern. Such justifications are also expected to affect the candidate's perceptions of allocator criteria, perhaps serving to rationalize a decision not to enter the explicit pool. Justifications for Withdrawal are also anticipated to be reciprocally related, negatively, with Percentage of Prior Losers. The more such losers there are who have decided to remain in the pool, the weaker the justifications for withdrawal. In the opposite direction, the more frequent the justifications for withdrawal, the smaller the number of prior losers who will be motivated to try again and to remain in the pool in question.

Here we are of course studying the causal linkages between justifications or excuses for prior failures and the persistence of prior losers in future competitions. Also, the greater the percentage of prior losers remaining in competition, the more likely a given potential candidate is to decide actually to enter the pool. There is also a presumed effect of Percentage of Prior Losers on Accuracy of Perceptions, although with an indeterminate sign depending on what the actual allocator criteria happen to be.

Prior Allocation Outcomes, as one might expect, play an important role in the model by affecting the perceptions and behaviors of current potential candidates. They are predicted to affect Justifications for Withdrawal, Perceived Allocator Criteria, Expected Probability of Failure, and Allocator Encouragement to Withdraw. The last of these postulated relationships is based on the presumption that allocators will be aware of previous outcomes and will incorporate these into their working theories concerning candidates of different types. Where they believe some of these to possess inferior qualifications, this is then expected to lead them to discourage such persons from entering the race.

Past Failures of individual potential candidates are expected to increase their expected probabilities of failure and also their motivation to withdraw from the competition. Obtaining Necessary Training is predicted to have a negative impact on one's expected probability of failing to the degree that the training concerned is perceived as relevant to one's competitive qualifications. There is also a reciprocal, positive relationship anticipated between the obtaining of necessary training and an individual's decision to enter the pool. Training should increase the probability of pool entry, again assuming the relevance of such training to one's qualifications. But earlier plans to enter such a pool should also increase a potential candidate's efforts to obtain training, under the assumption that such a person has a sufficiently longtime perspective to motivate such an action. In the case of the causal flow in this reverse direction, we therefore should ideally specify a temporal lag, the duration of which will depend on the nature and extensiveness of the required training.

Size of Applicant Pool is for obvious reasons predicted to have a positive effect on Amount of Discretion and a negative one on Allocator Costs of Withdrawal. In the case of the second of these relationships we anticipate a possible nonlinear relationship. Where a pool is extremely large, allocator costs of withdrawal are primarily a function of per person expenses of processing or evaluating a huge excess of candidates. As pool size becomes much smaller, however, costs will also be a function of the quality of lost applicants, especially so among those organizations having low status in a hierarchical setup. Once more, we assume that such organizations will display a greater sensitivity to total pool size (and composition) than will those closer to the top of the hierarchy.

Motivation to Withdraw is assumed to be affected by four variables but to affect (negatively) only the potential candidate's decision to enter the explicit pool. Amount of Discretion, which has appeared in earlier models, is assumed to affect Choice of Cutoff Points, Actual Allocator Policies, and Prior Allocation Outcomes, the last of these relationships under the assumption that discretion has remained relatively constant over the relevant period of time.

Expected Probability of Failure, which is assumed to be directly affected by four of the variables in our model, is rather naturally anticipated to have a negative impact on a potential candidate's decision to enter an explicit pool. Allocator Encouragement to Withdraw is predicted to have a positive effect on a potential candidate's motivation to withdraw and a negative one, as well, on that actor's decision to enter the pool. By allowing for such a direct effect, as well as the indirect one through motivation, we are admitting the possibility of additional unspecified mechanisms through which allocator encouragement to withdraw affects the behavior. One of these, perhaps, is by affecting the candidate's assessment of his or her realistic chances of success, quite apart from the motivational factor. Finally, our last intervening variable, Allocator Costs of Withdrawal, is assumed to have a negative impact on Allocator Encouragement to Withdraw.

## A Note on the Dependent Variables

Of the five dependent variables the last two, Choice of Cutoff Points and Concern About Fate of Dropouts, refer to allocators and are of only minor importance in the model. All three of the remainder are of major importance, however, and refer to the perceptions and decision behaviors of potential candidates. There are only two additional arrows linking these three variables, both being drawn from the perception variables to the ultimate dependent variable, Decision to Enter Pool. As previously noted, this "final" dependent variable is presumed to feed back to Obtaining Necessary Training, with the proviso that the decision has actually been made in time to permit the actual attainment of such training. Presumably, the strength of this particular feedback arrow will depend on the nature of the training needed, the time it requires, and the proportion of potential candidates who have had the foresight to plan ahead. None of these variables are contained in this very general model but would presumably need to be incorporated in more specific models of particular allocation processes.

In the following chapter we shall continue to deal with sequential pools but focus almost exclusively on allocator rather than candidate behaviors. Then, in Chapter 7, we shall return to candidate reactions when we consider matters relating to distributive justice.

## NOTES

1. This and the following two sections are basically elaborations on discussions contained in Blalock and Wilken (1979), Chapter 12.

2. Although not *necessarily* so, it will generally be the case that correlations based on aggregated data will be considerably larger than those involving the "same" variables measured at the individual level. This is so because persons tend to self-select themselves into internally homogeneous groupings. See Blalock (1964) and Hannan (1971).

# Decision Processes in Sequential Pools

Allocators responsible for impacting on pool entry processes at different stages of a sequential pool setup may of course have very different interests or may fail to communicate with one another as to the real criteria they have been using in the candidate selection process. Possibilities for such miscommunication are especially likely whenever there have been multiple sequential steps or whenever the allocators at some earlier stage are numerous and in only indirect contact with one another. Allocators at any given stage are likely to make incorrect assumptions about the true characteristics or qualifications of the candidates who have entered their explicit pools. Such faulty assumptions are especially serious in their implications to the degree that, for any reason, contemporary allocators are unable to make their own independent assessments of the candidates but must rely on records or judgments produced during prior pool competitive processes.

One rather obvious kind of situation is likely to arise in settings where potential competitors, or their agents, have a tight degree of control over the socialization or training of those who will be permitted to enter the ultimate explicit pool. In the case of apprenticeship programs controlled by craft-type labor unions, for example, large classes of potential competitors may be excluded on the basis of ascribed characteristics such as race, religion, age, or gender. In effect, the potential pool is being limited in a manner that is obviously to the advantage of those favored categories that control this part of the screening process. Often, but not always, such exclusive practices are accomplished with the connivance of allocators at the higher levels, as for example those who intend to employ the apprentices once they have been trained and become eligible.

This will not always be the case, however, as it will often be to an employer's advantage to increase the size of the explicit pool and to find ways of playing off one group of competitors against another. In the case of skilled labor pools controlled through an apprenticeship arrangement, employers may seek to undercut wage levels by locating previously excluded pools, such as a racial or ethnic minority, and either train them by other means or redefine the division of labor in such a way that most tasks could be carried out by persons having lesser skills and, presumably, lower pay. Edna Bonacich (1972, 1976) has discussed such split labor market situations, suggesting that the success of the more highly skilled labor force may depend, among other things, on their ability to exclude rival categories by other means, such as intimidation or restrictive immigration policies.

Perhaps more common are those situations in which allocators at different levels simply use diverse criteria based primarily on their own immediate interests. Those who are responsible for training members of a student cohort, for example, may be in sufficiently weak power positions or subject to conflicting pressures that they simply pass along nearly everyone, regardless of their performance levels. Where they have evolved either a double standard of performance that applies the same criteria differentially among categories of persons (such as blacks and whites), or where they have simply permitted blurred standards to obscure real differences in performance levels, it may be virtually impossible for allocators at subsequent levels to place much credence on their reports or evaluations. Whenever nearly all letters of reference contain glowing appraisals of all candidates to graduate schools or for academic positions, such letters may likewise have to be ignored in the subsequent decision process. Unless allocators at these subsequent levels can develop their own independent criteria for evaluation, they must engage in a guessing game concerning the relative credentials of the candidates they are appraising. More than likely, the criteria they actually rely on will have to be based on short-term performances or relatively superficial judgments made in interview situations.

If an allocator at a later stage is attempting to assess potential, so as to estimate whether candidates will improve their current performance levels, that allocator is very likely to rely on a "working theory" concerning the handicaps that various competitors have been under, as well as the nature of prior efforts to help them overcome such handicaps. One such working theory, for example, may be that minority candidates will tend to have relatively greater potentials because of the fact that they have successfully overcome such handicaps, largely on their own initiative. A contrasting set of beliefs may be that minority individuals have already been the beneficiaries of affirmative action programs that have actually placed them at a competitive advantage or provided them with evaluations that are inflated judgments of their true performance potentials.

Ambiguous situations of this sort provide obvious opportunities for allocator biases to operate, so much so that allocators may be placed in a "no-win" situation if their decisions are later opened to public scrutiny. In effect, critics of opposite persuasions may rely on very different criteria for evaluating "potential." If so, the path of least resistance for the allocator may be that of biasing his or her decisions in favor of whichever parties are expected to exercise the most power in challenging the outcome, or whichever outcome is expected to be least likely to raise a public outcry. Weak allocators will be especially vulnerable in such situations and therefore most likely to bend their operating criteria in the least damaging directions. This may entail the playing of a numbers game, in which outcome frequencies are made to match very closely the distributions of eligible pool applicants. Indeed, governmental or other third-party regulations may virtually assure such a matching operation in those instances where quotas or targets have been set.

An important aspect of allocators' working theories will be their assumptions concerning the nature and extent of prior help provided to candidates of different sorts. Ideally, the allocator might like to know just how much a given candidate's performance is due to his or her own efforts, net of such outside help. Realistically, however, such information will practically never be available, and that which is provided is likely to be subject to considerable dispute. If the allocator adopts a universalistic perspective, basing the decision strictly on actual performance, regardless of the purported explanations for such a performance, such a decision is likely to be favored by those who would tend to be winners but opposed by those categories that tend to score lower on the criterion being used. In effect, outcome inequalities that might be attributed to a lack of *distributive justice* may be perceived by some as involving a lack of *procedural justice*. If so, the kinds of distinctions often made between these two kinds of defects in a justice system will be difficult to disentangle and will depend upon the working assumptions of those who are evaluating it from differing perspectives.

In the remainder of the chapter we shall discuss different kinds of allocation decision processes that in large part reflect the relative power positions of different kinds of allocators in sequential pool setups. We begin by examining situations in which some of the potential competitors, or their agents, have a high degree of control over the processes by which members of a given pool are passed along to the next level.

## POOLS CONTROLLED BY COMPETITORS OR THEIR AGENTS

Consider a relatively simple but yet rather common type of situation in which agents of potential competitors have a direct impact in controlling the nature of the ultimate explicit pool of candidates. Perhaps the most familiar such situation is that of the craft-type labor union that controls the flow of applicants through a monopolistic type apprenticeship program. In the extreme case, successful apprentices may even be guaranteed a position in some local market, perhaps the same organization in which the apprentice is being trained. The essential features of this type of situation are that not only are the numbers of successful candidates tightly controlled by their future competitors, but the nature of their training or apprenticeship is also determined by such persons, so that there are excellent opportunities to observe the apprentices in settings highly similar to the ultimate work setting and to socialize them so as to make it highly probable that they will become loyal members of the guild.

Rigid controls, as for example through apprenticeship programs, enable competitors to restrict pool entry to certain categories, provided that category membership can be easily identified. Racial or gender exclusion practices are obvious cases in point, but in some instances pool entry may also require that a person be recommended by a present member, so that the system may become wide open to the use of particularistic criteria of many different kinds. The ultimate allocators may still select among those who have been made eligible through an apprenticeship program, and if they are reasonably satisfied with performance levels produced in this fashion may actually welcome such a prior selective mechanism as a cost-saving device and as a mechanism for helping to assure the loyalty of new recruits who have been selected. Recruitment is kept within the family, so to speak. It presumes, of course, a high degree of cooperation between the ultimate allocators and those who control the pool entry process in this type of setup.

A looser form of entry control is exercised by some professional organizations that have a somewhat weaker connection with a delegated set of socializing agents, but who may control the total number of successful candidates through some sort of licensing procedure. In the fields of medicine, dentistry, and law, for example, there are limited numbers of universities permitted to grant appropriate degrees, some reasonably well agreed upon norms concerning the numbers of "apprentices" to be accepted, the programs of study to which they will be exposed, and a set of standards by which they will be evaluated. As an ultimate control on numbers, there may also be a set of licensing procedures, as for example within each state, that may be either loosened or tightened according to the current supply of professionals in the area and the anticipated demand.

A still looser socialization mechanism, but one that is still influenced by members of the profession that candidates will ultimately join, is one that is characteristic of most academic but nonprofessional fields. We may take sociology as an example. Here, as in the case of medical faculty, the socializing agents represent a relatively small but elite subset of the entire membership, namely the faculty at research universities of varying levels of stature. Although they may have a general stake in the competitive position of their entire discipline, these agents typically have their own agendas that operate to maintain a certain minimum level of graduate student enrollments, regardless of the local or national market demand. Graduate seminars must be filled, new research-oriented faculty attracted to the department, and a steady flow of freshly minted Ph.D.s produced so as to enhance the reputation of the department. Furthermore, there is little or no control by the profession itself over the number of Ph.D. granting institutions, with expansive pressures developing among ambitious departments that wish to start up new degree programs in order to enhance their own local standings. As a result, the control of both numbers and quality is relatively weak in spite of the fact that basic curricula may be subject to normative standards within the profession.

Obviously, the greater the degree of control over the flow of potential pool applicants that can be exercised by their future peers, the less the discretion available to the ultimate allocators. This will be true not only with respect to the absolute size of the explicit pool but also its quality and homogeneity. In craft-type setups such homogeneity may be extreme, or at least there will be the appearance of homogeneity to the ultimate allocating agents who may be virtually forced to accept candidates on a seniority basis. In other instances, the ultimate decision makers may be highly dependent on the word of the socializing agents, as is usually the case in connection with the hiring of newly minted Ph.D.s.

Where the degree granting institution can guarantee only a certain minimum level of competence and where the decision maker also recognizes that there will be a substantial range of variability above this minimum, the reputation of the socializing agent will be especially critical. This is certainly the case in academia, where a strong endorsement from a highly regarded member of the profession carries considerable weight. What happens in sociology, for example, is that a rather long list of job applicants is narrowed considerably, largely on the basis of such recommendations, until the "short list" of candidates is sufficiently homogeneous that the ultimate judges can break the ties primarily on the basis of job interviews or the candidate's presentation of a colloquium talk. In effect, only rather weak evidence can be used at this late point in the allocation process, given the presumed homogeneity of the smaller subset of candidates who remain in the explicit pool. There is a definite choice made by the ultimate allocators, but it often comes close to being a mere flip of the coin.

As noted, the interests of the socializing agents and the larger group of principals whom they supposedly represent are often only loosely coupled. In theory, the agents are looking to the interests of the profession as a whole, both with respect to regulating numbers and perhaps the pattern of ascribed characteristics as well. They are also supposedly delegated the responsibility of assuring quality control. Yet the agents have their own interests, which include personal aggrandizement, possible exploitation of trainees, and assuring a competitive advantage vis-à-vis other similar agents. Sociology departments, for example, typically operate to admit and produce a rather even flow of graduate students, so as to maintain the stability of teaching and research assistants and seminar enrollees. The fact that the demand for academicians may have fluctuated much more radically may either be conveniently ignored, treated as someone else's problem, or rationalized away by postulating some as yet undetermined future demand, as for example by business firms or government agencies.

In this connection it is useful to distinguish between those situations in which the market is local and capable of being supplied with minimal lag periods, and those in which it is more remote both in time and space. In the former case, those who help to socialize apprentices may expect to become their immediate competitors, with the possibility that such younger recruits will be in a position to undercut them in the local market. Where training periods are also relatively brief, it will also be much easier to predict local demand and, perhaps, to adjust the flow of apprentices into such a market. Where competitors are indeed in a power position to gain a local monopoly with respect to such socialization processes, we would expect a relatively tight system of apprenticeship and control, as compared with the previously discussed situation in which socialization agents produce for a much broader market that is expected to have only a limited impact on their own competitive positions.

It may also be useful to distinguish those situations in which apprenticeships involve closely supervised one-on-one relationships with their mentors from those in which they are trained much more on a "batch" basis. The former kind of training, being more labor-intensive, will be wasteful to the extent that there are substantial numbers of dropouts from the program, either because of strains within the training program itself or an anticipated weakening of the job market. Whenever the market is geographically widespread, whenever anticipated dropouts are numerous or whenever the size of the market is difficult to predict, we would anticipate that a batch-type socialization program would be more likely.

As an intermediate situation, we might expect to find batch socialization during the initial portions of a training program, followed by more intensive "practicum" programs toward the final stages when, presumably, relatively few additional dropouts are anticipated. Programs in education, and in schools of nursing and social work, may be cases in point. Given the high percentage of women in such fields, it used to be the case that—especially before professional commitments had been developed—attenuation rates were high in spite of the need for more closely supervised training at some point of the process. In such situations, it may even become a deliberate policy to admit relatively large numbers of applicants and then to expect high percentages of dropouts during the initial stages of the process. Such a "padding" of numbers also has the function of keeping up enrollment figures even in the presence of reduced demand at the ultimate stage. Somewhat the same kind of process seems to occur within the humanities, where there has until recently been a large surplus of Ph.D.s.

If the prestige of the occupation is high and the pay is also at an appropriate level, then we would expect that the entry pool from which apprentices or trainees are selected will be large. If so, it becomes critical to develop highly accurate predictors of performance, especially so if training is to follow the one-on-one apprenticeship model. In medical schools, for example, the actual failure and dropout rates are relatively low, so that much will depend upon the adequacy of the initial screening process. Unless candidates have previously been in a setting that is closely similar to that in which they will later be evaluated, however, it may be exceedingly difficult to make such accurate predictions. One possibility, of course, is to admit very large numbers and then to screen them rather quickly before intensive training has begun. Another is to rely very heavily on one or two standardized but difficult pre-screening courses, such as a biochemistry course in the case of medicine or a thermodynamics course in the case of engineering. Calculus courses often serve as more generalized screening courses for the sciences as a whole, and indeed the so-called math bottleneck has been identified as a major hurdle for female students who wish to enter these fields.

If those who do the actual socializing of potential candidates are only indirectly connected with the job market in their local areas, or if there are outside socializing agents (e.g., foreign medical schools) capable of flooding that market, the ultimate control over numbers may involve some sort of centrally administered examination in which the percentages of those who pass can be more carefully controlled. In such instances there may be an effective division of labor between the actual socializing agents, who may form close attachments to and vested interests in specific individuals, and the ultimate screening agents who utilize blind testing procedures to control numbers and assure a minimum quality level. Such a division of labor has the advantage of removing some of the inherent strains that arise whenever the same persons must serve as senior colleagues and even patrons of their students, while nevertheless evaluating them differentially. Collegial relationships among fellow training agents may also be protected by placing the ultimate competitive stage beyond their own immediate control.

## ALLOCATOR CONTROLS OVER PRIOR PROCESSES

In sequential pool setups the question naturally arises as to the degree to which allocators at any given level affect, directly or indirectly, the decisions made at prior stages, either by the allocators at these levels or by the potential candidates themselves. Conspiracy theorists and liberals may, for example, tend to assume that allocators at the very top of the sequential hierarchy actively control those at lower levels, so that they also effectively control the entire process. Conservatives and pluralists may, in contrast, assume that decision processes at any given level are virtually independent of those that take place at another. In most instances, the truth will undoubtedly lie somewhere in between, but it becomes important to try to specify the general conditions under which either the one version or the other is more appropriate.

Why attempt to control prior allocation decisions? First, in many instances there will be cost savings whenever prescreening can be done by others, at their own or someone else's expense. It is clearly to an allocator's advantage to weed out the weakest contenders as efficiently as possible, and this can sometimes be accomplished by making one's criteria reasonably clear to those who are responsible for passing along a set of individuals to the next higher pool. Real estate agents, for example, are typically well enough informed about mortgage lender criteria that it will be both to their own and the bankers' interests to eliminate those who would obviously be unqualified for an appropriate loan. Certain criteria may be only informally communicated to such prior allocators, as for example the unwillingness to make loans to blacks except in specified sections of a city. Similarly, teachers and career counselors in school settings may have a very good idea as to what kinds of jobs will be available to candidates with particular qualifications.

There need be no coercion involved in such relationships among allocators at different levels. Indeed, to the degree to which they have been socialized to apply much the same standards of evaluation, those who in effect serve as prescreeners may perceive themselves as simply being realistic in helping potential pool members make wise decisions. Obviously, if this sort of working cooperative relationship is to be effective from the standpoint of the ultimate allocating agents, there must be a reasonably high degree of predictability between performance criteria at the prior level and those that will be relevant for the ultimate decision. If, for example, student evaluations are based primarily on test scores that are largely irrelevant for later job performance, there will be sufficient slippage in the prescreening stage that too large a number of highly eligible candidates will inadvertently be ruled out of the competition.

A second advantage to a multistage screening process is that the blame for poor, discriminatory, or otherwise controversial decisions cannot as easily be laid at the doorstep of the ultimate allocators. If certain types of candidates have been previously eliminated, say by being discouraged from applying, then the ultimate allocators can readily point to a shortage of applicants from that category. "We received only a handful of qualified black applicants" is a common claim, which may in fact be technically correct but partially misleading if prior allocation decisions, as well as informal advising mechanisms, were taken into consideration. If those processes are under the control of completely different parties, however, it becomes possible to place the blame farther down in the sequential process. Those who wish to reform the process will find it difficult to do so, especially when the "official" criteria being proclaimed for public relations do not coincide with the unofficial ones that are believed to be the operative ones by those who have the primary responsibility for passing candidates along to the next higher level. If "everyone knows" that black or women candidates will not receive careful attention, but if such a belief cannot readily be pinpointed as to its source, buck-passing will become the primary means by which responsibility is disclaimed. The less obvious and direct the connections between allocators at each level, the more difficult it will be to challenge such practices.

In examining variations in the degree to which there are direct linkages among allocators at several different levels, let us consider a number of different kinds of examples. Perhaps the most clearcut case occurs where all allocating agents are hired (and fired) by the same parties, or where the allocators at one level have themselves been graduated through the system. Military promotions represent an obvious illustration, but so do many other instances in which personnel are promoted through the ranks, or where a so-called internal labor market exists.[1] It is full professors who make decisions regarding the promotion of associate and assistant professors, associate professors who pass judgments on assistant professors, and all three levels make allocation decisions regarding new hires and, of course, graduate students. Given such close linkages among allocators at each level, it would seem almost absurd to try to argue that decision criteria are independent across levels, or even that, say, the early promotion of a given candidate has no bearing whatsoever on the later evaluations of this person.

Most cases involving sequential pools are not this simple, however. The allocating agents at some levels are much more likely to be distinct parties that are only partly influenced by those at higher levels. Furthermore, they may use protective devices, such as secrecy, to prevent the close surveillance of their decision processes. As long as decisions fall within certain bounds, and are not considered outrageous by those in superior positions, such decisions may indeed be relatively independent of these other parties. But although their individual decisions may be characterized in this way, the *numbers* who are permitted to "graduate" may indeed be controlled by higher up authorities or by policies heavily influenced by them.

Consider, for example, the nature of the education that was permitted for blacks in the South in the early 20th century (Fisher, 1970; Franklin, 1967; Frazier, 1957; Meier, Rudwick, and Broderick, 1971). At that time, Booker T. Washington gained considerable influence among white elites in both the South and North by enunciating a policy stressing that blacks should receive only technical training that would prepare them for selected occupations well below those occupied by influential whites (although comparable in level with those of many poorer Southern whites of his day). This orientation was seriously disputed by W. E. B. Dubois, who in effect argued in favor of what we would today refer to as a liberal arts education for the "Talented Tenth," who would presumably become members of a black elite capable of directly challenging their white counterparts.

In terms of the implementation of actual policy regarding the education of blacks in the South, it was not until much later, during the 1950s and 1960s, that Washington's "appealing" philosophy was gradually discredited. In the meantime, black youth continued to receive educations that, in terms of both quantity and quality, were far inferior to those of their white peers. Blacks were in effect being trained to enter only those occupational pools for which they were deemed to be suited, namely those near the very bottom of the status and power hierarchies. Southern black educators out of necessity followed the Washington line, since their very jobs depended on it. Black colleges were also controlled by white trustees, who tended to appoint highly conservative presidents who, in turn, exercised almost authoritarian control over their faculties. Here, it does not require conspiracy theories to arrive at the conclusion that those who controlled the economy also rather tightly controlled educational policies as they applied to blacks in the South.

Although the degree of control today is nowhere near as complete, it has been argued that the educational establishment in the United States and other Western democracies is beholden to economic elites in much the same way (Bowles and Gintis, 1976). The emphasis may not be placed on holding back blacks or other minorities, so much as it is in preparing students to enter selected labor markets by virtue of the curricula they are encouraged to pursue. Clearly, there are severe constraints placed on school principals and teachers in terms of certain taboo subjects that they are not permitted to discuss, the advocacy or serious discussion of Marxist thinking being a case in point. Control may go far beyond this, however, as for example the channeling of young women into secretarial or clerical positions and away from mathematics and the sciences, the active discouragement of minorities from attempting to apply to elite universities, or the encouragement of substantial numbers of students into a "General Curriculum" that usually leads to dead-end positions in the occupational arena.

Rarely, moreover, does one find school principals or superintendents taking courageous stances in favor of more controversial educational policies. In effect, the entire administrative apparatus is basically status-quo oriented, consisting of highly vulnerable individuals who can be, and are, regularly replaced if they become too controversial. The operative controls are somewhat more subtle than those employed within a single hierarchical organization, but their indirect effects on the students are nevertheless real. The fact that exceptions occur, and that allocational decisions are never rigid, permits easy rationalizations to the effect that controls are nonexistent, whereas the statistical patternings that result are often very clearcut.

In many instances of this sort, allocation roles are also somewhat nebulous, so that it is difficult to pinpoint responsibilities for whatever frequency distributions ultimately emerge. In a very real sense, teachers can be considered to be "allocating" grades and other rewards and punishments, but usually in such a way that no single person is deemed responsible for a given student's successes or failures. The student begins to develop an intellectual self-image, however, that may heavily depend on a series of grade allocation decisions that cumulatively result in an overall grade point average and acceptance into selected curricula. Perhaps it would be reasonable to replace the word *allocation* with the notion of *steering* or *guiding*, with the proviso that formal grades also may result in a student's being denied access to some later potential pool. Regardless, it remains that those who are in a position to provide officially approved rewards and punishments are basically serving in an allocating role, even where responsibilities are spread out and somewhat diffuse.

Diffuse allocation, such as exists in our educational system, does mean, however, that each individual allocator will be somewhat protected from higher authorities even though he or she is technically in a vulnerable situation. Protective devices, such as disguising one's allocation criteria and using blurred standards of student performance, would seem to be especially characteristic of such allocators who are simultaneously in weak power positions but also in a setting in which responsibilities are diffuse. In the extreme allocators may attempt to make no real allocation decisions at all, as occurs whenever all students are automatically passed along to the next stage with innocuous "satisfactory" ratings or an extremely truncated distribution of grades.

Whenever candidates have experienced multiple allocation decisions that are difficult to unravel, the simplifying assumption is likely to be that any biases in such decisions (say, about a student's abilities) tend to cancel one another out, so that the ultimate qualifications they possess are basically due to their own capabilities or efforts. That is, the responsibility for subsequent pool entry and performances is placed squarely on the individual concerned, rather than those who have made a series of prior allocation decisions. This is especially likely whenever each individual "decision" is deemed to be rather more a piece of advice (say, whether or not to try harder) than an actual allocation (say, the awarding of an A grade). The more remote and numerous such decisions have been, the more likely that responsibilities will be assigned to the individual recipient, under the assumption that there is essentially no patterning to these decisions that could be attributed to the recipient's gender, race, or socioeconomic background. Pool entry decisions are thus assumed to be individually made, with prior experiences being deemed irrelevant. In view of the obvious costs that would be involved if one were to attempt to track down all such relatively minor impacts on each individual candidate, such an extreme simplifying assumption—even where inaccurate— may indeed be the most efficient one that a current allocator can make.

Allocators in prior sequential pools may have been constrained in other ways, which may also be a function of decisions that have been influenced by those who control processes at higher or subsequent levels. This is especially the case whenever the relative *numbers* of winners and losers can be affected by other parties. Governments, for example, often control the sizes of training programs of different types, as well as in some cases the nature of the examination system used to evaluate the candidates. Where such exams must be taken at a rather early point in a child's schooling, and where an important allocation decision is then made as to which students qualify for the next stage, the advantage usually falls to those whose parents have been in a position to give them a head start or specialized tutoring. In Japan and a number of European countries, for example, there are extreme pressures placed on rather young adolescents to perform well on examinations that virtually predetermine their life chances. As already noted, the ancient Chinese examination system, by requiring a mastery of a highly complex writing system and the memorization of classical works, also gave a decided advantage to those whose families were in a position to afford the luxury of prolonged study.

In the United States, public higher education priorities are heavily controlled by state legislators, governors, and appointed trustees. Not only are the relative enrollment quotas often set by these parties, but somewhat more subtle pressures often prevail that send a clear message to university presidents that certain kinds of professional schools are to be favored at the expense, say, of the humanities. There may even be special funding for favored projects, such as high-tech research centers or institutes designed to promote trade with other countries. In a real sense, those few courageous college and university presidents who take strong stances in opposition to such projects may take the risk of alienating their bosses, the governor and board of regents. Their provosts and deans may also discover that "politics" prevent their allocating scarce resources to programs that do not enjoy the support of important alumni, business leaders, or key members of a state legislature. Thus internal allocation priorities based on such outside pressures may determine the relative fates of schools of business, sociology departments, and art history. These in turn will partly affect the relative numbers of faculty and students in each area.

Another characteristic of diffuse allocation processes is that potential pool applicants are likely to have a very unclear idea about their actual qualifications, apart from those that are officially designated (e.g., the possession of a high school degree). To the degree that previous allocation decisions have all been highly consistent in the case of any particular individual, this may result in a subjective probability of success that falls within an unrealistically restricted range and perhaps is close to either zero or unity. If we assume that most persons evaluate themselves in terms of some comparison group, a consistency of prior decisions may imply that they are either clearly well above or decidedly below average for such comparison groups. Whether or not they enter the ultimate pool with realistic expectations will then depend upon how similar the previous comparison groups are to other members of the ultimate pool. It is also possible that if potential candidates have been accustomed to evaluate themselves in accord with a "frog pond" setup (Davies, 1962), they may for example consider themselves either to be clearly superior to or inferior to others in the pool they are about to enter. Those who are accustomed to being well below average, as compared to others they have competed with in prior settings, may decide not to apply at all for the pool in question, even where their actual qualifications would make them highly competitive in such a pool.

As a general rule, we would expect that the more informal and diffuse prior allocation experiences have been, the less clear the expectations will be in a later competitive situation, and perhaps the more reluctant the individual will be to enter the explicit pool. Given such a lack of clarity, we would also expect that such factors as rumor, peer gossip, weak network ties, stereotypes, unrealistic assumptions made by socializing agents, the presence or absence of role models, and myths concerning secret allocation criteria will be relatively important in influencing the final decision of the individual. Such situations are likely to impact adversely on those categories of persons who are currently underrepresented, both in the pool composition itself and among the membership of winners from previous pools.

Finally, whenever prior allocation decisions have been numerous and individually unimportant, or where previous allocators are difficult to identify or perhaps different for each candidate being considered, conspiracy theories that attempt to link one such set of allocators to another become untenable. This is in contrast, for example, with clearly defined sequential pools such as those involved when students are passed from one grade to another or where employees are moved (or not moved) up an occupational hierarchy within the same firm. Lacking such relatively simple conspiracy theories, analysts may instead take the opposite tack of assuming essentially a random process with respect to pool entry and therefore very similar distributions of relevant characteristics within the applicant pool. As previously discussed, this, in turn, may lead to the temptation to treat simple measures of *inequality* as indicators of allocator *discrimination*.

## SHIFTING STANDARDS
## IN SEQUENTIAL POOL SETUPS[2]

Depending on the circumstances, allocators may either raise or lower standards, make use of double standards, or attempt to blur their standards so as to afford increased flexibility. The allocation strategies considered in the present section are especially likely whenever allocators are in weak power positions and are expected to pass along a certain number or percentage of candidates, while also being in a position to use subjectively determined standards that are not easily scrutinized by outsiders or by allocators in subsequent pools. We shall focus primarily on the example of educational standards set by school principals and teachers or by faculty members at colleges and universities.

Frequently, allocators who are in weak power positions are placed in situations involving incompatible demands that cannot easily be satisfied. Consider the problem of so-called grade inflation that became visible during the 1960s, a decade during which simultaneous demands were placed on teachers to provide "quality education" but also to pass along nearly all students and to make sure that minority students were not disproportionately failed or subjected to differential treatment with respect to disciplinary measures. The short-term saving grace for teachers was that students could be passed along and awarded reasonably high grades without parents or local students being aware of any changes in standards. It was only much later, once it became clear that functional illiterates were receiving high school degrees, that the issue of changing standards was seriously raised by the general public.

What alternatives did teachers, as allocators, have under the circumstances? One possibility would have been to redefine the minimal passing grade, so that students would be permitted to graduate with D minus averages, and perhaps might then automatically be admissable under "open enrollment" policies to certain colleges and universities. Such an arrangement would have entailed an explicit policy change, however. It turned out to be much simpler to inflate students' grades by awarding D level work a C grade, and so forth. Actually, such grade inflation really amounted to grade truncation or compression, as students who would ordinarily have been awarded A grades could go no higher. As a result, nearly everyone could pass according to the previously designated standards, with parents and local community members being none the wiser.

A second alternative, under such circumstances, is to apply an explicit double standard through which students with a specified handicap are in effect awarded extra points so as to enable them to achieve what appears to be the same level of performance. Whenever such double standards are used, this amounts to designating distinct applicant pools with different cutoff points being used to place them in the successful group of candidates. Such double standards, or awarding of handicap points, have been made explicit in the case of points awarded to veterans on Civil Service exams. On occasion they were also used by some medical, dental, and law schools in order to meet formal or informal quotas of minority students. As long as the public and the courts are willing to accept such a practice—as they have done in the case of veterans and Civil Service exams—such an overt use of the double standard becomes a rather simple way of resolving the dilemma.

More frequently the use of double standards is likely to be kept secret, or at least not openly acknowledged. Where competitors are familiar with one another's performances, however, it becomes much more difficult to hide such differential standards from view. Students are likely to be well aware of each other's general performance levels, since much classroom work is essentially public. The same applies to work associates competing for promotions.

Under many circumstances, then, the use of double standards will be difficult to justify and may, if known to beneficiary groups, lead to feelings of guilt or self-doubt as to their real performance levels. Therefore it must be rationalized in some way. In the case of handicap points being awarded to minorities, the practice may be justified as being merely a temporary expedient necessary to compensate for prior inequities. But how temporary is temporary? And how many points should be awarded to which categories? Should the point differential be reduced over time? How can one persuade the beneficiaries that such a double standard should either be reduced or eliminated by a specific target date? And, perhaps most difficult of all, how can those who are being penalized by the double standard be made to accept its application when they, as individuals, may have had no responsibility for the prior handicaps of the currently favored group? All of these problems have surfaced over and over again, in connection with affirmative action and other compensatory allocation practices.

One more subtle means of employing a double standard in a justifiable manner is to base rewards on changes or *improvements* in performance, rather than on the actual performance levels themselves. In such a fashion, those who begin with low performance levels, or who may have entered with specific handicaps, have approximately the same opportunities to improve their scores as do those who begin near the top. Actually, if there are performance ceilings at work, those who begin with high scores will find themselves handicapped as compared with those who have nowhere to go except upward. If candidates are aware, however, that it is only improvement that counts, and if they can control their initial performance levels, they will have a vested interest in beginning low, so that they have considerable room for improvement.

Knowing this, the allocators concerned may elect to reward partly on the basis of performance levels and partly on the basis of improvement scores. We suspect that such a practice is indeed common among teachers and others who have initially elected to reward improvement. That there is a possible double standard at work, here, is obscured by the inclusion of a second type of evaluation criterion. The latter may also be justified under the assumption that relative rates of improvement will continue, so that those with initial handicaps will not only catch up but perhaps ultimately surpass those who began ahead of them. The tortoises will win the footrace with the hares, so why not encourage them early in the game?

In many instances it may be simpler to adopt *blurred* rather than double standards. In the case of double standards, the candidate's performance is carefully measured, but different cutoff points are used for members of the selected categories. In contrast, when standards are blurred it becomes much more a matter of subjective judgment to decide which candidates to accept. Let us suppose that a selection committee is choosing among a number of candidates to graduate school. There will be available the students' grade point averages, some knowledge of the relative quality of their undergraduate institutions, performances on standardized exams such as the Graduate Record Exam (GRE), letters of recommendation, and perhaps student statements as to their objectives or reasons for applying to graduate school. Both grade point averages and GRE scores are quantified and may be explicitly weighted and placed into a regression equation to predict later academic success. If one wishes, double standards may be applied by introducing categorical memberships as dummy variables, thereby giving them relative weights that would affect intercepts and thus the overall point score.

When standards are blurred, however, the most "discriminating" criteria are either ignored or given very small weights. Thus if GRE scores are claimed to be biased against blacks, information about such scores may be totally discarded or not even requested. Similarly, if grades are considered to be "punitive" or also discriminatory, or if they are thought to depend more on the quality of the undergraduate institution than on "objective" performance, they too may be disregarded. More likely, a minimum GPA may be used as a cutoff point, but with such a minimum being set at a low enough level that virtually all candidates qualify by that particular standard. Instead, such things as letters of recommendation and student essays may be used, together with the allocators' judgments concerning "potential," "suitability," or other similarly vague criteria. In effect, the allocators' subjective judgments are allowed to determine, almost completely, the candidates' relative standing, with few or no objective measures being used as checks on these judgments. Those who question such judgments may simply be told that the allocators based their decisions on the "total picture" or on special considerations that cannot be easily codified.

Whenever allocators are held accountable for candidates' future performance, as for example if they are being promoted through the ranks and expected to perform important duties for the unit to which the allocator is directly attached, we would anticipate that the modification of standards in any of these manners will be subjected to the scrutiny of the principals whom the allocators represent. If the allocators are simply passing candidates along to the next higher level, however, and are not directly subject to the control of those responsible for screening at these higher levels, the use of shifting standards would seem more likely. This will be especially the case whenever allocators are under pressure to pass a certain (usually high) percentage of candidates, regardless of their actual performance levels. If equality of outcomes is demanded, for example, there may be careful scrutiny of data concerning percentages of passes and failures but very little concern about the *processes* that have led to these outcomes. In other words, the concern for distributive justice may be much greater than that for procedural justice. If so, the easiest thing for allocators to do is to modify their standards so as to achieve the demanded outcomes.

The use of lowered, double, or blurred standards creates problems for future allocators, however, unless the latter are well aware of what has taken place and are in a position to know the actual criteria that have been used. If students have nearly all been graduated from high schools with C averages or better, college admissions officers may be misled into accepting persons who are nearly functionally illiterate or who are at least very poorly prepared for more advanced work. If employers cannot rely on grades because there has been very pronounced inflation or suspected double standards, they may either be forced to devise their own screening criteria or to rely on much less useful information such as (also inflated) letters of recommendation. If the allocators within these subsequent pools apply changed standards, inadequately prepared individuals may simply be passed along until they reach a point where performance levels are really critical to some ultimate set of allocators, say those charged with the responsibility of selecting from a number of job candidates.

There may be other instances where the allocators at one level, say college admissions officers, are indeed aware of performance differentials at lower levels but elect to admit certain applicants as high risk candidates. If such persons are then treated in a universalistic fashion by unsuspecting future allocators, say college faculty, it may indeed turn out that they experience higher failure rates. Charges of discrimination may then be leveled at the latter allocators on the grounds that outcome differentials ought to be small under the assumption that there were no systematic differences at the outset. In other words, the fact that certain students have been selectively admitted as high risk students is conveniently ignored, both by the faculty concerned and their potential critics. There may be available few or no compensatory programs such as special tutoring or remedial courses, since the use of a double standard at the initial entry level was either unknown to the appropriate persons or simply deemed to be irrelevant.

There may also be rather obvious impacts on the candidates themselves, who may be unaware of the fact that they have been the beneficiaries of the prior use of double or blurred standards. Minority high school graduates may enter an elite college or university under the assumption that their past performance levels are comparable to those of their competitors, only to experience a shock if the standards of comparison are suddenly very different. They may then experience severe problems produced by sharply reduced self-esteem, low morale among their minority peers, or patterned temptations to escape a threatening situation.

A somewhat similar difficulty may occur if participants in a setting involving lowered standards are receiving mixed signals regarding their performance. Their grades, for example, may appear highly satisfactory and well above the official standard for passing. At one prestigious Ivy League college, for example, a student was not flunked out unless his overall grade point average fell below 70. Yet, in each individual course instructors were basically told that the lowest passing grade for the particular course was also 70, meaning that it would be virtually impossible for a student's grades to *average* to 70. Indeed, overall grade point averages were in the mid 80s, suggesting that "average" students were doing nearly honors work.

Suppose that below average students are to be discouraged, say from applying to graduate school or to doctoral programs, once having completed their master's work. If all of their official grades are high, how can the poorer ones be weeded out? Often, it is by informal devices such as word of mouth suggestions from their advisors. Those who are not properly attuned to such signals, or who have taken their official record at face value, may simply refuse to give up, so that mere perseverance becomes the overriding criterion of survival. In effect, the allocating agents will have sidestepped their responsibilities to make differential evaluations. They may merely be hoping that any resulting mistakes will be corrected later on.

Discouraging weak though officially passing candidates from entering subsequent pools may also be important to preserve the allocator's reputation. Clearly, if allocators in subsequent pools apply much higher standards than previous allocators, or if they find the applicants' qualifications have been misrepresented because of unknown double or diffuse standards, they may come to disregard the official credentials among those applicants who have passed through the prior screening process. And if the candidates themselves discover that some allocators have applied reduced or blurred standards, there may develop a self-selection mechanism through which the best candidates refuse to participate in that previous process, leaving only the weakest ones with the pool.

This sort of mechanism may well be at work in connection with the self-selection of weaker students into such fields as elementary education and some of the "softer" social sciences and humanities. It is well known, for example, that SAT and GRE scores of students entering the physical sciences and mathematics are considerably higher than those in many other fields. Mathematics performance is also much easier to evaluate, in the sense of discriminating between very good and very weak performances, than is the case where evaluations must be made on the basis of essay exams or student papers. Those who are capable of performing well in settings involving high standards of evaluation will therefore expect to benefit relatively more than would be the case if they had to take their chances with evaluators whose standards are blurred. Those who do poorly in mathematics will also be given very clear, nonambiguous signals concerning their chances of success in more advanced courses. Most will simply drop out and elect other options. As a result, those fields that insist on the most demanding standards will tend to attract the highest quality applicant pools.

A similar sort of phenomenon may take place *within* a single unit, such as an academic department in which the faculty apply different standards. Those who gain the reputation of being stiff graders will tend to attract the best students, but they may also suffer an attenuation of their effective pools. Therefore, the initial abilities of students in two instructors' classes may differ. If they then apply the same grading curve it may be rather difficult for outsiders to assess their relative standards. The easy grader's classes may be larger, however, giving the impression that in spite of apparently equally tough grading standards, the job performance of the easy grader is superior to that of the one who is actually applying the higher set of standards. The possibility of student self-selection may either be ignored altogether or treated as an unmeasured variable.

Finally, we note that the use of double standards, especially, creates a long-term difficulty if there is any expectation of returning to a single standard at some later point in time. Obviously, some parties will have a strong vested interest in retaining the double standard and are likely to attempt to develop highly persuasive arguments for maintaining the practice "just a bit longer" or "until previous handicaps have been overcome." The temptation will then be to delay implementation of a single standard, especially in those instances where the allocators concerned are in weak power positions vis-à-vis those who display a strong vested interest in retaining the dual standard. It is also possible that other categories of persons may attempt to get themselves designated as "disadvantaged" so as to take advantage of the double standard of evaluation. If blacks and Hispanics are considered disadvantaged, why not Chinese- and Japanese-Americans or other Asian ethnic groups? In India there has been an apparently peculiar phenomenon of *relatively* lower caste groups attempting to obtain "protected" status designations, so as to improve their own chances of succeeding in situations in which caste quotas have been initially

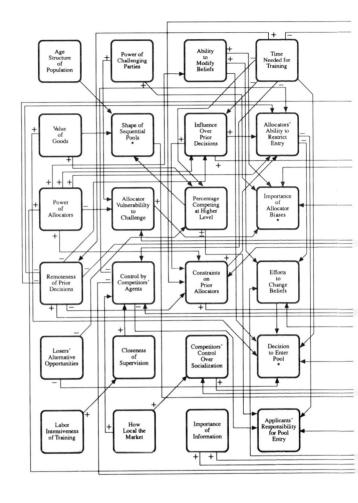

**Figure 6.1.** Model VII: Decision Processes in Sequential Pools

designed to compensate for membership in so-called scheduled castes.

The more general point in this connection is that once a double standard situation has become evident, although perhaps officially denied, it may be exceedingly difficult to return to one involving a

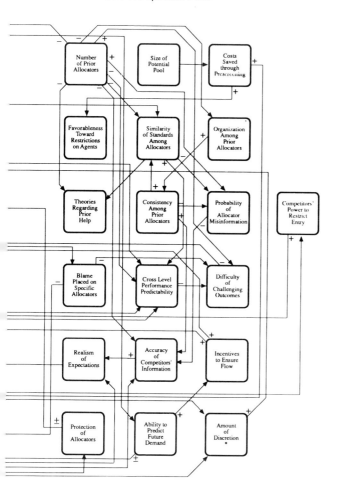

single standard of evaluation. Ideally, one can imagine moving toward such a single standard gradually over a number of years or perhaps by insisting on more even levels of performance as candidates pass through a sequential pool situation. But since many of the allocators will be primarily concerned with short-term consequences and their own security, there may be little incentive for them either to divulge the nature of the standards they have been applying or to work toward a gradual modification in them. What seemed to be a workable short-term resolution may have unanticipated long-term consequences. This indeed seems to be the present-day situation with respect to academic standards in our public schools.

## CAUSAL MODEL VII:
## DECISION PROCESSES IN SEQUENTIAL POOLS

The model of Figure 6.1 refers to any given stage in a sequential pool setup although the reader may prefer to focus on the final or ultimate stage of the process. Because the model for this chapter contains 43 variables and therefore requires a double page, the locations of exogenous, intervening, and dependent variables are somewhat different from those of previous diagrams. Exogenous variables continue to be placed across the top, down the left-hand column and in the second and third columns of the bottom row. The 7 dependent variables are located toward the center of the figure, however, 5 being in column four and 2 in column five, the columns that serve to break the diagram into two portions. Intervening variables appear in the final column and elsewhere toward the center of the figure. Once more, we proceed by listing each of the three types of variables and then turning to brief discussions of the assumed causal linkages.

### The Exogenous Variables

As noted, the 13 exogenous variables are listed, in order, by going across the first six columns of the top row, then down the left column, and finally part of the way across the bottom row.

(1) The age structure of the population from which the several pools are drawn (Age Structure of Population)
(2) The power of parties, including losing competitors, who are likely to challenge allocator decisions (Power of Challenging Parties)
(3) The ability of allocators to modify beliefs of competitors and their allies (Ability to Modify Beliefs)

(4) The amount of time needed by candidates to obtain the training necessary for pool entry at a given level (Time Needed for Training)

(5) The number of different allocators whose decisions have influenced the candidates entering a given pool (Number of Prior Allocators)

(6) The size of a potential pool at a given level (Size of Potential Pool)

(7) The value of goods or positions to potential candidates at a given level (Value of Goods)

(8) The power of allocators at a given level, vis-à-vis both prior allocators and potential candidates (Power of Allocators)

(9) The remoteness in time and space between prior allocation decisions and current ones (Remoteness of Prior Decisions)

(10) The alternative opportunities for losers to join other pools or otherwise be compensated (Losers' Alternative Opportunities)

(11) The degree to which training of candidates is labor intensive (Labor Intensiveness of Training)

(12) The degree to which the market for candidates is local or temporally proximate to trainers (How Local the Market)

(13) The importance to allocators of outside information regarding candidates' qualifications (Importance of Information)

## The Intervening Variables

The first of the 23 intervening variables appears at the extreme right top corner of Figure 6.1. We then proceed across each row, skipping the dependent variables appearing in columns 4 and 5.

(1) The degree to which allocators' costs are reduced through pre-screening by prior allocators (Costs Saved Through Prescreening)

(2) *(Shape of Sequential Pools)

(3) The degree to which allocators at a given stage can influence decisions at prior stages (Influence Over Prior Decisions)

(4) The degree to which allocators at different stages use similar standards (Similarity of Standards Among Allocators)

(5) The degree to which allocators in prior pools are organized or coordinate their decisions (Organization Among Prior Allocators)

(6) The degree to which allocators at a given stage are vulnerable to challenges (Allocator Vulnerability to Challenge)

(7) The percentage completing a given stage who enter the explicit pool at next higher stage (Percentage Competing at Higher Level)

(8) The degree to which criteria used by prior allocators are consistent with one another (Consistency Among Prior Allocators)

(9) The probability that allocators at different levels miscommunicate with one another (Probability of Allocator Miscommunication)

(10) The degree to which competitors have the power to restrict entry to subsequent pools (Competitors' Power to Restrict Entry)

(11) The degree to which competitors' own agents actually control entry to subsequent pools (Control by Competitors' Agents)

(12) The degree to which allocators in prior pools have been constrained in their decisions (Constraints on Prior Allocators)

(13) The degree to which blame can be placed on specific sets of allocators in prior pools (Blame Placed on Specific Allocators)

(14) The degree to which performances at one level are predictive of performances at others (Cross-Level Performance Predictability)

(15) The degree to which outcomes of decisions at a given stage can be successfully challenged (Difficulty of Challenging Outcomes)

(16) The degree to which allocators at a given level are closely supervised or monitored (Closeness of Supervision)

(17) The degree to which a set of competitors control the socialization of pool entrants (Competitors' Control Over Socialization)

(18) The degree to which potential candidates have realistic expectations about needed qualifications (Realism of Expectations)

(19) The degree of accuracy of information competitors have about each other's qualifications (Accuracy of Competitors' Information)

(20) The degree to which allocators have incentives to assure a steady flow of applicants to higher levels (Incentives to Ensure Flow)

(21) The degree to which allocators at a given level are protected from the losing candidates or their allies (Protection of Allocators)

(22) The degree to which allocators at a given level can predict future demand for recipients (Ability to Predict Future Demand)

(23) *(Amount of Discretion)

## The Dependent Variables

The seven dependent variables are listed in order, going down the fourth column, beginning with the second row, and then going to the two dependent variables in the fifth column. Two of these variables, denoted by asterisks, have appeared in prior models.

(1) The degree to which allocators have the ability to restrict entry to their explicit pools (Allocators' Ability to Restrict Entry)
(2) *(Importance of Allocator Biases)
(3) The degree to which allocators actually make efforts to change the beliefs of potential or losing candidates (Efforts to Change Beliefs)
(4) *(Decision to Enter Pool)
(5) The degree to which potential applicants are believed to be responsible for pool entry (Applicants' Responsibility for Pool Entry)
(6) The degree to which allocators favor placing restrictions on competitors' agents (Favorableness Toward Restrictions on Agents)
(7) Allocators' working theories regarding degree to which potential candidates have received prior help (Theories Regarding Prior Help).


*Discussion of Model:*
*Effects of the Exogenous Variables*


Certain of the exogenous factors in the model refer to structural characteristics of the setting, whereas others refer to properties of allocators or other parties that are taken as givens. As usual, we proceed across the top row and then down the left column.

Age structure of population is assumed to affect the shape of the pyramid of sequential pools. For example, if there is an unusually large number of persons of high school age this may reduce the probability that each one has of entering college or of obtaining a job. The Power of Challenging Parties is postulated to have positive direct effects on two variables, the allocators' vulnerability to such challenges and the importance of allocator biases in affecting the ultimate decisions. In the latter instance we assume that allocators will adjust their biases to conform to the interests of powerful challengers, though there may be circumstances where such individual biases may operate in the opposite direction. If so, the sign of this particular relationship would become negative.

Ability to Modify Beliefs is presumed to have positive effects on the importance of allocator biases by increasing the tendency for such biases to induce allocators to attempt to influence potential candidates either to enter or withdraw from competition. Such abilities should therefore also impact positively on allocators' actual efforts to change potential candidates' beliefs. The third variable directly impacted by ability to modify beliefs is the candidate's actual decisions regarding pool entry.

Time Needed for Training is assumed to affect, directly, six other variables in the model, basically through the mechanism of temporal delays as candidates move through a sequential pool setup. It is expected to have a negative impact on the percentage of persons completing any given stage who then go on to subsequent stages, if only because some persons will fail to have sufficiently long time perspectives to motivate them to obtain the necessary subsequent training. Time Needed for Training is also expected to have a negative effect on allocators' influence over prior decisions and on control over entry processes by competitors' agents.

Time Needed for Training is also predicted to affect potential candidates' decisions as to whether or not to enter a given explicit pool and to have a negative impact on allocators' abilities to predict future demands for additional candidates in time to assure such needed training by sufficient numbers of potential candidates. Finally, required training time is expected to have a positive effect on the remoteness of decisions made by prior allocators. Basically, a prolonged period of training time means that the whole prolonged allocative system becomes loosened and therefore subject to fewer controls by allocators in the ultimate pools in the sequence.

Number of Prior Allocators is expected to affect directly eight other variables in the model, making it one of our key exogenous factors. It is predicted to have a negative effect on the constraints placed on such allocators unless, of course, nearly all such prior allocators are closely associated with one another as for example would be the case if they were all teachers at the same school. Number of allocators is also assumed to reduce the accuracy of the information that competitors have of one another's qualifications. Negative impacts are also anticipated on the similarity of evaluation standards across allocators, this being especially the case if each allocator is at a different stage in a sequential setup. Similarly, a negative effect is expected on Cross-Level Performance Predictability if only because a very large number of allocators are likely to have evaluated (and reported) performances in a diversity of ways.

Large numbers of allocators should also tend to confuse allocators in subsequent pools, thereby affecting their working theories regarding the nature and extent of prior help given to competitors of different sorts. Given the multidimensionality of such theories, however, it is not meaningful to assign a sign to this particular relationship. Number of allocators is, however, expected to have a positive impact on the probability of miscommunication between allocators and also on the difficulty outsiders have of challenging any particular allocation decision because of the ambiguities involved in assigning responsibility to any one allocator. Finally, a large number of distinct prior allocators is expected to impact negatively on the degree to which they are able to organize themselves, this being especially so whenever they are at different levels in a sequential process.

The sixth exogenous variable, Size of Potential Pool, is expected to affect allocators' costs through prescreening mechanisms. In general, if a potential pool is very large it will be to allocators' advantage to screen out many of these persons so that they do not actually enter the explicit pool. This will depend, however, on the adequacy of the prescreening tools and the cooperation received from allocators at prior levels, who are presumably in the best position to do such prescreening. So the sign of this particular relationship may be difficult to predict.

Value of Goods is expected to affect the shape of the sequential pool pyramid, though in ways that are difficult to specify because of the fact that screening at prior levels may be more or less rigorous. If the value of the goods or positions at the very final stage is high, as for example an M.D. degree, this will generally mean that large numbers will enter the earlier pools. But it is then difficult to predict what proportions will be screened out at subsequent levels, as this will depend in part on the interests of allocators (e.g., chemistry professors) at these levels. In general, also, the greater the value of the goods at the ultimate level, the higher the percentage of graduates from prior levels who will attempt to compete at higher levels (Percentage Competing at Higher Levels). Finally, there is expected to be a positive effect on any potential candidate's decision to enter the higher pool.

Power of Allocators is predicted to affect six variables and is thus another important exogenous variable. It is expected to have positive effects on allocators' ability to modify the beliefs of both winning and losing candidates, as well as potential candidates considering entry from lower pools. It should also positively affect allocators' influence over the prior decisions of allocators in lower pools and on allocators' ability to restrict the entry of potential candidates having various characteristics. Allocator power is expected to reduce allocator vulnerability to challenge but to increase the constraints placed on prior allocators. Finally, it is predicted to increase allocators' protection from a diversity of actors, including losing candidates, third parties, and the allocators' own principals.

Remoteness of Prior Decisions, the ninth exogenous variable, is assumed to have direct effects on six variables and, as already noted, will generally be affected by Time Needed for Training. The more remote the prior decisions the less the ability of current allocators to restrict potential candidates' entry into an explicit pool. Also the less the similarity of standards among allocators at different stages. Similarly, it will ordinarily be more difficult to predict performance at one level by means of that in prior (remote) levels, and therefore the expected sign of this relationship is positive. Remoteness is expected to reduce the constraints on prior allocators under the assumption that allocators at higher levels will have less contact with and influence over those at lower levels. Also, increased remoteness is presumed to make it less likely that blame can reasonably be placed on specific allocators, so that buck-passing becomes both simpler and more difficult to challenge. Finally, and consistent with all of the above relationships, increased remoteness is expected to reduce the ultimate allocators' influence over prior allocation decisions.

Losers' Alternative Opportunities is presumed to affect only two variables, both negatively. The greater the number and value attached to alternatives, the smaller the percentage of potential candidates who will be willing to compete at higher levels and the fewer who will decide to actually enter the explicit pools at such levels. Labor Intensiveness of Training is expected to affect closeness of supervision, as we have already discussed. How Local the Market is postulated to have positive effects on the control that competitors' agents have over the numbers and kinds of individuals who are actually permitted to pass upward in the system. Similarly, the more local the labor or other type of market the greater the opportunities for at least some groups of competitors to control their own socializing agents, as illustrated by the example of craftlike labor unions. Finally, Importance of Information is predicted to have positive effects on two variables, the degree to which potential candidates can develop realistic expectations of their own chances for success and the accuracy of competitors' information about one another. This assumes, of course, that such important information is accurately conveyed to all parties and is not subject to distortion. Where deception is pronounced or information is false the signs of these two postulated relationships may be reversed.

This completes our discussion of the effects of exogenous variables. We turn next to a consideration of the effects of the much larger number of intervening variables.

*Discussion of the Model:*
*Effects of the Intervening Variables*

We begin with the single intervening variable in the top row, which appears in the final column. Then, as before, we move across each row and downward, skipping the dependent variables appearing in columns four and five.

Costs Saved Through Prescreening is assumed to have positive effects on the degree to which competitors are allowed to control the socialization of pool entrants, the presumption being that competitors' agents are in a position to select and train desirable candidates at minimal cost to the organization in question. At the same time, however, this intervening variable is also expected to have positive effects on the degree to which allocators favor placing certain restrictions on such agents.

Shape of Sequential Pools is expected to affect the degree to which allocators have discretion in selecting among candidates. A steep pyramid implies relatively small explicit pools at each stage, meaning that allocators will only be able to weed out a small proportion of applicants at each level. A flatter pyramid, however, means a larger surplus from which to select and therefore greater allocator discretion.

Influence Over Prior Decisions is predicted to have positive effects on three variables, one of which is Constraints on Prior Allocators. The second is allocators' ability to predict performances across levels, the presumption being that to the degree that allocators can control the decisions made by allocators in prior pools, they will also be in a position to help set performance standards at those levels. Their ability to influence prior decisions also implies that they will also be in a better position to restrict the entry of potential candidates at these lower levels, and also to the particular pool with which they are directly concerned.

Similarity of Standards Among Allocators is postulated to affect three variables, the first of which is allocators' working theories regarding the nature and extent of prior help received by candidates. It is also assumed to reduce the probability of miscommunication among allocators at different levels and to increase Cross-Level Performance Predictability. These three relationships are based on the assumption that allocators at each level employ sharply defined rather than blurred standards, however. Organization Among Prior Allocators, the fifth of our intervening variables, is expected to have a positive effect on Consistency Among Prior Allocators.

Allocator Vulnerability to Challenge is anticipated to have a positive effect on allocators' biases by encouraging them to bend in the direction of favoring relatively more powerful groups of competitors or those who can induce powerful third parties to intervene on their behalf. Percentage Competing at Higher Level will obviously affect the shape of the sequential pool pyramid. It is also expected to affect the degree to which applicants are believed to be personally responsible for failing to enter high-level pools. The sign attached to this predicted relationship is taken to be indeterminate. Sometimes, perhaps usually, a high percentage will lead to favorable stereotypes of the category in question and, especially, to the belief that they are highly motivated and well trained. On the other hand, there may be other occasions when a high percentage, especially of weakish candidates, may suggest precisely the opposite, namely that they are being pushed into applying for positions that are over their heads. We do predict, however, that allocator beliefs will be influenced, one way or another, by the percentage compositions of their respective pools.

Consistency Among Prior Allocators is anticipated to have positive effects on the degree to which they apply similar standards, and indeed one may even define *consistency* in such a way that similarity of standards is one of the overriding criteria for comparison. However, it is always possible that there may be a high degree of "consistency" in the use of criteria (say, high school grades) and yet the standards themselves may vary considerably by level (say, differing cutoff points). Consistency Among Prior Allocators, however, is definitely expected to reduce the probability of miscommunication among them unless, of course, deception is involved. Consistency should also increase the degree to which competitors have accurate information about each other's qualifications, again with the same condition that deception can be ruled out.

The ninth intervening variable, Probability of Miscommunication, is predicted to have a negative impact on a single variable, the accuracy of the information that competitors have of one another.

Competitors' Power to Restrict Entry likewise is assumed to have a positive effect on a single variable, Control by Competitors' Agents. These two variables may seem to be virtually identical, but we must recall that power may not always be exercised whereas the second of these two variables refers to the actual behaviors of these agents. Such control is, in turn, predicted to have negative effects on three variables: Applicants' Responsibility for Pool Entry, Amount of (allocator) Discretion, and Allocators' Ability to Restrict Entry.

Constraints on Prior Allocators is taken as having positive effects on two variables. The first of these is allocators' ability to restrict the entry to their respective pools, the assumption being that it is these allocators who are helping to place such constraints on prior allocators. If not, then the postulated relationship may be very weak or nonexistent. The second variable is Cross-Level Performance Predictability under the assumption that the constraints imposed are such as to increase the similarity of tasks and evaluation tools across levels. Again, under some circumstances this may be an inappropriate assumption.

Blame Placed on Specific Allocators, the 13th intervening variable, is expected to have a negative effect on Difficulty of Challenging Outcomes in that, whenever blame can be placed unambiguously, legal or other mechanisms for challenging outcomes will be easier to implement. Whenever such blame can be pinpointed to one or another allocator this is predicted to reduce the degree to which applicants, themselves, are held personally responsible for pool entry. In effect, the decision is at least partially taken out of their hands, whereas whenever responsibility among allocators is diffuse there is predicted to be a greater tendency to blame candidates themselves for the decision.

Cross-Level Performance Predictability is anticipated to have a negative effect on Difficulty of Challenging Outcomes, this being especially the case whenever performances are readily visible to outsiders and whenever the performances are essentially identical across levels (as in the case of athletics). Difficulty of Challenging Outcomes, in turn, is expected to have a negative impact on

Allocator Vulnerability to Challenge for rather obvious reasons. Closeness of Supervision, likewise, is anticipated to affect positively only a single variable, Control by Competitors' Agents. This is of course under the assumption that such agents are either the supervisors themselves or that they are in a position to receive accurate information from such supervisors. Conceivably, however, those who do the supervising or monitoring may supply false information to these agents.

Competitors' Control Over Socialization, the 17th intervening variable, is expected to have a positive impact on their power to restrict the entry into a subsequent pool since by controlling socialization one generally also controls the numbers and kinds of persons who pass into subsequent pools. The realism of potential candidates' expectations (and knowledge) is predicted to affect their decision to enter any given pool, but with the sign of this relationship depending on their perceptions as to their chances of success. Accuracy of Competitors' Information, in turn, is presumed to affect positively their realism unless, of course, they either distort such information or disbelieve it.

Incentives to ensure the flow of applicants are predicted to motivate allocators to place constraints on prior allocators in terms of the numbers and kinds of individuals they pass along to higher levels, although this of course does not assure that they will actually be successful in doing so. Such a need for a steady flow can also be expected to increase allocators' efforts to modify the beliefs of potential candidates, with the sign of this relationship depending on whether or not the expected flow is above or below the desired level.

Protection of Allocators is expected to affect Allocator Bias by permitting such biases to operate freely if they are present or to be of minimal importance if they are nearly absent. In other words, a high degree of allocator protection is expected to amplify the impact of any biases that exist but also to enable unbiased allocators to be free from the impact of potential outside sources of bias. Ability to Predict Future Demand is postulated to increase Incentives to Ensure Flow, as might be expected. Finally, Amount of

Discretion is presumed to have a positive impact on Allocator Bias by allowing such biases more room to operate.

## A Note on the Dependent Variables

Once more, our discussion of the seven dependent variables can be very brief since the causes of these variables have already been discussed. Allocators' Ability to Restrict Entry is predicted to have negative impacts on two of the other dependent variables, namely Efforts to Change Beliefs and Applicants' Responsibility for Pool Entry. In the first instance the presumption is that if allocators already have the ability to restrict entry there will be little or no need for them to expend the effort to modify the belief systems of potential candidates, except possibly in those instances where too few applicants are expected. Efforts to Change Beliefs is also predicted to affect candidates' decisions to enter explicit pools, presuming that such efforts are actually successful. The remaining five dependent variables are assumed to be strictly dependent, having no causal connections with each other.

Our discussion of this somewhat more complex model is now complete. In Chapter 7 we shall also confront a similarly complex model, as we focus primarily on the reactions of winning and losing competitors and the notions of distributive and procedural justice.

## NOTES

1. For discussions of internal labor markets see Doeringer and Piore (1971), Hodson (1983), Hodson and Kaufman (1982), Smith (1983), and Thurow (1975).

2. This section represents a modified version of a discussion in Blalock (1979), Chapter 4.

# Reactive Processes: Equity and Distributive Justice

In considering the reactions of the several parties to any allocation process we need to take into consideration their perceptions and interpretations concerning the fairness of both the *procedures* that have apparently been used and also the *outcomes* or resultants of these procedures. The first of these topics has been termed *procedural justice* and includes such things as the qualifications of the allocators, the rules they have followed, the timing of the process, and the measures and weights used in evaluating the qualifications of the candidates (Deutsch and Steil, 1988; Thibaut and Walker, 1975; Tyler, 1990). Also, by implication, procedural justice requires that all candidates be fully aware of the nature of the information they are to provide and that they be given equal opportunities of appearing on the explicit list of applicants being evaluated.

*Distributive justice,* in contrast, refers to the actual distribution of outcomes. This does not necessarily require that all categories of candidates be proportionately represented among the winners, since their relative qualifications, inputs, or investments may also be taken into consideration. In America the notion that all persons have equal "opportunities" presumably refers to procedural justice, the assumption being that under such circumstances all individuals will have been treated fairly. It does not necessarily imply equality of outcomes, however. One of the basic practical issues that often arises whenever procedures cannot be directly observed is whether or not the presence or absence of equal outcomes implies that there has also been procedural justice. Perhaps, but then again, perhaps not. The two ideas are theoretically distinct, though in practice they are often confused.

It is clearly recognized by virtually everyone who has studied the subject that justice is in the eyes of the beholder and that perceptions of both procedural and distributive justice are basically subjective in nature. Of course this does not mean that there are no observable phenomena on which these judgments are based or that there cannot be a reasonable degree of consensus on the amount of justice existing in any given situation. As we shall shortly see, however, there will inevitably be differential evaluations based on the criteria actors impose on these objective phenomena.

We begin with the widely accepted position that actors are for the most part characterized by selfish interests and that there will tend to be a self-serving bias operative that ordinarily gives the greatest weight to factors that afford an advantage to whatever actor is making the evaluative judgment. Such a self-serving bias has been noted in the literature on attribution processes, as for example the tendency to credit oneself for positive outcomes but to blame others for those outcomes deemed negative (Jones and Davis, 1965; Jones and Nisbett, 1971; Kelley, 1971). Social psychologists likewise argue that a similar process is at work whenever actors assess whether or not a distributive allocation process has been fair (Mesick and Cook, 1983; Walster, Walster, and Berscheid, 1978).

## EQUALITY AND NEED
## AS CRITERIA FOR ALLOCATION

One very simple criterion defining the fairness of an outcome is that strict equality must be preserved. That is, regardless of any of the candidates' other characteristics, all goods are to be apportioned equally among them. Such a criterion is of course easy to apply in the case of goods that can be subdivided, but it may also be applied in instances where goods are nondivisible. If there are multiple contests, the allocator may make sure that each person wins an equal number of times. If not, a random device may at least be used to assure an equal probability of all candidates' winning. Whenever allocators lack the information necessary to distinguish among candidates' qualifications, whenever decisions must be made in rapid succession, or whenever it is a matter of indifference to the allocator which candidates win, we would generally expect the equality principle to prevail. It has also been noted that the principle of equality as a basis for allocation decisions tends to promote solidarity among group members (Walster et al., 1978). Also, consistent with the above-noted self-serving bias, we would expect poorly qualified candidates, or those who are accustomed to losing most of the time, to favor this equality principle, as it will tend to increase their overall chances of success. In contrast, those with superior qualifications will tend to favor another equity principle that takes these qualifications into consideration.

A second principle on which allocations could be based is that of "need," as defined in some manner. If persons having the greatest objective needs, say for food, shelter, or clothing, are also perceived as being in such a position through no fault of their own, as for example as a result of chance mechanisms or situational factors beyond their control, then such a need principle may meet with general approval, and especially among those who expect to benefit from the use of this criterion. Rawls (1971), for example, argues (without empirical evidence) that totally disinterested parties would naturally agree on a distribution principle "maximum" that maximizes the outcomes for the least favored members of the group. That is, it endorses the highest possible floor or "safety net" position as one of the two overriding principles of justice, the other being the maximization of individual freedoms consistent with the freedom of other members. Need also constitutes a justice criterion stressed in the Judeo-Christian tradition and, indeed, most other religions in which a special recognition is given to the obligation of charity.

The need and equality principles may, on occasion, be virtually identical. Lenski (1966), among others, argues that one generally finds egalitarian distributive systems in simple hunting and gathering societies, in which there is very little surplus beyond actual need. His basic argument is that considerations of power will only begin to predominate to the degree that there are surpluses that can safely be extracted from producing agents, with powerful individuals attempting to extract as much of such a surplus as they can. Whenever basic survival is at stake and only minimal biological needs can be met with existing resources, such a need criterion will result in nearly equal distributions unless, of course, there are certain classes of individuals (such as the very young or old) whose "needs" are defined as less important than average. Even in such instances of minimal surpluses, however, we may expect to encounter certain self-serving biases in defining just what such minimal survival needs are and what constitutes "surplus." In our own society, this definitional problem becomes even more difficult.

The need principle obviously encounters resistance on the part of those (self-serving) individuals who hold the needy responsible for their own fate. Why did they become needy in the first place? Was it because of a lack of foresight, saving, or prior effort? The notion that it is only the "deserving poor" who should be helped is also a common one in our own society. But who decides on who is "deserving," and how does one know exactly why a given individual is currently experiencing need? How does one draw the line between the "needy" and the "nonneedy?" What criteria does one use to establish an official poverty line? Those who might expect to pay out the most to help the needy may have a vested interest in drawing the line so low that virtually no one is eligible for inclusion. Potential recipients have a vested interest in drawing the line slightly above their own position.

In the current American scene we witness a number of social debates concerning the meaning of the term *disadvantaged*, precisely how many homeless persons there are, who are the elderly poor, and so forth. There are also strong differences of opinion concerning the responsibilities of persons who become school dropouts, homosexuals, drug addicts, unwed mothers, AIDS victims, or members of other stigmatized categories. Are gay men and women biologically predetermined to lead "deviant" sex lives, or do they self-select themselves voluntarily into life-styles that are stigmatized? Are girls who drop out of school and become teenaged mothers simply "victims" of the social system, or are they behaving irresponsibly on the basis of their immediate interests? If they are indeed victims, then they may be defined as having legitimate needs that deserve sympathy and justify remedial action. If not, then they have only themselves to blame.

The causal variables affecting these and other social processes are indeed complex and operate with varying lag periods. It therefore becomes possible to select out whatever subset of explanatory factors is most compatible with one's vested interests or ideological biases so as to decide which kinds of persons "in need" are indeed deserving of receiving a slice of whatever pie is being allocated.

## EQUITY AS THE CRITERION FOR ALLOCATION

The third allocative principle involved in distributive justice considerations is that of *equity,* which, following Adams (1965), Blau (1964), and Homans (1974), is usually defined in terms of the ratio of inputs or investments to outcomes. Although there have been several technical discussions of the difficulties of constructing an adequate equity formula (Harris, 1983; Jasso, 1978), we may for simplicity say that distributive justice requires that each person's outcomes be proportional to his or her inputs or investments. The major problem, of course, then becomes that of deciding just what constitutes the latter.

A number of authors have pointed to severe ambiguities in this regard. Cook and Yamagishi (1983), for example, note that inputs in real-life situations are likely to be multidimensional and that, in particular, it becomes important to distinguish between *attributes* and *contributions,* as well as the relevance of each of the outcomes involved. Along similar lines, Camerer and MacCrimmon (1983) point out that a group's outcomes are sometimes dependent on total productivity, which means that each party's individual contributions (if measurable) become relevant to the total quantity of goods to be distributed. In contrast, there will be other kinds of situations where the outcomes are predetermined and do not depend upon performance levels. In such a case, individuals' attributes may more readily be considered as relevant investments to be differentially rewarded. Additionally, as noted by Camerer and MacCrimmon (1983), one's performance may be partly based on controllable inputs, such as effort, and partly on those, such as ability or physical strength, that cannot be easily controlled by the actor.

Given the wide variety of potentially relevant inputs or investments, one would therefore expect self-serving biases to operate to favor those criteria that are possessed by the actor concerned and a rejection, as "irrelevant," of those that would favor one's opponents in the allocation process. In particular, those categories of persons who are favored by having high generalized status characteristics are likely to consider these as important "investments," whereas those whose performance levels or contributions give them the advantage will tend to argue in favor of actual contributions as "inputs."

Persons with power are likely to predominate in the selection of input criteria, and especially so whenever they are either the allocators' principals or in a position to influence the allocators' decision processes. In many instances, neither the recipients nor the nonrecipients will be in a position to know or evaluate each other's inputs and, indeed, there will almost inevitably be an asymmetry with respect to such knowledge. People will be much more aware of their own characteristics and contributions than they will of others', except in the case of extremely simple laboratory experiments in which they are provided with such information.

In an experimental study involving American college students, Cook (1975) found that whenever such knowledge regarding inputs is unavailable, there is a strong tendency to believe that allocations have, in fact, been made in order to preserve equity, so as to make outcomes proportional to inputs. Such a conservative tendency may be peculiar to this type of setting, which of course does not involve either long-term allocative processes or prolonged experiences as consistent losers. Yet it appears compatible with a number of other accounts involving nonexperimental allocation situations. It also suggests an important reason why allocators usually attempt to withhold crucial information concerning the relative qualifications of winners and losers. The latter seem more willing to accept unfavorable outcomes whenever they are not in a position to evaluate their rivals' credentials.

In general, one of the important factors that can be expected to influence competitors' overall reactions to the allocation process is the degree to which they *believe* themselves to be in possession of accurate and complete information. Some characteristics and contributions will be easier than others for competitors to evaluate, however, and this will be especially true to the degree to which they have been in previous contact. For instance one's race, gender, and approximate age will often be readily apparent, much more so than latent characteristics such as abilities, motivation, or "personality." So too may be one's formal credentials, such as high school or college graduation, in comparison with the skills or quality of training one has really obtained in the process of putting in time in an educational institution.

Where prior performance has been visible to a wider public, as for example in the case of college or professional athletes, it will be nearly impossible for allocators to keep such information secret from one's competitors. Coworkers will have had numerous opportunities to evaluate each other's performances and may in fact be much better informed than are the allocators who are passing judgments on their relative merits. Given that other more subtle types of information are likely to be costly to obtain, it is the more highly visible attributes or performance levels that are likely to predominate in any evaluations concerning distributive justice. It may indeed be difficult for allocators to convince the losing candidates that, in fact, any really important additional information has been used in the decision process.

Walster et al. (1978), among others, stress that in any situation judged to involve an inequitable distribution, all actors involved will experience discomfort and will make some effort to restore equity. We would naturally expect the greatest discomfort among the losing competitors, but Walster et al. argue that even the recipients and the allocators themselves will also attempt to restore equity, at least to some degree. It may be far less costly for them to restore "psychic equity," however, rather than to redistribute the actual goods to their own disadvantage. Since equity judgments are basically subjective, psychic equity may be restored by the winners either by exaggerating their own inputs or deflating their estimates of those of the losers. Alternatively, they may come to believe that the winners' outcomes were really not all that valuable as compared with those of the losers.

Thus the winners may perceive themselves as really having made additional investments or having contributed more than was readily apparent. Or perhaps the losers may be perceived as having contributed negatively to the outcome or as being lacking in some previously unnoticed desired attribute. Therefore, without there being any real changes in the true inputs or outcomes, the evaluator can adjust his or her perceptions so as to restore apparent equity. As previously noted, Walster et al. (1978) also postulate that such perceptual distortions used to restore psychic equity are likely to be in line with the actor's own self-interest, namely in exaggerating one's own inputs or devaluing one's relative outcomes.

Discomfort with inequitable exchange systems is emphasized by those social psychologists who tend to favor explanations stressing the need for cognitive consistency. Indeed, this was the thrust of Adams's (1965) early discussion of the notion of distributive justice (see also, Wilke, 1983). Thus the postulated corrective mechanism involves the assumption of a psychic strain toward consistency, in this case involving a consistency between inputs and outcomes, effort and rewards, or a kind of intellectual honesty on the part of the allocator. Just how important this kind of psychic process is in the case of allocation decisions involving highly valued goods—such as jobs or other means of economic livelihood, choices of marital partners, governmental contracts, titles of nobility, or major academic rewards—remains to be seen. One suspects that the actual restoration of equity will be of much greater concern to winners whenever the goods or benefits under consideration are of only relatively minor importance to them. Still, since the restoration of psychic equity may be a relatively cost-free exercise, we anticipate that whatever discomfort has arisen from an initially perceived inequitable decision can be counteracted by modifications of one's subjective assessments of one or more of the parameters involved.

Exchange theorists seem more likely to stress another mechanism responsible for the restoration of equity, namely the need in ongoing relationships for continued coordination or cooperation among competitors as well as a reduction in the chances of creating overt conflict (Blau, 1964; Homans, 1974). This is the orientation that we shall stress, admitting that the restoration of psychic equity is also likely to accompany any such concern that an exchange system be perceived by all parties as reasonably equitable in some objective sense. A restoration of psychic equity, from this viewpoint, will at most help to serve as a rationalization as to what has taken place. Unfortunately, however, whatever self-serving perceptions that losers may have are likely to be very different from those developed by the winners, or perhaps by the allocators whose decisions have favored the latter category. This obviously means, then, that there will be a diversity of assessments of both relative investments and relative outcomes. In turn, this implies that there will ordinarily be differing opinions as to whether or not there has been distributive justice in any given instance.

Martin and Murray (1983) point out that equity and distributive justice formulations have much in common with arguments that stress the notions of relative deprivation and reference groups. The latter arguments, they claim, are less likely to be conservative in orientation and more likely to emphasize what Runciman (1966) referred to as "fraternal" rather than "egoistic" comparison processes. At issue in this connection is the problem of just what kinds of comparisons the actor makes. One may compare one's outcomes with those that were expected on the basis of one's own prior outcomes or at least those of persons who are very similar to oneself. If so, the response is predicted to be basically conservative. In contrast, one may compare oneself with highly dissimilar others, as for example when black applicants compare themselves with whites, or females contrast their outcomes with those of male applicants.

The essential argument is that whenever competitors compare themselves only with those who are highly similar, or their near equals, they will tend to perceive inequities in personal terms and thus their responses will tend to be individualistic. They may indeed blame themselves if they fail, or possibly even blame the allocators for idiosyncratic biases or perhaps the neglect of some particular one of their inputs. They are much less likely than those who make dissimilar comparisons, however, to perceive the decision-making process as being systematically biased against people like themselves. In so-called fraternal comparison processes, in contrast, upward comparisons are more likely. That is, losers will tend to compare their entire category or group with those who are in more favored positions. Blacks may perceive a systematic bias favoring whites, females one that favors males, and so forth. If so, there is at least the potential for a more organized response as well as a tendency to discredit the whole allocation *system* as being biased against their own group or category.

The literature is rather inconclusive, however, as to the nature of the conditions under which either egoistic or fraternal comparison processes will be more likely. Runciman (1966), who places a heavy stress on the notion of relative deprivation, is also cautious not to imply that fraternal type comparisons nearly always lead to organized protest. In fact, his own survey data of British workers suggest precisely the contrary. As the Tillys (Tilly, Tilly, and Tilly, 1975) have also pointed out, it is true as well that the overwhelming proportion of social protest movements in 19th- and early 20th-century England, France, and Italy were local, rather uneventful, and basically peaceful in nature. Nelson (1982) has made a similar point in connection with the American scene. There may have been a rather large number of organized protests involving narrowly based claims or efforts to improve workers' immediate situations, but these resulted in virtually no overall change in measures of system inequality. What all these authors seem to be saying, then, is that even where fraternal comparisons are used and form the basis for some type of collective action, it is relatively rare that the basic allocation system itself is challenged.

The findings of equity research, much of which has involved experimental studies with college students in settings that are of short duration and that entail allocations of relatively minor rewards, also point in a similar direction, although it is usually the case in these studies that a fraternalistic comparison process is unlikely to be considered by such subjects. As already noted, Cook (1975) found a tendency to accept allocation outcomes as just whenever relative inputs were unknown to the subjects. More generally, the implication is that unless there is evidence to the contrary, many persons simply accept recurrent allocation decisions as just. Basically, then, they tend to trust the allocators unless there is specific evidence of bias. They can do so, of course, because it is relatively easy to restore psychic equity by reassessing one's own or one's opponent's relative inputs or outcomes.

Walster et al. (1978), whose work in equity theory has focused primarily on micro-level processes, argue that people's discomfort with inequitable exchanges often makes it easier for them to make psychological adjustments in their perceptions, rather than admitting that they have been victims of an inequitable exchange process. Writing from a macro perspective, however, Bergel (1962) makes virtually the opposite argument, namely that persons or classes that consistently find themselves at the bottom of a social hierarchy will find it much easier to blame a faulty distributive system rather than their own failings, poor performances, or lack of ability. Obviously, in many instances both temptations will be at work and therefore the important question becomes that of specifying the conditions under which blame is placed primarily on the individual allocator, on the allocation *system,* or on the self.

Here organizational factors, resource mobilization, and belief systems come into play. It is beyond the scope of the present work to discuss the conflict process, and the author's own thinking on the subject has been presented elsewhere (Blalock, 1989b). Clearly, however, certain minimal conditions must be met if there is to be an organized response on the part of those who are dissatisfied with any particular allocation process. First, the outcomes must be *patterned* and *visible* to those who would be expected to form the potentially organizable segment of the population. Thus if blacks are consistently turned down for jobs for which they believe themselves qualified, a fraternalistic comparison process *may* become predominant. If so, there will be a feeling that *we* are being discriminated against by *them,* presumably either by the allocators or their principals or by an organized group of competitors capable of influencing the allocation decisions.

Second, there must be some hope, or nonnegligible subjective probability, that the system can be modified by some specified form of action, which may include coalition formation with powerful allies. Even though the utility or value attached to reform may be high, subjective expected utility theory takes the probability of actual behavior (to modify the system) as a function of the *product* of subjective probabilities and utilities. If so, then if either component is near zero, there will be virtually no protest behavior regardless of the level of the other variable.

Third, this hope for success will be a function of the group's current level of organization and its ability to mobilize resources in some reasonably coordinated manner (McAdam, 1982; McCarthy and Zald, 1977; Oberschall, 1973; Zald and McCarthy, 1979). It has frequently been pointed out that mere discontent is not enough. Seldom, for example, do disorganized and mutually isolated peasants engage in successful rebellions. It is usually not those at the very bottom of a social hierarchy who initially rebel against an unfair system, as they are usually far too consumed with efforts merely to survive from one day to the next. Major social revolutions have usually built upon massive discontent, or high utilities for change, but it has generally required actions on the part of discontented intellectuals or elements of the elite to provide both the initial impetus and organizational skills needed to turn egoistic comparison processes into fraternalistic ones.[1]

Finally, as just noted, organized efforts to achieve a solidarity base among otherwise disconnected individuals practically always require a supportive ideological system that makes such individuals aware of their common plight, the nature of the allocation system being employed against them, and the benefits being (unfairly) awarded to their competitors. In particular, ideological systems that are both simplistic and ethnocentric and that place the blame on other parties rather than the self will be well suited to such organizational efforts. Fatalistic belief systems, which are often encouraged by dominant parties, will tend to inhibit effective organization. These and other ideological dimensions may then combine with other setting variables to influence the degree to which persistent losers in allocation contests are able to organize themselves, collectively, so as to modify the outcomes of those contests (Blalock, 1989b).

## ALLOCATOR DEFENSES

It is the thesis of Walster et al. (1978) that, given that the self-interest assumption applies both to allocators and competitors, social systems usually evolve methods of rewarding those allocators who adhere to the principle of distributive justice and of punishing those who do not. The problem then becomes that of convincing relevant parties that the distributional system has, in fact, been fair. As we have just noted, this may be relatively easy whenever the allocators are successful in hiding both their selection criteria and the credentials of all other competing parties. If this is possible, then the tendency may be for others to assume that outcomes are automatically proportional to the unknown inputs, and thus that distributive justice holds.

What more specific kinds of protective devices can be used by allocators to reduce the risk that the system will be challenged? One device is to deny that there are any real losers, or at least that losing individuals can be identified with any specific category that might form the basis for a fraternally coordinated response. Consider, for example, those affirmative action policies that encourage or require that numerical quotas or targets be set aside for minority or women job candidates. If, indeed, women or minorities are hired disproportionately to their actual numbers in some explicit pool, then in any zero-sum game setup (such as a hiring situation) this will of course mean that relatively fewer white males will be hired. The system is then biased against the latter *individual* candidates, but this may in fact be denied by resort to what may amount to a redefinition of the fraternal category used by those white males who may have been adversely affected. These latter may define the bounds of the fraternal category to include only those white males who have taken part in the *current* job competition, whereas the broadened definition used by the allocator may also include those white males who have been beneficiaries of *past* practices that indeed favored persons like themselves. Current practices are seen by the allocators and their supporters as being corrective actions needed to compensate for previous wrongs. Since the more inclusive category of past and present white male competitors may even have come out ahead in the frequency count (depending, of course, on how far back into the past one wishes to go), a continuation of affirmative action practices can thus be justified. We have here an instance where the choice of the boundaries of one's fraternal category can affect the numbers used to justify a given set of outcomes.

As we discussed in the previous chapter, allocators may also modify the selection criteria they use so as to justify their actions. Rather than use a double standard, they may use blurred standards that require subjective interpretations that, presumably, only the allocators are qualified to make. Rather than using scores on objective tests, for example, they may select among a pool of college applicants by attempting to evaluate "potential" or "maturity," or by substituting "relevant" experience. Those losers who challenge the selection system by pointing to their own superior test scores may be told that this is merely one among a number of (unspecified) qualities that have been used in the judgmental process. In effect, the concept of "inputs" becomes broadened to permit additional discretion on the part of allocators privy to more complete information than can be made available to the competitors themselves.

Allocators and their allies may also attempt to influence the belief systems prevalent among competitors, especially those competitors most likely to be tempted to perceive the distribution system in fraternal terms. First, they may try to create a "good loser" mentality, similar to that espoused in connection with sporting contests. Those who lose in such contests are supposed to praise the superior performance of their opponents and then quietly go home to improve their own skills in preparation for the next encounter. In such settings those who protest what they perceive to be unfair decisions are more likely to be castigated as poor sports and to suffer an even greater loss of esteem than that caused by the initial loss.

Similarly, in other situations that are perceived by the general public as being basically fair competitions presided over by impartial judges the costs of protest are likely to be perceived to outweigh the potential gains of a successful challenge. Since many losing competitors who are not already organized are also likely to believe that it is wiser to follow the "good sport" tack, it will ordinarily be difficult for those who do wish to challenge the outcome to coordinate their activities with those of other losing candidates. It may even be believed, perhaps on the basis of prior test cases, that those who complain too vociferously will be disqualified from future competitions. The system, whether fair or not, then remains unchallenged.

As previously noted, losers may perceive outcomes either on an egoistic or on a fraternalistic basis depending on the nature of the others with whom they compare themselves. If allocators prefer individualistic rather than organized challenges to their decisions as we would generally expect to be the case, it will obviously be to

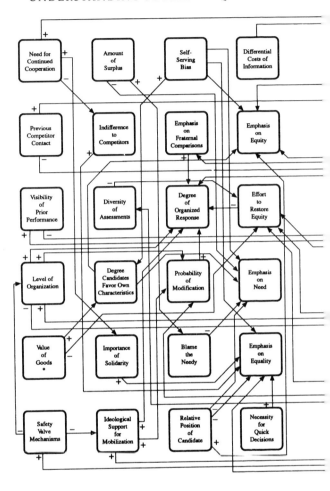

**Figure 7.1.** Model VIII: Reactive Processes and Distributive Justice

their advantage to encourage competitors to make comparisons only with their own near-equals or with highly similar categories of persons. To the extent that an ideology stressing the acceptance of supposedly permanent or inevitable differential advantages can be evolved, such that women compare themselves only with other women, slaves with other slaves, manual workers with other manual workers, and so forth, this will tend to inhibit the formation of

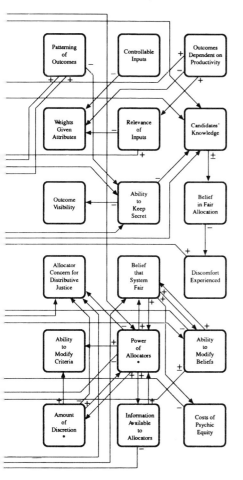

collective responses among such parties. Mason (1970), for example, has noted that gross inequalities between ethnic or caste groups can be maintained for very long periods of time, without conflict or the use of force, provided that the disadvantaged parties are socialized to accept input and outcome differences as inevitable. In the case of the Indian caste system, such outcome differences are believed to be the result of some unobservable and inscrutable process occurring during the actors' prior lives.

If allocators can encourage certain kinds of safety-valve mechanisms that drain off hostility and inhibit organized responses it will generally be to their advantage to do so. If, for example, losing candidates can take advantage of somewhat less satisfactory alternatives, such as lower paying jobs or less prestigious colleges, they may be counseled by allocators to look into such opportunities. Emigration from the local area may also be encouraged. Where an incipient organization of losers is anticipated, it may sometimes be possible to coopt potential leadership elements by giving them token positions as members of a board of advisors, by urging them to seek out better, more qualified candidates, or even by including them among a small group of winning candidates. Backup safety net programs, such as food bank programs, emergency shelters, and public welfare may also be modestly supported so as to discourage organized protests. Where such programs come to be defined as entitlements, any dissatisfactions among substantial numbers of persons within a given category may then be deflected toward those who are failing to provide adequate levels of such entitlements, rather than those allocating agents who have discriminated against them in the first place.

As noted, there will be many allocation situations in which competitors are not in prior contact with one another or even aware of how many such persons there are. If competitors can be processed one at a time, say by interviewers in a private office, it becomes possible to withhold substantial amounts of information while at the same time giving sufficient encouragement to each applicant so that he or she leaves the scene believing that the allocator is genuinely interested in fair play. Where awards are privately announced it is also less likely that a collective response will occur or that losers will be motivated to employ a fraternal type comparison process. Therefore, whenever feasible, it will be to the allocators' advantage to individualize the screening process as much as possible. Application by mail or the submission of personal résumés may have much the same result of mutually isolating individual competitors.

Finally, we should take note of the obvious point that very powerful allocators hardly need to be concerned about distributive or procedural justice at all, except possibly to salve their own consciences. Lenski (1966) notes that in both advanced horticultural and agrarian societies the major allocation decisions are often almost totally in the hands of powerful chieftains or kings and that the distinction between their own private wealth and property and those of the state is usually blurred. Such powerful individuals could, and usually did, employ entirely self-serving criteria to attempt to ensure dependence and loyalty among awardees. This was accomplished by retaining control over the land and offices being allocated, so that hereditary rights did not evolve. The only "justice" in such allocative systems tended to be defined in terms of the divine right of kings or of traditional authority based on lineage or religious beliefs. Basically, it was the allocator's right to make final decisions, given a social system oriented to satisfying the wishes of a ruling elite and backed by the necessary power resources to put down organized revolt. Such social systems serve as reminders that Western civilization may represent a very atypical case among a huge variety of social systems, many of which give far less weight to considerations of distributive justice.

## CAUSAL MODEL VIII: REACTIVE PROCESSES AND DISTRIBUTIVE JUSTICE

Our final causal model (Figure 7.1) is also larger than those of earlier chapters and requires a double page for presentation. Therefore we follow the same scheme as used for the previous model, namely locating the dependent variables toward the center of the figure. There are 42 variables in all, 16 exogenous, 16 intervening, and 10 dependent variables. We again use the format of first listing the variables and then turning to a discussion of the causal relationships among them. In examining the nature of these exogenous variables it should be specifically noted that many refer to situations in which positions or rewards are being given either for prior contributions or for investments of candidates. Thus the scope of the model's application may be somewhat narrower than in the case of earlier models.

*The Exogenous Variables*

The exogenous variables are listed in order, first going across the top row, then down the left column, and finally across the bottom row, excluding the final two columns.

(1) The degree to which there is a need for continued cooperation among competitors (Need for Continued Cooperation)

(2) The degree to which there is a surplus of goods in the larger social system (Amount of Surplus)

(3) The degree to which allocators or competitors are subject to self-serving biases (Self-Serving Bias)

(4) The degree to which there are differential costs to competitors in obtaining information (Differential Costs of Information)

(5) The degree to which outcomes of allocator decisions are obviously patterned or unequally distributed (Patterning of Outcomes)

(6) The degree to which competitors can actually control their own inputs in contributing to group outcomes (Controllable Inputs)

(7) The degree to which a group's outcomes are dependent on the productivity of its members (Outcomes Dependent on Productivity)

(8) The amount of previous contact among competitors (Previous Competitor Contact)

(9) The degree to which competitors' prior performances are visible to other competitors or the public (Visibility of Prior Performance)

(10) The current degree or level of organization among competitors (Level of Organization)

(11) *(Value of Goods)

(12) The degree to which there are safety valve mechanisms to drain off hostility of losing candidates (Safety Valve Mechanisms)

(13) The degree of ideological support for the mobilization of losing candidates (Ideological Support for Mobilization)

(14) A candidate's relative position in terms of competitive qualifications (Relative Position of Candidate)

(15) The degree to which allocators find it necessary to make quick decisions (Necessity for Quick Decisions)

(16) *(Amount of Discretion)

## The Intervening Variables

The 16 intervening variables are listed, in order, by going across rows, beginning with the second row. Since the dependent variables appear in the fourth and fifth columns, as well as there being two in the third and fourth rows of the third column, these variables are skipped as one reads across the figure.

(1) The degree to which allocators are indifferent as to which types of competitors are selected (Indifference to Competitors)

(2) The degree to which losing candidates are inclined to make fraternalistic comparisons (Emphasis on Fraternal Comparisons)

(3) The degree to which candidates' relative inputs are considered by allocators in making evaluations (Relevance of Inputs)

(4) The degree to which candidates have knowledge about each other's inputs or characteristics (Candidates' Knowledge)

(5) The degree of diversity of assessments among competitors regarding fairness of outcomes (Diversity of Assessments)

(6) The degree to which allocators have the ability to keep criteria or results secret (Ability to Keep Secret)

(7) The degree to which allocation procedures and outcomes are generally believed to be fair (Belief in Fair Allocation)

(8) The degree to which candidates favor their own characteristics as most important (Degree Candidates Favor Own Characteristics)

(9) The degree to which there is general belief that the allocation *system* is fair (Belief That System Fair)

(10) The degree to which allocators or competitors experience discomfort with decisions made (Discomfort Experienced)

(11) The importance of achieving solidarity among losing candidates (Importance of Solidarity)

(12) The degree to which the needy are generally blamed or held responsible for their own condition (Blame the Needy)

(13) *(Power of Allocators)

(14) *(Ability to Modify Beliefs)

(15) The amount of information available to allocators about competitors' characteristics (Information Available to Allocators)

(16) The amount of costs to allocators or competitors of restoring psychic equity (Costs of Psychic Equity)

## The Dependent Variables

The 10 dependent variables are ordered by first going down the third column, taking the third and fourth rows, then using the middle four rows of the fourth and fifth columns respectively. It should specifically be noted that in this and certain other listings of variables, it is entirely possible that allocators and winning and losing competitors will have differing perspectives or priorities, meaning that additional dependent variables may be required if one wishes to distinguish among the levels for each of these types of actors.

(1) The degree to which there is or is expected to be an organized response by losing candidates (Degree of Organized Response)
(2) The probability that the system can be modified by an organized response by losers (Probability of Modification)
(3) The degree to which the equity principle is emphasized by allocators and competitors (Emphasis on Equity)
(4) The degree to which there are efforts to restore equity by allocators or competitors (Effort to Restore Equity)
(5) The degree to which the need principle is emphasized by allocators and competitors (Emphasis on Need)
(6) The degree to which the equality principle is emphasized by allocators and competitors (Emphasis on Equality)
(7) The relative weights given by allocators and competitors to attributes as compared to contributions (Weights Given Attributes)
(8) The degree to which allocation outcomes are visible to competitors (Outcome Visibility)
(9) The degree to which allocators are concerned about principles of distributive justice (Allocator Concern for Distributive Justice)
(10) The degree to which allocators have the ability to modify selection criteria (Ability to Modify Criteria)

*Discussion of the Model:*
*Effects of the Exogenous Variables*

Once more, we discuss the effects of the exogenous variables in the order in which they have been listed, beginning with the top row of the figure.

Need for Continued Cooperation is assumed to affect three variables, the first of which is allocators' indifference to competitors. The idea is that the greater the need for cooperation among some of the competitors, the more concerned allocators will be about their possible collective responses and therefore the less indifferent allocators will be to them. The greater the need for cooperation the greater, also, should be the importance of solidarity among the respective groups of competitors. This relationship seems almost true by definition, but we must remember that there can be instances where cooperation does not necessarily require solidarity or a fraternalistic orientation on the part of the relevant parties. Finally, need for continued cooperation is expected to have a positive impact on Power of Allocators, since a high degree of need means that it is difficult for losing candidates to challenge the power of allocators.

The amount of surplus in a system is anticipated to have a positive impact on tendencies to blame the needy for their disadvantaged positions and to have a negative effect on Emphasis on Need as a criterion for the distribution of goods or positions. As we argued previously, systems in which there is very little surplus are expected to place a greater emphasis on need than on equity as the predominant distributive criterion.

Self-serving biases are postulated to affect four variables in the model. Rather obviously, these should have a positive effect on the degree to which candidates favor giving greater weights to characteristics they, themselves, possess and lesser weights to those possessed by their rivals. Such self-serving biases are also expected to affect the degree to which individuals favor equity principles over those based on either need or equality, but we cannot tell the direction of this relationship without knowing the degree to which inputs of such individuals are above or below average. Arrows are also drawn from Self-Serving Bias to Emphasis on Need and Emphasis on Equality for the same reasons.

Differential Costs of Information are expected to affect candidates' knowledge of each other's qualifications, with only the most obvious information being available to those who are in the poorest positions to invest in obtaining less obvious information. The degree to which outcomes are highly patterned is predicted to have a negative impact on allocators' ability to keep such information secret. A high degree of patterning is anticipated to have positive effects, however, on both the degree to which losers tend to emphasize fraternalistic comparisons and also on the degree to which their responses are organized.

Controllable Inputs, the sixth exogenous variable, is predicted to have a negative effect on a single dependent variable, Weights Given Attributes, under the assumption that whenever an individual's contributions are thought to be under that person's control, such contributions will be given greater weights than will attributes, which are generally not subject to such control. Not indicated in the figure is the assumption that it has already been established that equity principles will override equality and need principles in order for such controllable inputs to have an impact on allocators' decisions.

Outcomes Dependent on Productivity is expected to increase the relevance of a person's inputs or contributions, as compared with the weights given to attributes or ascribed characteristics. It is also expected to have a positive impact on Emphasis on Equity, and of course a corresponding decrease in that given to either equality or need. In other words, when a person's actual contributions are both highly visible and also important in affecting a group's outcomes, these will tend to be rewarded in the allocation process. This assumes, of course, that the allocators involved actually desire positive outcomes for the group in question.

Previous Competitor Contact is expected to have positive effects on candidates' knowledge of each others' qualifications and contributions. Likewise, it is predicted to have a negative impact on allocators' ability to keep such information secret from fellow competitors.

Visibility of Prior Performance is rather obviously expected to have a negative impact on allocators' ability to keep selection criteria or restults secret from competitors. Likewise it is predicted to have a positive effect on candidates' knowledge of each others' qualifications.

Level of Organization is anticipated to have a negative effect on allocators' ability to influence competitor beliefs but a positive effect on three other variables. The first of these is allocators' concern for distributive justice, the assumption being that a high degree of organization among at least some competitors will motivate allocators to take their concerns seriously and to justify any decisions made in terms of competitors' relative inputs. Level of Organization is, secondly, expected to have a positive impact on the degree to which competitors' responses are organized. Finally, it is also predicted to have a positive effect on the probability that the system can be modified by an organized response by losing competitors.

Value of Goods, which we have previously encountered as an exogenous variable, is anticipated to have a positive effect on the degree to which candidates favor their own characteristics. The assumption, here, is that the more valuable the prize the more tempted persons will be to employ self-serving strategies that emphasize those traits that they, themselves, possess at the expense of those possessed by their competitors. By the same token, Value of Goods is expected to have a negative effect on winners' efforts to restore equity under the assumption that they will strongly prefer to retain valuable prizes, as contrasted with ones of lesser importance. Here we are referring to the actual restoration of equity at a cost to winners, rather than the mere restoration of psychic equity.

The existence of safety valve mechanisms is predicted to have a negative impact on Level of Organization under the assumption that the presence of safety valve mechanisms will foster an individualistic as contrasted with a fraternalistic comparison process and that it will therefore be more difficult to organize those losers who are in a position to take advantage of such mechanisms. Likewise, the existence of satisfactory safety valve mechanisms should reduce the ideological support for mobilization among losers. Given such compensatory mechanisms this is also predicted to increase beliefs that the overall allocative system is fair. It is in situations where there are few if any alternatives for losers that we would expect beliefs in the system's fairness to become weakened and, possibly, be replaced by a counterideology supporting rebellion or some other type of organized response.

Ideological Support for Mobilization, in turn, is predicted to have a positive impact on allocators' concern for distributive justice, if only as a protective device against such mobilization. Ideological Support for Mobilization is likewise predicted to affect, positively, both Degree of Organized Response and Probability of Modification.

The relative position of a given candidate in terms of his or her qualifications or contributions is expected to affect that candidate's preference for the kind of allocator priority system to be employed. Persons having strong qualifications should prefer an equity based distributional system and to play down or attempt to discredit both the principles of need and equality. This assumes, of course, a self-serving bias at work, a factor that has been predicted to be more likely to be operative whenever the positions at stake are highly valued. The necessity for quick decisions on the part of allocators is expected to affect only a single variable in the model, namely the emphasis that such allocators place on the principle of equality. The assumption, here, is that an equality principle is simpler to employ than one based either on need or on equity, both of which require allocators to seek out more information about each candidate.

Our last exogenous variable, Amount of Discretion, has also appeared in previous models. It is expected to have a positive effect on the ability of allocators to modify selection criteria but a negative one on the degree to which allocators find it necessary or desirable to be concerned about adhering to principles of distributive justice in making their decisions. This latter relationship assumes, of course, that one of the major constraining factors likely to operate on allocators with little or no discretion is that distributive justice criteria are to be taken seriously. There may be circumstances, however, under which such constraining factors may operate against distributive justice and toward biasing allocation criteria in the direction of one or another type of candidate. If so, increased allocator discretion may actually favor the introduction of distributive justice criteria, so that the sign of the relationship would be reversed. Finally, allocator discretion is expected to have a positive reciprocal relationship with Power of Allocator. Powerful allocators will be able to employ more discretion and, in turn, increases in discretion will tend to increase allocator power.

This completes our discussion of the effects of exogenous variables. We therefore turn to a consideration of the impacts of the 16 intervening variables.

*Discussion of the Model:*
*Effects of the Intervening Variables*

Proceeding across each row, beginning with the second and skipping dependent variables, we locate the first intervening variable, Indifference to Competitors. Where allocators are truly indifferent as to which competitors they select we expect them to emphasize equality as a distributional principle. Therefore we have drawn in a positively signed arrow between these two variables.

Emphasis on Fraternal Comparisons is predicted to have a positive impact on a single variable, namely the degree to which losers' responses are organized. The degree to which candidates' relative inputs are considered by allocators is anticipated to have a negative effect on Weights Given Attributes under the assumption that there is an inverse relationship between the weights assigned to inputs or actual contributions, on the one hand, and attributes or ascribed characteristics, on the other hand. Relevance of Inputs is, however, expected to have an overall positive effect on the degree to which allocators (and competitors) tend to emphasize equity principles over both strict equality and need.

Candidates' Knowledge is predicted to affect the single variable Belief in Fair Allocation, but with an indeterminate sign depending on the content of such knowledge. Diversity of Assessments also is expected to affect a single variable, namely allocators' efforts to restore equity. The reasoning, here, is that a high degree of diversity means that allocators will be under little systematic or sustained pressure to think seriously about their decision processes or the outcomes of these decisions.

Ability to Keep Secret is postulated to have negative impacts on two variables, Outcome Visibility and Candidates' Knowledge, both for rather obvious reasons. Belief in Fair Allocation is expected to have a negative effect on the degree to which both allocators and winning candidates are likely to experience discomfort with decisions that have been made, thereby reducing their interest in finding ways to restore equity in those situations where fairness might be in doubt. Losers who believe the decision has been fair may, however, experience discomfort to the degree that they blame themselves for their failure. Therefore, if one is talking primarily about losing candidates, a sign reversal may be necessary.

The eighth intervening variable, the degree to which candidates favor their own characteristics as being most important, is predicted to affect Emphasis on Need in either direction, depending on whether or not such candidates find themselves near the very bottom of the pile in terms of need. By the same token, a favoring of one's own characteristics should affect Emphasis on Equity, with the sign again depending on the relevant characteristics of the candidate in question.

The degree to which there is a general belief that the allocation system as a whole is fair needs to be distinguished from the apparently similar intervening variable, Belief in Fair Allocation, which refers to a specific allocation outcome. Belief That System Fair is predicted to have a reciprocal positive linkage with allocators' ability to modify the beliefs of specific competitors. On the one hand, a generalized belief in the system's fairness should make it easier for allocators to convince losers that they, also, have been treated fairly. On the other hand, allocators' abilities to modify specific sets of candidates (especially the losers) is expected to reinforce the generalized belief in the overall system's fairness. Similarly, a generalized belief in the system's fairness is predicted to have a positive reciprocal relationship with Power of Allocators for much the same reason. Allocators' power will be enhanced to the degree that there is overall confidence in the system, and powerful allocators will be in a position to convince the general public of the system's fairness. In addition, a general belief in the system's fairness is predicted to increase the costs of restoring psychic equity in those instances where it is initially believed that a specific allocation outcome has been unfair. This should be especially true for losing candidates who may find it more difficult to explain the fact that, in a fair system, they have lost out to superior candidates.

Discomfort Experienced is expected to have a positive impact on a single variable, Effort to Restore Equity. The presumption is that without at least some discomfort or guilt experienced, there will be little or no motivation to restore equity. The importance of achieving solidarity among losing candidates is predicted to effect, positively, the emphasis placed on equality. The reasoning, here, is that it is least difficult to achieve solidarity among members whenever equality of members is the overriding principle and whenever the relatively more divisive principles of need or equity based on inputs is invoked. In the interest of simplicity, however, no arrows have been drawn from Importance of Solidarity to either Emphasis on Equity or Emphasis on Need. Had these arrows been introduced, the signs would of course have been negative.

236ding

INEQUALTY

Blame the Needy is likewise expected to have a negative impact on the emphasis placed on need. As in the previous case, arrows could also have been drawn to emphasis on equity and equality, but with positive signs.

Power of Allocators, which has appeared in prior models, is an important intervening variable in the model. It is assumed to be reciprocally and positively related to Information Available to Allocators for obvious reasons. It is similarly presumed to be reciprocally linked to Amount of Discretion, which has also appeared in prior models. As previously noted, there is also a postulated reciprocal linkage with the general belief that the system is fair. Power of Allocators is likewise expected to decrease their concern about conforming to the norms of distributive justice, to increase their ability to modify the criteria used in the allocation process, and to decrease the probability that the system can be modified by an organized response on the part of losing candidates.

Ability to Modify Beliefs, as already noted, is assumed to be linked reciprocally and positively to the general public's beliefs that the overall system is fair. It is also predicted to have a negative impact on allocators' efforts to restore equity, presumably because there will be less need for them to do so to the degree that they can modify the beliefs held by others. Ability to Modify Beliefs is also expected to affect Diversity of Assessments, but with an indeterminate sign. Sometimes it may be to allocator's advantage to encourage such a diversity, so as to play one group of candidates off against another. Perhaps more often, however, allocators will attempt to create a homogeneity of assessments favoring their own legitimacy and the overall fairness of the distributive system.

Information Available to Allocators, as noted, is expected to be reciprocally related to the amount of power they possess. Additionally, information available to them is predicted to have a negative impact on the degree to which they place an emphasis on equality as the primary criterion for allocation. We have argued, in this instance, that it is when information about competitors is scarce or unreliable that the equality principle works as well as any other and is less likely to result in negative reactions to the decision process. Finally, the degree to which the restoration of psychic equity is costly is expected to have a negative effect on efforts to employ this equilibrating tactic. We have argued, however, that in general such costs will tend to be relatively low as compared with the actual restoration of equity.

This completes our discussion of the assumed effects of the 16 intervening variables. As before, we can now turn to a much more brief consideration of the 10 dependent variables, only a few of which are presumed to be causally connected with one another.

## A Note on the Dependent Variables

Most of the dependent variables in the model refer to behaviors or orientations of allocator, but two pertain primarily to the losing candidates. Also, as previously noted, the three variables Emphasis on Need, Emphasis on Equality, and Emphasis on Equity may refer either to allocators or competitors, as the case may be. Where these are expected to differ according to type of actor, it may therefore be advisable to make further distinctions and thus to add to the number of dependent variables.

Only two of these dependent variables are postulated to affect another dependent variable. Probability of Modification is assumed to have an obvious positive effect on Degree of Organized Response. The degree to which there are efforts by allocators to restore equity is expected to inhibit the degree of organized response, partly by making such a response unnecessary but also by indicating good faith on the part of such allocators. This presumes, of course, that such restorative efforts are visible to the relevant parties and that they are both reasonably substantial and immediate rather than delayed. If such efforts were to be perceived as being results of threats of an organized response, however, they might actually have the effect of further increasing the organized response.

Our discussions of all eight causal models are now completed. What needs to be stressed before we proceed with the concluding chapter is that all of these models should be treated as tentative. Certainly, when one focuses on special applications, as for example a particular kind of position being allocated, each model may be simplified by leaving out those variables considered to be irrelevant for that application or those that, in a given setting, can be treated as constants. Thus each specific application of the models can be simpler than the more general formulation in certain respects. It is also likely, however, that an augmented set of exogenous variables should at least be considered and that further distinctions among types of competitors or allocators may be required.

The important message to convey is that each of the models presented should be treated more as a starting point than as a definitive theory to be evaluated as it stands. Too rigid an orientation to the testing of any specific causal model may prove disadvantageous to the exploratory collective endeavor to develop a useful and reasonably complete explanation of any complex causal process. This is especially so whenever we lack good measures of most of the variables contained in such models. It is hoped that the heuristic value of these models, however, will be to serve as a stimulant to the development of more complete and more adequate models, as well as to the necessary data gathering effort needed to test them.

## NOTE

1. Students of social revolutions, while not referring specifically to fraternalistic versus individualistic or egoistic comparisons, make many of these same points. See, for example, Brinton (1938), Davies (1962), Gurr (1970), and Moore (1966).

EIGHT

# *Toward an Agenda for Research*

The theoretical arguments and models we have presented are intended to be very general, whereas research projects must inevitably be both narrower in scope and restricted with respect to the number of variables that can be studied. A number of questions must therefore be answered if any genuine program of research can be developed to address the many issues suggested by our discussions.

As stressed at the outset, this theoretical project was undertaken precisely because of the considerable gaps that exist in the empirical literature. Many of these gaps are the result of data collection problems, especially those encountered whenever survey research is the primary type of data-collection instrument. In particular, two- or multiparty interactions have typically been neglected, so that one is left studying only the results of such processes. As stressed on numerous occasions, many such resultants take the form of inequalities of various sorts. In order to infer the underlying causes, one is then tempted to make undue simplifications that hold only one party responsible for such outcomes. Sociologists commonly take this party to be the dominant one, thereby ignoring feedbacks from the behaviors of so-called victims of these dominant or stronger parties.

We must do much better than this if credible conclusions are to be reached, if only because critics will be unwilling to make the same simplifying assumptions as do social science investigators. This implies the need for considerable patience and a strategy that aims to fill in the puzzle, piece by piece. It also implies that empirical studies will need to deal with special cases of allocation processes, rather than a large number at any one time. Contexts will have to be delimited by time and space, meaning that in any given study many of the variables we have used may be considered constants for that particular setting.

For illustrative purposes suppose one is interested in studying the processes by which high school graduates make decisions and are then selected into various types of positions: jobs, entrance to college or other kinds of postsecondary educational institutions, military service, marriage and homemaking, and so forth. Obviously, certain characteristics of such graduates will be nearly constant: their ages and geographic locations, the school they have recently attended, and perhaps even the curricula to which they have been exposed and certain of their qualifications. Other variables will have truncated ranges: their job qualifications, the nature of the occupational and schooling alternatives they actually consider, and perhaps even some of the allocator characteristics and constraining factors discussed in Chapters 3 and 4.

All this may mean that some of the coefficients in a given model may be so close to zero that the corresponding linkages can be ignored. Obviously, whenever a variable becomes virtually a constant in a given study, one cannot estimate its impacts on other variables in the theoretical system. Furthermore, for the particular kind of allocation process being examined, certain of the exogenous or intervening variables in our models may turn out to be theoretically irrelevant. Positions awarded may be totally irrevocable, for instance.

The fundamental decision that must be faced in any given piece of empirical research is that of which variables to omit from the study. Often, this decision is made either in an ad hoc fashion, with very little prior thought or preliminary research, or largely on the basis of data availability considerations. Investigators may first decide on a method of data investigation or the use of a particular data source, and *then* on the variables they will study and the explicit model to be used. This is of course putting the empirical cart before the theoretical horse. If one also makes only a pro forma effort to state the assumptions needed in one's statistical tests or estimating equations, the damage is complete. Potentially embarrassing questions are never asked and hidden assumptions never unearthed.

Critical in all single-equation statistical procedures, such as analysis of variance, multiple regression, and loglinear analysis, is the assumption that omitted variables represented in disturbance terms are uncorrelated with all independent variables being employed. This is a strong assumption indeed, even in experimental designs in which randomization has been employed to take care of some but not all such disturbing influences.[1] But how can such an assumption about missing variables be justified without a more complete theory containing at least a substantial proportion of the relevant omitted variables? How does one decide, without a theory, whether such omitted factors have additive, multiplicative, or possibly other types of joint effects in conjunction with those few factors that have been explicitly included (Blalock, 1982)? And can one reasonably assume, without a theory, that variables that have been selected as "dependent" actually do not feed back to affect some of the supposedly "independent" variables in the equation? Conventional statistical methods commonly require one to make certain very simple assumptions, whether or not this is clearly recognized or conveniently ignored.

All of this of course implies the need for reasonably complete theories *before* data have been collected and analyzed. If, instead, investigators each make use of very partial theories that neglect different sets of variables, then each can be expected to involve unknown biases of differing types. The situation will be ripe for endless and nonproductive controversies. Worse still, if entire intellectual traditions systematically neglect certain variables, either because they are considered to "belong" to the domain of another discipline or because of patterned intellectual biases or blindspots, the biases concerned may go totally unrecognized—except, of course, by outsiders who reject such disciplinary-bound assumptions. As we have argued, this is precisely the kind of situation that students of stratification or race and gender discrimination find themselves in today.

With a relatively complete theory, one may then go about the necessary task of stating theoretically grounded justifications for omitting certain variables. For example, if one is willing to assume that certain exogenous factors directly affect only a single variable in a causal system, such antecedent variables can be omitted. Indeed, if this were not permissible it would be impossible to find a starting point for one's theory. It would be necessary to go back to Adam and Eve in every analysis. Suppose, however, that a given exogenous variable were a direct cause of two or more variables in the remainder of the system. This would mean that they would be spuriously related and, if the investigator were unaware of this fact, the conclusions reached could be highly misleading. Without a prior theory there would be no rational basis for deciding which factors among a variable's important causes could safely be omitted. A similar kind of argument applies to the omission of supposedly intervening variables. If there were feedback loops involving such omitted variables, misleading conclusions could easily result (Blalock, 1982). Again, without an inclusive and realistic theory one is left guessing as to the appropriateness of any particular decision to omit some variables but not others.

In applied research, especially, there may be a temptation to move prematurely to a focus on one's ultimate dependent variables by means of an atheoretical listing of possible independent variables whose interrelationships are left theoretically unspecified. If one then controls for each such variable in turn, or if one controls for all "relevant" variables simultaneously, the conclusion may be reached that those variables that "explain" the most variance statistically are also the most important ones theoretically. Such a theoretically blind practice may inadvertently uncover some of the most proximate causes, whereas the prior causes through which these intervening variables are operating are screened out. If multicollinearity or high intercorrelations among explanatory variables are ignored, one may also be misled whenever there are differential measurement errors or relatively small samples (Gordon, 1968). And, as already noted, such a practice does not permit one to come to grips with possible biasing effects of unmeasured variables.

A far better but more long-term strategy, given a nearly recursive setup, is to obtain prior variables, including some of one's intervening variables in the larger model. By proceeding recursively, equation by equation, one may eliminate postulated causal links that prove to be empirically weak, as well as adding others that may have been located through empirical investigations but not anticipated in the prior theory. Through a deliberately conceived series of investigations, one may then proceed recursively through the system of successive "dependent" variables and ultimately to those in which one is most interested. In terms of the several models we have presented, this would generally involve proceeding from left to right (and top to bottom) in the larger, more inclusive diagram, rather than immediately jumping to the ultimate dependent variables and a relatively small handful of their postulated causes.

Models such as those presented in Chapters 2 through 7 are intended to be highly general. Whenever one delimits a study to a specific kind of allocation process, say how teachers allocate time among students or how mortgage loan officials and real estate agents jointly influence what kinds of individuals locate in particular neighborhoods, any of our general models will need to be supplemented or otherwise modified. As illustrated in Blalock (1989b), it may therefore be necessary to develop specific submodels that elaborate on the more general ones, say by bringing in additional subjective factors or exogenous variables presumed to be relevant to specialized applications. Such submodels may also contain simplifications that involve the elimination of certain of the variables in the more general models, perhaps because their impacts are presumed to be of only minor importance or because prior studies have shown these variables to be only very weakly correlated with others in the system. Presumably, it is through the process of submodel development that important kinds of special cases can be analyzed and the general theory thereby elaborated and improved.

Finally, we should take note of the implications of our models for the kinds of research we conduct and, especially, how we organize ourselves to collaborate more effectively so as to provide more complete information to data analysts. As already implied, both research involving multiple methods and considerable preliminary or exploratory work need to become the prevailing norm, rather than the exception. Observational studies and unstructured interviews are obviously needed in order to investigate the allocator decision process in sufficient detail to fill in present gaps in our knowledge. Do they actually take into consideration such factors as relationships to their principals, expected reactions by losing candidates or any third parties supporting them, or the long-term implications of their decision processes for subsequent applicant pools? Under what conditions do they seek additional information or support from fellow allocators? What kinds of biases seem most relevant, and how do these actually impact on the final decisions being made?

Well-documented case studies are obviously needed, both to serve as reality checks on existing theory and to suggest additional variables that should be brought into our models. A premature leap to more quantitative or "objective" sorts of data is likely to result in the omission of many kinds of important intervening variables, as well as the factors that impact upon them.

Thus there is considerable need for small-scale research of the sort that can be conducted by individual researchers over a relatively short time span. The problem with such research, in general, is that it is rarely coordinated. Each piece of exploratory research tends to stand alone. Data-collection methods are so varied, and concepts so idiosyncratic to each investigator, that genuine cumulation of knowledge is made extremely difficult. Such small-scale research, especially, requires a much higher degree of coordination among investigators than is presently the practice. If each investigator goes off in a different direction, using a unique theoretical orientation or no theory at all, such small-scale exploratory work will result in a highly inefficient knowledge accumulation process, at best.

Eventually, much more coordinated, systematic efforts will be needed to collect data that can be pooled so as to provide analysts with reasonably complete data sets capable of testing models of at least the complexity of those we have presented. Since it is highly unlikely that a single data-collection method, such as survey research, can provide all such information, this implies a need for coordinated research involving multiple methods. In turn, this suggests the need for large-scale research institutes focused on particular kinds of *topics,* rather than those that employ a single data-collection strategy applied to a diversity of substantive problems. Clearly, we are not organized along such lines.

The point to be emphasized is that it is our *theories* that should guide our research strategies and collaborative efforts. For this reason, theory building efforts need to precede rather than follow data analyses. Perhaps more accurately, insights produced by exploratory studies must be formalized and systematized so as to facilitate the coordination of more serious, large-scale data-collection efforts. If we fail to develop the theory or to agree upon a reasonably common framework for coordinating our research, we will remain frustrated by meager results. The knowledge cumulation process will be seriously impeded.

## NOTE

1. For early statements of this position see Kish (1959) and Blalock (1964). Kish's (1987) more recent and much more thorough treatments of survey and experimental designs also stress these same points.

# References

Adams, J. S. 1965. "Inequity in Social Exchange." Pp. 267-299 in *Advances in Experimental Social Psychology, Vol. 2.*, edited by L. Berkowitz. New York: Academic Press.

Aigner, D. J., and G. G. Cain. 1977. "Statistical Theories of Discrimination in Labor Markets." *Industrial and Labor Relations Review* 30:175-187.

Antonovsky, A. 1960. "The Social Meaning of Discrimination." *Phylon* 21:81-95.

Arrow, K. J. 1973. "The Theory of Discrimination." Pp. 3-33 in *Discrimination in Labor Markets*, edited by O. Ashenfelter and A. Rees. Princeton, NJ: Princeton University Press.

Bergel, E. E. 1962. *Social Stratification.* New York: McGraw-Hill.

Bidwell, C. E., and J. D. Kasarda. 1975. "School District Organization and Student Achievement." *American Sociological Review* 40:55-70.

Blalock, H. M. 1964. *Causal Inferences in Nonexperimental Research.* Chapel Hill: University of North Carolina Press.

Blalock, H. M. 1967. *Toward a Theory of Minority Group Relations.* New York: John Wiley.

Blalock, H. M., 1969. *Theory Construction.* Englewood Cliffs, NJ: Prentice-Hall.

Blalock, H. M. 1979. *Black-White Relations in the 1980s: Toward a Long-Term Policy.* New York: Praeger.

Blalock, H. M. 1982. *Conceptualization and Measurement in the Social Sciences.* Beverly Hills, CA: Sage.

Blalock, H. M. 1989a. "Comparing Individual and Structural Levels of Analysis." In *Research in Sociology of Education and Socialization*, edited by K. Namboodiri and R. G. Corwin. Greenwich, CT: JAI Press.

Blalock, H. M. 1989b. *Power and Conflict: Toward a General Theory.* Newbury Park, CA: Sage.

Blalock, H. M., and P. H. Wilken. 1979. *Intergroup Processes: A Micro-Macro Perspective.* New York: Free Press.

Blau, P. M. 1964. *Exchange and Power in Social Life.* New York: John Wiley.

246

Blau, P. M. and O. D. Duncan. 1967. *The American Occupational Structure.* New York: John Wiley.

Bonacich, E. 1972. "A Theory of Ethnic Antagonism: The Split Labor Market." *American Sociological Review* 37:547-559.

Bonacich, E. 1976. "Advanced Capitalism and Black/White Relations in the United States: A Split Labor Market Interpretation." *American Sociological Review* 41:34-51.

Bowles, S., and H. Gintis. 1976. *Schooling in Capitalist America.* New York: Basic Books.

Braybrooke, D., and C. E. Lindblom. 1963. *A Strategy of Decision.* New York: Free Press.

Brinton, C. 1938. *The Anatomy of Revolution.* Englewood Cliffs, NJ: Prentice-Hall.

Camerer, C. F., and K. R. MacCrimmon. 1983. "Underground and Overpaid: Equity Theory in Practice." Chapter 10 in *Equity Theory: Psychological and Sociological Perspectives,* edited by D. M. Mesick and K. S. Cook. New York: Praeger.

Cook, K. S. 1975. "Expectations, Evaluations and Equity." *American Sociological Review* 40:372-388.

Cook, K. S., and T. Yamagishi. 1983. "Social Determinants of Equity Judgments: The Problem of Multidimensional Input." Chapter 5 in *Equity Theory: Psychological and Sociological Perspectives,* edited by D. M. Mesick and K. S. Cook. New York: Praeger.

Costner, H. L. 1969. "Theory, Deduction, and Rules of Correspondence." *American Journal of Sociology* 75:245-263.

Costner, H. L., and R. K. Leik. 1964. "Deductions From Axiomatic Theory." *American Sociological Review* 29:819-835.

Davies, J. C. 1962. "Toward a Theory of Revolution." *American Sociological Review* 27:5-19.

Deutsch, M., and J. M. Steil. 1988. "Awakening the Sense of Injustice." *Social Justice Research* 2:3-24.

Doeringer, P., and M. J. Piori. 1971. *Internal Labor Markets and Manpower Analysis.* Lexington, MA: Heath.

Downs, A. 1957. *An Economic Theory of Democracy.* New York: Harper & Row.

Duncan, O. D. 1975. *Introduction to Structural Equation Models.* New York: Academic Press.

Farley, J. E. 1988. *Majority-Minority Relations,* 2nd ed. Englewood Cliffs, NJ: Prentice-Hall.

Firebaugh, G. 1978. "A Rule for Inferring Individual-Level Relationships From Aggregate Data." *American Sociological Review* 43:557-572.

Fisher, F. 1966. *The Identification Problem in Econometrics.* New York: McGraw-Hill.

Fisher, S., ed. 1970. *Power and the Black Community.* New York: Random House.

Franklin, J. H., ed. 1967. *The Negro in 20th Century America.* New York: Vintage.

Frazier, E. F. 1957. *The Negro in the United States,* rev. ed. New York: Macmillan.

Gordon, R. A. 1968. "Issues in Multiple Regression." *American Journal of Sociology* 73:592-616.

Granovetter, M. 1974. *Getting a Job: A Study of Contacts and Careers.* Cambridge, MA: Harvard University Press.

Gurr, T. R. 1970. *Why Men Rebel.* Princeton, NJ: Princeton University Press.

Hamblin, R. L. 1971. "Ratio Measurement for the Social Sciences." *Social Forces* 50:191-206.

Hannan, M. T. 1971. *Aggregation and Disaggregation in Sociology*. Lexington, MA: Heath.

Hannan, M. T., and L. Burstein. 1974. "Estimation From Grouped Observations." *American Sociological Review* 39:374-392.

Hannan, M. T., J. H. Freeman, and J. W. Meyer. 1976. "Specification of Methods for Organizational Effectiveness: A Comment on Bidwell and Kasarda." *American Sociological Review* 41:136-143.

Hanushek, E. A., and J. E. Jackson. 1977. *Statistical Methods for Social Scientists*. New York: Academic Press.

Harris, R. J. 1983. "Pinning Down the Equity Formula." Chapter 8 in *Equity Theory: Psychological and Sociological Perspectives*, edited by D. M. Mesick and K. S. Cook. New York: Praeger.

Herting, J. R. 1985. "Multiple Indicator Models Using LISREL." Chapter 14 in *Causal Models in the Social Sciences*, 2nd ed., edited by H. M. Blalock. Hawthorne, NY: Aldine.

Hibbs, D. A. 1973. *Mass Political Violence*. New York: John Wiley.

Hodson, R. 1983. *Workers' Earnings and Corporate Economic Structure*. New York: Academic Press.

Hodson, R., and R. L. Kaufman. 1982. "Economic Dualism: A Critical Review." *American Sociological Review* 47:727-739.

Homans, G. C. 1974. *Social Behavior: Its Elementary Forms*, 2nd ed. New York: Harcourt, Brace & World.

Jasso, G. 1978. "On the Justice of Earnings: A New Specification of the Justice Evaluation Function." *American Journal of Sociology* 83:1398-1419.

Jaynes, G. D., and R. M. Williams, Jr., eds. 1989. *A Common Destiny: Blacks and American Society*. Washington, DC: National Research Council.

Johnston, J., 1984. *Econometric Methods*, 3rd ed. New York: McGraw-Hill.

Jones, E. E., and K. E. Davis. 1965. "From Acts to Dispositions: The Attribution Process in Person Perception." Pp. 219-266 in *Advances in Experimental Social Psychology, Vol. 2*, edited by L. Berkowitz. New York: Academic Press.

Jones, E. E., and R. E. Nisbett. 1971. *The Actor and the Observer: Divergent Perceptions of the Causes of Behavior*. Morristown, NJ: General Learning Press.

Kelley, H. H. 1971. *Attribution in Social Interaction*. Morristown, NJ: General Learning Press.

Kelley, H. H., and J. W. Thibaut. 1978. *Interpersonal Relations: A Theory of Interdependence*. New York: John Wiley.

Kish, L. 1959. "Some Statistical Problems in Research Design." *American Sociological Review* 24:328-338.

Kish, L. 1987. *Statistical Design for Research*. New York: John Wiley.

Langbein, L. I., and A. J. Lichtman. 1978. *Ecological Inference*. Beverly Hills, CA: Sage.

Lenski, G. E. 1966. *Power and Privilege*. New York: McGraw-Hill.

Lundberg, S. J., and R. Startz. 1983. "Private Discrimination and Social Intervention in Competitive Labor Markets." *American Economic Review* 73:340-347.

McAdam, D. 1982. *Political Process and the Development of Black Insurgency*. Chicago: University of Chicago Press.

McCarthy, J. D., and M. N. Zald. 1977. "Resource Mobilization and Social Movements: A Partial Theory." *American Journal of Sociology* 82:1212-1239.

March, J. G., and J. P. Olsen. 1976. *Ambiguity and Choice in Organizations*. Bergen, Norway: Universitetsforlaget.

March, J. G., and H. A. Simon. 1958. *Organizations.* New York: John Wiley.

Martin, J., and A. Murray. 1983. "Distributive Injustice and Unfair Exchange." Chapter 7 in *Equity Theory: Psychological and Sociological Perspectives,* edited by D. M. Mesick and K. S. Cook. New York: Praeger.

Mason, P. 1970. *Patterns of Dominance.* London: Oxford University Press.

Meier, A., E. Rudwick, and F. L. Broderick, eds. 1971. *Black Protest Thought in the Twentieth Century,* New York: Bobbs-Merrill.

Mesick, D. M., and K. S. Cook, eds. 1983. *Equity Theory: Psychological and Sociological Perspectives.* New York: Praeger.

Moore, B. 1966. *Social Origins of Dictatorship and Democracy.* Boston: Beacon.

Myrdal, G. 1944. *An American Dilemma.* New York: Harper.

Myrdal, G. 1972. *Asian Drama: An Inquiry Into the Poverty of Nations.* New York: Vintage.

Namboodiri, N. K., L. F. Carter, and H. M. Blalock. 1975. *Applied Multivariate Analysis and Experimental Designs.* New York: McGraw-Hill.

Nelson, J. 1982. *Economic Inequality: Conflict Without Change.* New York: Columbia University Press.

Oberschall, A. 1973. *Social Conflict and Social Movements.* Englewood Cliffs, NJ: Prentice-Hall.

Ogbu, J. U. 1978. *Minority Education and Caste: The American System in Cross-Cultural Perspective.* New York: Academic Press.

Ogbu, J. U. 1990. "Minority Status and Literacy in Comparative Perspective." *Daedalus* 119:141-168.

Pascal, A. H., and L. A. Rapping. 1972. "The Economics of Discrimination in Organized Baseball." Pp. 119-156 in *Racial Discrimination in Economic Life,* edited by A. H. Pascal. Lexington, MA: Heath.

Piven, F. F., and R. A. Cloward. 1971. *Regulating the Poor: The Functions of Public Welfare.* New York: Vintage.

Rawls, J. A. 1971. *A Theory of Justice.* Cambridge, MA: Harvard University Press.

Runciman, W. C. 1966. *Relative Deprivation and Social Justice.* Berkeley: University of California Press.

Smith, D. R. 1983. "Mobility in Professional Occupational-Internal Labor Markets: Stratification, Segmentation, and Vacancy Chains." *American Sociological Review* 48:289-305.

Thibaut, J., and L. Walker. 1975. *Procedural Justice: A Psychological Analysis.* Hillsdale, NJ: Lawrence Erlbaum.

Thurow, L. C. 1975. *Generating Inequality.* New York: Basic Books.

Tilly, C. 1979. "Repertoires of Contention in America and Britain, 1750-1830." Pp. 126-155 in *The Dynamics of Social Movements,* edited by M. N. Zald and J. D. McCarthy. Cambridge, MA: Winthrop.

Tilly, C., L. Tilly, and R. Tilly. 1975. *The Rebellious Century: 1830-1930.* Cambridge, MA: Harvard University Press.

Tyler, T. R. 1990. *Why People Obey the Law.* New Haven, CT: Yale University Press.

Vander Zanden, J. W. 1972. *American Minority Relations,* 3rd ed. New York: Ronald.

Walster, E., G. W. Walster, and E. Berscheid. 1978. *Equity: Theory and Research.* Boston: Allyn & Bacon.

Willhelm, S. M. 1971. *Who Needs the Negro?* Garden City, NY: Anchor Books.

Wilke, H. 1983. "Equity: Information and Effect Dependency." Chapter 3 in *Equity Theory: Psychological and Sociological Perspectives,* edited by D. M. Mesick and K. S. Cook. New York: Praeger.

Yinger, J. M. 1965. *A Minority Group in American Society.* New York: McGraw-Hill.

Zald, M. N., and J. D. McCarthy, eds. 1979. *The Dynamics of Social Movements.* Cambridge, MA: Winthrop.

# Author Index

# Subject Index

Affirmative action programs, 70, 106; beneficiaries of, 168; policies of, 38, 149, 220; procedures of, 108, 220

Aggregation biases, problem of, 13-19, 22

Allocated goods: academic degrees, 28; allocator control over, 119; allocator's energy, 28; allocator's time, 28; awards, 41-43; college admission, 28, 29, 35, 37; continuous versus discrete, 30-31, 51, 59; depletion of, 34; devaluation of, 35-36, 56; distributional, 43-46, 63; divisibility of, 29-30, 52, 56; effects of properties of, 46-63; generalized value of, 33, 51, 54-55; grades, 28, 29, 35, 138, 184-194; home mortgages, 28, 37; jobs, 28, 29, 37; membership in honorary societies, 41-43; membership in social organizations, 41-43; monopoly control of, 40-41, 52, 55-56; negatively valued, 37-39, 52, 57; positions on sports teams, 29; positively valued, 37, 52, 57, 58; prison sentences, 28; promotions, 28, 37; properties of,

28-66; recipients of sharing future power with allocators, 36-37, 52, 57; replenishment of, 34, 52, 55, 57, 59; retractability of, 31-32, 53, 56, 57, 60; salaries, 28, 35, 37; spatial locations, 28; wages, 28

Allocation decisions: amount of conflict after, 54, 63; appropriateness of awards in, 54, 59; costs of incorrect, 78; degree of devaluation in, 53, 56, 59, 61; degree of secrecy for, 39-40, 56, 58, 61, 63; distributional, 43; eligibility pools and, 132-165; equality as criterium for, 208-209, 210; equity considerations and, 78-80, 211-219; excess of replenishment over depletion in, 53, 59; general factors influencing, 68-99; homogeneity of applicant pool and, 89, 92; importance of performance to outcomes and, 89, 93; legal protection for candidates and, 53, 57, 61; made by allocators, 91; mutual contact among competitors and, 58; nature of applicant pool in, 54, 56, 57, 59, 62, 77; need as criterium for, 208, 209-210;

# About the Author

**Hubert M. Blalock, Jr.**, was Professor Emeritus at the University of Washington, having previously taught at the University of Michigan, Yale, and the University of North Carolina. He was past president of the American Sociological Association, a fellow in the American Academy of Arts and Sciences and the American Statistical Association, and a member of the National Academy of Sciences. His interests included applied statistics, conceptualization and measurement, race and ethnic relations, and sociological theory. His three most recent books, all published by Sage, are *Conceptualization and Measurement in the Social Sciences, Basic Dilemmas in the Social Sciences*, and *Power and Conflict*. He died February 8, 1991.